WHISPERINGS

$\mathcal{W}$HISPERINGS

God's voice to His people

Edna Hunt

XULON PRESS

Xulon Press
2301 Lucien Way #415
Maitland, FL 32751
407.339.4217
www.xulonpress.com

© 2021 by Edna Hunt

Paperback ISBN-13: 978-1-6628-3640-4
Hard Cover ISBN-13: 978-1-6628-3641-1
Ebook ISBN-13: 978-1-6628-3642-8

TABLE OF CONTENTS

Introduction xi

A Bag with Holes in It 1

A Finished Work 4

A Long Answer to a Short Question 8

A Matter of Trust 12

A Required Course 15

A Word God Never Uses 18

AHA! 21

All Dressed Up 24

All In or Halfway In 28

An Exact Representation 31

Attention Please! 35

Baa! Baa! Black Sheep 38

Bad News or Good News? 41

Baffled! 44

Be Sure to Wash Your Hands! 47

Been There, Done That, Bought the Tee Shirt 50

Between the Cross and the Crown 53

Blessed! 56

Boundaries: It's the Law! 59

Camping Out 63

Challenges 67

Chosen 70

Citizen of the Kingdom 74

Defend Yourself! 78

Did I Hear You Right? 81

Divide and Conquer Unite and Reign 85

"Do-Overs" 89

Does That Sound Familiar? 92

Do's and Don'ts Still Apply 95

Eat Heartily! 98

Entertaining or Vitally Important? 101

Equipped for the Times 104

Examining the Corners of One's Soul 107

Extending the boundaries of God's Garden 110

Eyewitness 113

Follow the Money 116

For One Sin 119

Formula for Success 122

Fractured World, Fractured People 125

Fragile Faith 128

Freedom Isn't Free 132

From Despair to Salvation 135

Getting Back to Plan A 139

Gift Wrapped 142

God Bless You! 146

God My Exceeding Joy 149

God's Billboards 152

Good Grief 155

Graded By God 159

Graded by God 162

Great Expectations 165

Here Comes the Judge 168

History Repeated 172

Home Improvement 175

How Do You View the World? 179

How Many Times Must I Tell You? 182

How Will You Say Goodbye? 185

I Doubt It! 188

I Hope So! 191

I Promise 194

I'm Just So Angry! 197

I'm So Tired! 200

Important Recall 203

In the Meantime 206

Intimacy 209

Into the Storm 212

Into the Storm 215

Is it Free? 218

It Is Finished! 221

It's About Time 224

Kindling Fires 227

Know Your Source 230

Let There Be Light! 233

Life is Relationships 237

Listening Skills 241

Loneliness 244

Longsuffering 247

Markers 250

My Inheritance 253

Never Fatherless 256

Not a Double to Be Found 259

Organic Food 262

Our One Need 265

Out of Step 268

Overexposed or Underdeveloped 271

Pivotal Moments 274

Planning Ahead 277

Power of Attorney 280

Poverty 283

Powerless or Powerful? 286

Press On! 289

Priorities 292

Processed Food 295

Productive or Reproductive? 298

Protect Your Treasure 302

Read the Signs 305

Recruited 309

Regarding Others 312

Restored! 316

Scaredy Cat! 319

Searching for Treasure 322

Seeing Beyond the Veil 326

Self- Medicated Christianity 329

Someone is Watching You! 332

Spiritual Refraction 335

Standing at the Jordan 338

Strengthen the Brethren 341

Take a Walk 344

Take Root! 348

Testing Your Resolve 351

That Doesn't Make Sense! 354

That's My Dad! 357

The Best Day of My Life 360

The Benefits of Imprisonment 363
The Aliens Have Landed 366
The Art of Letter Writing 369
The Disastrous Exchange. 372
The Family Business 375
The Greatest Dream of All 378
The Impertinence of Arguing with Father. 381
The Kingdom of Me 384
The Measuring Stick 387
The Owner 390
The Proof is in the Tasting. 393
The Returns and Complaints Department 396
The Samson Syndrome. 400
The Whole Truth. 404
The WOW Factor 407
Three Little Words 410
Time to Plant My Garden 413
To What Shall I Compare This Generation? 416
Traditions 419
Transitions. 422
What Answer Will You Give? 425
What's Your Passion? 428
What Can a Nickel Buy? 431
What Happened to Simon? 434
What is the Purpose? 438
What Kind of House Will You Build For Me? 441
What Language Was That? 445
Where Did That Come From? 449
Where Do You Belong? 453
Which Path Shall I Take? 456
Who Cares? 460

Why the Reaction? 463
Wilderness Skills 467
Will it Never End! 470
Winning is Everything 473
Words Matter 476
Your Personal Trainer 480

INTRODUCTION

*I*n the early hours before the break of dawn, the house is quiet. I sit in the corner of my room, Bible in my lap, reading and thinking about what truth is there for me to understand. In the quiet, God whispers. The words I have read leap to life as He shares His truth. Each whisper is encouraging me on my walk with Him. I sense His great love for me and His desire that I get to know Him more and more. I dare not stir lest I miss any word He may share, so precious are these moments. Often there are tears as I feel His presence so deeply and sense His caring heart.

These encounters remind me of Elijah's visit from God as he huddled in the cave. He had hidden in fear of bodily harm from an evil queen just after one of the greatest revelations of God's presence recorded in the Old Testament. As Elijah waited, there came an earthquake, then fire and then a great wind. But God was not present [n any of those. Then God spoke in a whisper to Elijah, addressing his fear and need for reliance in Him. You can find the entire account in 1 Kings 19.

As I pondered Elijah's encounter, I couldn't help wondering how many ways God chooses to get our attention. I am certain there is an endless number of means which He uses, many often missed by us as we hurry through our lives unaware. That is a cause to ask for forgiveness!

There is no greater blessing for me as a Christian than to know God's great love for me as He shares Himself through His Word. It makes me hunger to know Him at a deeper intimacy, to listen more attentively as He reveals Himself, and to share what I learn with other hungry believers. This I have done through the years as a teacher of the things God has provided through His Word. Each time I am humbled by the opportunity to see what God does as seeds of truth are planted.

From those delicious whispers through the years has come this book. It is my humble effort to share with you some of what has blessed and strengthened my walk with Him through some seventy-five years as a Christian. I hope that as you read, God will speak into your heart what He has for you in ways that will also strengthen your desire to please Him.

There is no particular order to the arrangement of subjects. Each is a new entry into the mind of God for us as we live out in the challenges and issues of our everyday pilgrimage through this fallen world. I think we often forget that God is the same even though what we may encounter differs from the accounts in His Word. All are based on an incident in the scriptures of both Old and New Testaments in which God has dealt with those He created in His image.

At the end of each reading there is a question, challenge, or something to consider in the hope you will take the opportunity to jot down what you have heard God whisper to you. I offer this book for no other reason than in obedience to God's direction, and in faith that He will use it as He wills.

It is my prayer that you will meet the perfect God and that this imperfect author will be hidden. To God be the glory!

A BAG WITH HOLES IN IT

Have you ever picked up a bag full of purchases only to find that the hole in the bag has allowed some merchandise to escape? Perhaps you located your favorite tote to carry your possessions, only to discover it had been torn at the bottom? Frustrating, isn't it and useless as well. Such was the condition of God's people in the time of the Prophet Haggai.

Haggai records that sense of dismay from God's point of view.

"Thus says the Lord of Hosts, 'Consider your ways. You have sown much but harvest little. You eat, but there is no satisfaction in it. You drink but not enough to become drunk. You put on clothing, but no one is warm enough. And he who earns wages puts them in a bag with holes in it.'" (Haggai 1:5-8)

Are these thoughts familiar? How often do we think of our lack in spite of our efforts? Where does all my money go? My pocket seems to have a hole in it. Why can't I ever seem to get ahead? The food we eat leaves us craving something more. The clothes we wear are threadbare or out of current style. Satisfaction seems illusive and frustration abounds like "a bag with holes in it".

This same dissatisfaction can be applied to our church going. How often do we come away as empty as when we arrived? The lack of spiritual food leaves us wanting. The rituals of religion, two songs and a prayer, a sermon that seems more like a pep talk, all promote emptiness of heart. There seems to be an absence of the Spirit of God.

Haggai continued to record God's assessment of the condition of His people.

"You look for much, but it comes to little. When you bring it home, I blow it away. Why?', declares the Lord of Hosts (Haggai 1:9)

God answers His own question by pointing out the self-satisfaction that has invaded the hearts of His people. Instead of focusing on God's priorities, they were selfishly putting self wants first. Their own personal wants took precedence over God's plans for them. Preoccupation with their own plans left no time to consider God's desires for them. It left them empty. Because of their neglect of God's commands and their preoccupation with self-interests, God withheld His blessings from them.

At the beginning and end of His assessment, the Lord said that we should "consider our ways." That means we must pause and take stock of our situation, assess our habits, resources, our whole lives. When doing so, we may discover the reason for a "holey bag".

Jesus echoes the concerns of His Father as He says,

"Do not worry what you will eat or what you will drink, nor for your body as to what you will wear. ...for your Heavenly Father knows you need all these things. Seek first the Kingdom of God and His righteousness, and all these things will be added to you(Matthew 6:33)

This can be well said of our own lives. It is time to consider whether our concentration on what we want takes precedence over God's agenda. Is our focus on building up our own lives or building up the Kingdom of God? Jesus continued to emphasize the importance of our focus and to reassure us.

"So do not worry about tomorrow, for tomorrow will take care of itself. Each day has enough trouble of its own." (Matthew 6:34)

In clear words, "Put first things first". And as we all have discovered, our days bring unwanted troubles of one kind or another, some large and some small. Having understood that our first priority is not things or status, God reminds us to consider His ways! He wants to assess the condition of our heart to see where our priorities lie. Check our "bags" for holes! Having done that on a regular basis, we then are able to align our priorities with His.

Consider: Check your "bag" for holes. What is the cause of the holes?

A FINISHED WORK

Day after day a young man labored on a piece of work his master had assigned him. One day a lady came into the shop and spied the work of art the young man was making. "Oh, how beautiful!", she exclaimed. "May I purchase it?"

"It is not yet finished", the young man replied.

"Oh, but it looks finished to me! she exclaimed.

"Yes, Madam", he replied. "But it is not finished until my master says it is."

Most of us have stared at unfinished projects, chores, or challenges. There are a myriad of things which cause such delays. Most fall into the category of neglect, but some are due to the difficulty of the task. Neither of those reasons justify the delay. More likely, they define the person.

The only time in history when anyone could truly say "My work here is finished" is found in the cry of Jesus on the cross when He declared, "It is finished!" (John 19:30) The work God had assigned His Son was complete. Sacrifice for the sins of mankind had been paid. All that His Father had given Him to do, He had accomplished.

Jesus said, "I glorified You on earth having accomplished the work You gave Me to do." (John 17:4)

The writer of Hebrews some years later proclaimed this admonition.

"Let us fix our eyes on Jesus, the Author and Perfecter of faith, who, for the joy set before Him, endured the cross, despising the shame, and has sat down at the right hand of the throne of God." (Hebrews 13:2-3)

Jesus did His assigned work obediently and without complaint! He could truly say that He had finished His assignment.

What does that mean for us? Jesus, speaking to the people of His day in what we now call The Sermon on the Mount, gave us the answer.

"Therefore, you must be perfect as your Father in heaven is perfect." (Matthew 5:48)

What? We are to be perfect, a complete work? No way! I will never make that standard of measurement!

Yes, we must,because it is God's desire for us. Even though we so often feel like an unfinished work, flawed in so many areas, we ponder that statement. Who of us has not made a mess of some attempt to be God's hands, feet, and voice in our daily lives? Or felt a failure when the wished for success seemed illusive? The challenges we face to "be perfect" loom large until we stop to consider the challenges Jesus met every day of His earthly ministry. Remember, He came as a man and was subjected to all the challenges of being human. It is humbling to consider!

The Apostle Paul, speaking during what was his last meeting with the elders of the Church at Ephesus, he said the same.

"I do not consider my life of any account to myself, so that I may <u>finish</u> my course, the ministry which I received from the Lord Jesus, to testify solemnly to the grace of God." (Acts 20:24)

Paul wanted to complete what the Lord had called him to do in such a manner as to be seen as a "finisher", one faithful to the very end.

Paul's words from prison to his young protégé, Timothy, are those we hope to be able to say.

"I have fought a good fight, I have finished the course, I have kept the faith. In the future there is laid up for me a crown of righteousness which the Lord, the righteous Judge, will award to me on that day, and not only me but also to all who have loved His appearing." (2 Timothy 4:7-8)

The sincere desire of our hearts is to reach the finish line having run the race faithfully. We are waiting to hear God say, "Well done, good and faithful servant. You have finished well!"

Question: How are you "running the race" before God? Do you have hope for final victory?

A Long Answer to a Short Question

Matthew 24-25

As Jesus was coming out of the Temple with is disciples, He made a remark that caused the disciples to ask a question. He had said that the Temple would be destroyed so that only a pile of rubble would remain.

"When will these things happen and what will be the sign of Your coming at the end of the age?" (Matthew 24:3)

They wanted to be prepared for such an event as it would be life-changing. We know that it was near the time of the Passover when Jesus would partake of the last meal with His disciples before His crucifixion. The disciples had no idea what lay ahead. They failed to understand the many times Jesus had told them about what was to come for Him.

Instead of dismissing their question, Jesus began with a warning.

"Don't be fooled by those you may see who come claiming to be Me." (Matthew 24:4-5)

Then He launched into a description of what would occur before His return. Remember that they still did not understand that Jesus would actually leave them.

Jesus continued with a list of instructions for those who would be living during the time when what the Prophet Daniel called "the abomination of desolation". He was telling them in advance to prepare them. But there was also a promise to give them hope.

"All who remain faithful to the end will be saved." (Matthew 24:13)

Jesus wasn't finished. He had only begun to prepare them – and us- as He used stories and parables to drive home His message. Some terms mystify us. For example "the abomination of desolation". the prophet Daniel spoke of in the "70 weeks" passage.(Daniel 9:27; 11:31; 12:1) We don't know if it is a "who" or a "what" but we do know it will be a very hard time. Jesus spoke of "a great tribulation which has never before occurred and never will again". He spoke of the false Christs who would even perform signs and wonders. After this period of the tribulation the heavens will be shaken. Stars, sun, and moon will be darkened. It makes us shudder to think of such a time. 2

Then came the great news!!! Jesus, the Son of Man, will come on the clouds with great glory. Angels will announce His coming! They will gather the elect from wherever they are.

As if to ease the wonder and awe of His listeners, Jesus told a parable. The fig tree life cycle is paralleled with His coming.

Jesus declared, "No one will know, not even the angels or Me. Just be ready! Be on the alert/" (Matthew 24:36,42)

Jesus will come again at a time we do not expect. He told a short parable about a faithful slave who is ready and one who is not. Needless to say, the cruel and unfaithful servant's demise was not a pleasant one.

"Who is the faithful slave the master put in charge of his household to give them their food at the proper time? Blessed is the slave whom his master finds so doing when he comes." (Matthew 24:45-46)

The message is clear. Don't wait idly for My return. Be busy about the Kingdom business. The end for the lazy is dire!

Jesus concluded His teaching with great hope. We see the separation of believers and unbelievers. To illustrate what we who live now must be about during this time, Jesus made it personal. As we minister to others we are doing it for Him. Those who turn a deaf ear will end up in eternal punishment.

Even though we do not hear any response from the disciples, we may put ourselves in their place and ask, "Do I measure up? Am I doing as Jesus has directed me We must be ready.

- Be alert
- Be busy about Kingdom business

- Beware of falsehoods
- Be strong in the promises of the Lord

It was indeed a long answer to a short question, but one of increasing importance as the time of Jesus' return draws nearer.

Question: Are you ready?

A MATTER OF TRUST

Some years ago while conversing with a friend, she made this statement. "I don't trust anyone." Questioning her, I asked, "Not even your husband or closest friend?" Same answer. "No one" At the time I thought it to be a harsh statement and very exclusive. I mean, who doesn't want to be trusted. I think myself trustworthy, don't you?

Knowing the heart of my friend, however, I realized that as a sincere Christian, one who has lived out her strong beliefs through the years, there was no malice or bitterness involved in the statement. It was not based on perceived slights or long held grudges. So, why would she say such a thing? What was the basis for such a statement?

I knew this must have a Biblical base to it. And so, my own search to discover the truth began with the Word of God. What was written there to offer such a wide-reaching scope? Here is my discovery.

Setting the stage in John's Gospel account, we find Jesus early in His ministry attending the Passover celebration in Jerusalem. Entering the Temple He found money changers exchanging the coinage of other countries in preparation to buy a sacrifice to offer. Sellers of oxen, sheep, and doves were present to offer their goods, often with inflated prices. Jesus' immediate response to the desecration of the Temple was to drive the moneychangers and sellers of animals out of the Holy place God ordained as holy unto Him.

Jesus addressed them. "Take these things away. Stop making My Father's house a place of business." (John 2:13-16)

The narrative continued as Jesus remained in Jerusalem for Passover. Many during that time began to believe in Him as Messiah because of the signs He was doing. We are not told the exact nature of what they saw, but it was convincing enough to penetrate their hearts. The words that led me to this passage was John's recording of what he knew Jesus' response to the crowd was.

"But Jesus, on His part, was not entrusting Himself to them for He knew all men...for He Himself knew what was in the heart of men." (John 2:24-25)

This theme of the untrustworthiness of man is echoed throughout scripture, beginning with a sin free man named Adam. Not long after the flood when Noah and his family had emerged safely from the refuge of the ark, Noah responded by offering a sacrifice of thanksgiving to God. God's response is a commentary on the reliability of man to be trusted. God knew what we must recognize as true.

"The Lord said to Himself, 'I will never again curse the ground on account of man, for the intent of man's heart is evil from his youth...'" (Genesis 8:21)

Many years later the Prophet Jeremiah echoed this truth.

"Let everyone be on guard against his neighbor, and do not trust any brother, because every brother deals craftily, and every neighbor goes about as a slanderer...I know, O Lord, that a man's way is not in himself; nor is it in man to direct his own steps." Jeremiah 9:4;10:23)

This statement speaks of the fallen state of mankind. Though we embrace Jesus' sacrifice to redeem us and through Him to be made new, there remains in each of us the dregs of the old Adamic nature. Jesus did not seek to bring condemnation to anyone but to call attention to our desperate need to be washed clean within as well as without. The warnings in scripture about the untrustworthiness of man serve as a warning to be discerning as to the things and people we trust.

If we humans are all not to be trusted, it seems we may be viewed as cynical, but those who have not yet experienced this untrustworthiness firsthand. There is a reason U.S money says "In God we trust". He alone is trustworthy. He never reneges on His promises. He is faithful to act on our behalf even when we think ourselves unworthy. It is to God that we entrust our lives when we profess faith in Jesus as Savior.

I have often been glad I heard the truth of God's Word spoken through my dear friend. Let God speak to you through His Word.

Consider: What does it mean to trust God completely, all the time, and in every situation?

A Required Course

During our school years we all discovered that there were certain courses that were required in order to complete the grade level and get that coveted diploma. Often these courses were not so much to our liking, not as much fun as those in the areas of our interest. In fact, these required courses were just plain hard!

As if that was the end of required courses we soon learned that we had to take a Drivers' Ed course, a proficiency course in the occupation of our choosing, a SAT, GRE, APT etc. all of which required effort. Sometimes painful effort!. Some occupations even require courses at intervals during our work life.

In the Christian arena there is a "required course" It is called TESTING. It is one we take and retake a number of times as we journey through the tangles of life. It may require hardship, pain, loss, sleepless nights and restless days as we face the kind of testing that purifies.

Jesus, eating with His disciples at what would be His last meal with them, was speaking to them about their discussion as to which among them was the greatest. When He had addressed their lack of humility, Jesus turned His attention to Peter, the disciple who felt he would be strong to the end. Calling him by his given name, Simon, not as Peter, the rock, Jesus spoke prophetic words which Peter recalled later.

"Simon, Simon, Satan has demanded permission to sift you like wheat; but I have prayed for you that your faith may not fail. And you, once you have turned again, strengthen your brothers." (Luke 22:31-32)

To this Peter protested vigorously that he was with his Messiah all the way to prison and even death. Both Jesus' warning and Peter's protests were fulfilled, though not as Peter expected. Jesus did not say, "If you fail". He said, "When you fail". Jesus knew Peter was going to enter the required course called "Testing". because He knew the places in Peter that were in need of repair.

We know how the story unfolds. Peter denied he knew Jesus three times as Jesus was on trial before the religious elders. We can only imagine the pain in Peter's heart when he understood what he had just done as the rooster signaled his denials.

We know how Jesus met Peter by the Sea of Galilee and restored him to fellowship as Peter had a big dose of humility. It was then that Jesus gave Peter his assignment. Three times, one for each betrayal, Jesus said to Peter, "Feed My sheep."

Jesus' admonition was lived out in the rest of Peter's life, beginning shortly after the crucifixion when we find Peter in a leadership role among the eleven disciples. Not long after that, on the Day of

Pentecost, the Spirit of the Living God filled all of the disciples, and Peter took the pulpit to explain Jesus' fulfillment of the Old Testament prophecies. With boldness and clarity this former fisherman became the leader of the many new converts who heeded his message of truth. Had Peter not been through the "Testing course" he would not have understood where the source of his strength lay. It was in Jesus, his Lord, not in Peter. Peter faithfully ministered for the rest of his life; and we are told that he was crucified like his Savior.

There are a number of lessons for us in this, none the least of which is Peter's lesson in humble grace. We often believe we know how we will react in a given situation. But when the testing comes and our feet are held to the fire, what then? God has chosen to allow each of us to enter the required course of "Testing", knowing that we will proceed one of two ways. We will give up the effort as too hard, or we will, like Peter, allow Jesus to bring us to our knees so He can raise us up to new strength and usefulness

Question: Will you pass the test, or do you require a trial of your faith to discover how much faith you lack?

A WORD GOD NEVER USES

"Oops! I spilled the milk!" "Oops! I forgot to mail that birthday card!." "Oops! I failed to keep my doctor's appointment." Whether we belong to the "Clutzes' Club" or not, life gives us plenty of opportunities to say "oops". In fact, sometimes those come in bunches and on successive days.

Such occurrences may not be viewed as sins, but rather just annoying human glitches whose origin may be attributed to a myriad of causes. Carelessness. Negligence. Poor time management. Taking on too much to do. Mismanagement of time or effort. These are just a few causes. While it seems as if we are all destined to commit these "oops" moments, there is One who has never and will never utter that word.

He is God! Sometimes we may hear a person say, "Wow, God really committed a big "oops" when He gave man free will. Look what we have done with that!" Rest assured, friend, God knew what He was doing and why. Think about it. Who would want someone to honor and praise someone out of coercion?

When God encountered Adam and Eve cowering naked in the Garden after their disobedience, God didn't say "Oops. I shouldn't have created that tree!" He continued His relationship with them on a different basis, that of of mercy and redemption.

Throughout the history of man surely God has been grieved by the sinful disobedience of those He created to reflect and embody His Image. He hasn't said "oops, I was wrong to let them have free will." Instead, He continues to pursues us with the sole intent of drawing us to Himself.

One of the saddest pictures of "oops" moments is found in the book of Job. Everyone, from Job's wife to all of his friends, was certain Job had committed an "oops" which had made God retaliate by destroying Job's life. According to them, this was the "BIG OOPS", irredeemable in its severity. They had no idea that God was engineering the events and in control of every situation. As these so-called friends continued to pour out their assessment and advice to Job, he continued to protest his innocence

To his wife Job said, "Shall we indeed accept good from God and not accept adversity?" (Job 2:10)

Answering his friends Job said, "It is still my consolation, and I rejoice in unsparing pain that I have not denied the words of the Holy One." (Job 6:10)

There came a day when God answered Job and revealed with certainty just Who He is and what He is capable of doing. In all of that there is not one "oops". The result for Job was a fresh understanding of his God followed by a complete restoration of all he had lost.

Job answered God. "I know You can do all things and that no purpose of Yours can be thwarted... I have heard of You by the hearing of the ear, but now my eyes see You." (Job 42:2,5)

The post script to Job's trial of faith is this.

"The Lord blessed the latter days of Job more than his beginning." (Job 42:12)

The truth for each of us is that our "oops" moments are redeemable by God. He sees and mercifully uses those, if we allow Him, to draw us closer to Him. The in-between times may come with struggle, but they are cathartic in that they urge us to rely on the only One who knows our beginning and our end.

Question: What confession will you make to God of your "oops moments"?

AHA!

*A*ll of us throughout life, beginning very early after we leave the womb, have those moments when we suddenly become aware of a new truth, and our minds, even subconsciously, say "AHA!". If I cry, Mama will come and tend to my needs. A baby discovers the ability to crawl. A preschooler discovers that the ABCs have the power to form words. A "would be" inventor solves the riddle that makes his project come to fruition.

Why are these times important? It is because each one unlocks a new door we are able to enter. It may mean a new skill, a change of direction, a fresh beginning, an awesome bit of knowledge, a light on the path forward. To ignore such moments or to set them aside as trivial often results in stagnation, a missed opportunity for growth, a door that remains closed due to fear of the new.

This is certainly true of the Christian life. When God shows us from His Word an "AHA" moment, if we take it lightly or fail to heed the new revelation, our growth is halted, and a lukewarm approach to living the life God has designed for each of us 0ccurs. God's Word urges us to consider each new truth for what it means to our lives individually as well as collectively. The "AHA" moments are meant to promote new growth, change a destructive habit, consider a new way of thinking, reach out to a new challenge with vigor. We must not ignore any "AHA" moment.

The Bible is filled with just such moments. Here are a few examples.

- Gideon discovered he could win the battle with only 300 men. Judges 6-8.
- David discovered that the armor of God is sufficient to battle the giant Goliath. We find his story in 1 Samuel 17.
- Moses saw a burning bush and stopped to see what it meant Exodus 2.
- Isaiah heeded the call of God and offered himself Isaiah 6:8
- Peter discovered he could walk on water. Matthew 14.
- The Apostle Paul met on the Damascus Road the Savior he had adamantly rejected, and as a result, gained new sight. Acts 9.

Think what would be different if any one of them had ignored that important revelation, that "AHA" event. The battle would have been lost. The Philistines would have conquered Israel. The Hebrews would have been leaderless. The wonderful prophesies about the Messiah to come would be absent from scripture. Peter would have missed a "new skill". And we would not have all of the God inspired lessons from the letters of Paul.

Each of these and so many others heeded God's "AHA" times. Their lives were forever changed as a result. History was set on a new path. The world in which they lived, and ours as well, was impacted.

There are many instances as well when people ignored the truth before them and with disastrous results. One has only to consider as an example the lives of the Hebrews on the Exodus journey to find a classic case of dismissing all of the "AHA" moments God gave them as they journeyed toward the Promised Land. The Exodus generation all died never having entered the land God had sworn to give them as their permanent home.

The greatest "AHA" moment anyone can ever experience is the revelation of the cost Jesus paid for us to have new life as a citizen of the Heavenly Kingdom. The penalty for ignoring this moment is certain eternal death,. But the willingness to accept the Savior's gift is eternal life!

Whatever your "AHA" moments are, ask God to show you what it means for you. Then step out with courage to pursue His direction. He walks with you as challenges arise, detours lurk, voices discourage, or self gets in the way. And they will. Our adversary does not want us to act on those special moments lest we discover the absolute and eternal faithfulness of our God. He is the greatest "AHA" we will ever have!

Question: Have you ever has a spiritual "AHA" moment? Did it change your life? If so, how?

ALL DRESSED UP

As the saying goes, "Clothes make the man". In other words, how you dress may identify your status. You've climbed the ladder of success. You are a "working joe". You belong to the ranks of the very poor. To emphasize the point, just look at any magazine, TV commercial, or clothing store ad. We are constantly reminded to buy the latest clothing style, look a certain way, choose a finer quality brand – which of course, costs much more. Clothing can designate more than social status. It may also identify your profession, employment, club membership, or athletic team. Military attire is specific to branch and rank. And of course, those who dress like a star are among the elite of our day.

From the very beginning of the story of man, the purpose of clothing or body covering was meant to cover up something. We read in Genesis 3 that Adam and Eve, after transgressing the command of God, sought to cover themselves with fig leaves to hide their shame. God addressed their sin and became the first earthly tailor. He made them clothing of animal skins, covering their nudity as a symbolic way to show the change in their relationship with Him.

It is symbolic because we know that clothing only hides the exterior but does nothing to address the sinful heart.

Throughout the Bible clothing is used to tell a story, reveal a truth, describe human behavior, speak of rank or status, or characterize a holy life. Priests wore special clothing as they ministered before in the Temple. Prayer shawls were adorned with tassels. Lepers wore rags as befitted their condition. Kings wore crowns as a symbol of their power and status. John the Baptizer wore camel hair garments and a leather belt, and he was unshaven in his status as a Nazarite. Women were forbidden to wear men's clothing and men were forbidden to clothe themselves in women's garments.

Often clothing was used to emphasize a truth, offer instruction, or give a warning.

"Beware of false prophets who come to you dressed in sheep's clothing, but inside they are devouring wolves." (Matthew 7:15)

"Put on the whole armor of God that you may be able to stand your ground on the evil day. Tighten the belt of truth around your waist. Put on the breastplate of integrity and cover your feet in preparation to meet the enemy... Lift up as covering the shield of faith to ward off the fiery darts of the enemy. Put on the helmet of salvation and take up the sword of the Spirit which is the Word of God. (Ephesians 6:13-27)

James, the leader of the church in Jerusalem, perhaps recalling Jesus' words had this warning.

"Brothers and sisters, pay no regard to people as if to practice your faith with snobbery. For if a person comes into your midst wearing splendid clothes and you give him preferential treatment while the poor man stands in the back or sits at your feet, are you not discriminating and becoming critical judges with wrong motives?" (James 2:2-4)

The Apostle Peter, remembering the occasion when Jesus stooped to wash His disciples' feet, reminds us to "be clothed with humility". (!1Peter 5:5)

When did we get so clothes conscious, so fixated on the latest style or best brand? When did we arrive at the point at which we must have a different outfit for every occasion? Or such a change of season wardrobe? And when did society begin to condone scantily clad or revealing clothes as .as proper wear?

Perhaps take a look at a man who lived many years ago who was privileged to witness a scene of God upon His throne in all of His glory. The Prophet Isaiah even heard the angels cry out "Holy, holy, holy is the Lord of Hosts! The whole earth is filled with His glory!" (Isaiah 6:1-3)\

In that moment Isaiah understood the awesomeness of God and felt, as Adam and Eve had, naked before Holy God. Listen to his response.

"Woe is me, for I am ruined, a man of unclean lips, and I live among a people of unclean lips; for my eyes have seen the King, the Lord of Hosts!" (Isaiah 6:5)

The best news is that Isaiah began to understanding his unworthiness and God's acceptance of man as we are clothed with Him.

"I will greatly rejoice in the Lord; my soul will exult in my God. For He has clothed me with garments of salvation. He has covered me with the robe of righteousness as a bridegroom decks himself out with a garland, and a bride adorns herself with jewels." (Isaiah 61:10)

Question: What are you wearing? We, as children of the King, wear robes of righteousness made possible by the sacrifice of Jesus on the cross. Clothing does make the man and woman!

All In or Halfway In

"*Y*ou did a halfway job! Why didn't you finish completely?" This reprimand could come from a parent, teacher, boss, teammate or a friend. Someone has noted that you did a poor job at whatever you were assigned to do or had attempted to do. (Grace extended here for those of us who are a bit messy) The causes of such halfway attempts are numerous. Too lazy. In a hurry to be done. Too hard. Not enough time. Don't care attitude. Attempt to displease the assigner of the task. The list of reasons is long.

The real reason lies with the attitude of the one attempting the task. The desire to do a quality job is missing because it did not matter to the one doing it. Granted, some of us are better at certain things than others due to lack of skill or ability, but these are not reasons for doing a halfway job. Nor is the lack of praise or reward a reason for not attempting to do a thorough job. You can still be "all in".

This same principle applies to our belief system . We either must believe with certainty, or we are "halfway in". That is another way of saying that when we aren't sure or are hesitant to commit to something, we are numbered among the "don't believers". Such was the crowd which followed Jesus through His earthly journey and attended His last entry into Jerusalem.

We call this the Triumphal Entry because Jesus came riding on a donkey as befitting one who would be king. This had been prophesied many years before by Zechariah.

"Behold, your King is coming to you. He is just and endowed with salvation, humble and mounted on a donkey..." (Zechariah 9:9)

Matthew recorded the scene for us. The crowd was so excited, thinking Jesus would be the one to occupy the throne of David and restore the kingdom. They spread palm branches on the roadway to honor Him and shouted out their praise.

"Hosannah to the son of David! Blessed is He who comes in the Name of the Lord! Hosannah in the highest!" (Matthew 22:9)

Their voices continued to tell all within earshot about this "prophet, Jesus from Nazareth". Jesus lamented over the blindness of His city, Jerusalem. He knew that the crowd was only halfway believing the truth they spoke. We know this because not long after this triumphant entry, the same crowd revealed their lack of belief. We must pause to note that the crowd did not call Jesus "Lord" or "Messiah" but "one who comes in the name of the Lord".

Jesus stood before the religious leaders and Pilate, never once denying His identity. Yet the crowd cast aside their enthusiasm, and replaced it with their true belief when asked by Pilate what should be done with this innocent man.

"So they cried out, 'Away with Him! Crucify Him! We have no king but Caesar!' " (John 19:15)

Why was there such a lack of being "all in" for the Messiah? Surely the oppressive reign by Rome would have been reason enough to commit to Jesus. The answers may be numerous. The impetus on the road was focused on personal gain, not on faith in Messiah. They had missed the message amidst the awe over Jesus' miracles. The cost would have been too great if they fully committed to this One their religious leaders hated. Fear of ridicule or being ostracized by friends or family was too hard to bear.

All of these may hold the reasons we,,too, are reluctant to go "all in" for Jesus instead of just giving lip service to what we actually believe. The sheer thought of being captive to God in body, soul, and strength has awesome implications. It means we must be "all in", firm in our resolve to be wholly His regardless of the cost.

Question: Are you "all in" or just halfway in?

An Exact Representation

One day an artist of some renown was commissioned to paint a portrait of a man's wife. For days he painted portrait after portrait, each resembling her in some way. Each time the man came to see the artist's work, he would exclaim, "That is very good, but it is not quite right! Please try again." And so the artist would begin anew to try to capture the perfect image. One day he just knew he had the portrait right. When the man rushed in to see the finished work, he excitedly exclaimed, "You've done it! This is the exact representation of my wife!"

At first glance we may say, "But all of the portraits look just alike," Yet what the artist had come to realize is that the man was looking for some inner quality rather indefinable to the human eye but present to the soul. That was the missing element. At last he had seen beyond her outer appearance to who she really was within, and he expressed it on canvas...

Perhaps we have had similar thoughts while walking through an art gallery. There might be a number of canvases portraying flower gardens, but we come to one awash with color and meticulously

painted to view every flower as if it was alive. The artist captured it
so well that we could almost smell the fragrances. "What beauty!",
we exclaim.

Often a father or mother will hear someone say, "Your children look
just like you!" We smile and glow with pleasure at the thought. They
may even say, "Your children are so kind. I know they learned that
from you." Reflected in our offspring are family traits, some obvious
and some more subtle. But they bear our DNA and are representa-
tions of who we are.

An exact representation! This is a phrase with eternal meaning. The
writer of Hebrews said of Jesus, "He is the exact representation of
His Father."

"In the last days God has spoken to us in His Son whom He appointed
heir of all things through Whom He also made the world. He is the
radiance of His glory and the exact representation of His nature..."
(Hebrews 1:2-3)

The truth of this statement is staggering in scope. Jesus, the Son of
God, is in every aspect just like His Father. In love. In power. In
mercy. In grace, forgiveness, provision, judgment. On and on we
may list the awesome array of attributes of Father God perfectly
portrayed in His Son.

As Jesus walked the earth, He portrayed honesty, purity, justice,
morality, humility, honor. He longed to be accepted, believed and
loved for who He was. He desired to give the riches of His Father
to the world. He mourned loss and grieved over mankind's state.

He responded to the needs before Him and listened as hearts cried out for release from their burdens. He gave freely, listening to His Father's words of instruction. That only. No less. The Obedient Representation of Father God was indeed God in human flesh, the exact representation.

The thought does not end there. We who are His followers, children of God and joint heirs with Jesus, are told to emulate the same pattern in our lives. We who are made in the image and likeness of God are to portray that likeness every day. Granted, we never achieve the perfection of the Son, but we are commanded to try. We are to love with His love. To forgive because we have been forgiven. To serve as a model of servant Jesus portrayed. To extend mercy and grace because that is God's way. To be patient and kind to those who are "sandpaper people" in our world. You know that kind. They are the abrasive, cruel, antagonistic ones who rub us the wrong way. We are to attend to the needs in front of us with the guidance of the Father in our ear. We are to go when and where He commands without delay or whining. Will we always be successful at such an array of characteristics? No. Jesus, though perfect, had times when He was rejected. His message fell on deaf ears. His kindness was misunderstood. His words did not penetrate hardened hearts .In the end He was scorned, abused, cursed, betrayed. In the end He was crucified because He was the exact representation of His Father.

Probably, no one will ever say about us, "You are the exact representation of God." After all, we aren't. But some may think we resemble Him. I would like that! How about you?

Question: How much do you resemble God in your daily life? On a scale of 1 to 10, rate yourself.

ATTENTION PLEASE!

There are many ways to call attention to something or someone. A shout like "Hey, you!". An emphatic "Stop!" A clearing of the throat, "Ahem". An outlandish outfit we wear or less clothed than we should be. Some antic we perform. Or perhaps just a simple, "May I have your attention?" Whatever the method, the intention is to capture one's focus for the moment, to draw us away from the matter at hand.

Perhaps there is a cautionary warning like "Watch your step." It could be a desire to share something not for public hearing. Or the meeting will begin in five minutes. It may be a matter of great importance or small. Both demand that we listen to the speaker. and give some response.

So loud or intrusive are these attention-getters that they all but drown out the Voice of the One who most seeks our attention. God. His voice may come in a whisper rather than a shout, though at times God used both to call His people to attend to Him. God has expressed His message with blessing and with judgment. He really wants our attention. He has much in His heart to share.

The ways He chooses to get our attention are varied and sometimes rather startling. As God sought the attention of His people on their journey out of captivity, scripture gives us this amazing insight into an event when His people gathered at the base of Mount Sinai.

"So, it came about on the morning of the third day the thunder and lightning flashed, and a thick cloud was upon the mountain, and a loud trumpet sounded...Mount Sinai was al smoke since the Lord had ascended upon it in fire. The whole mountain shook violently. When the sound of the trumpet grew louder and louder, Moses spoke and God answered him with thunder." (Exodus 19:16-19)

Now that was surely an attention-getter! We are told that the people shook with terror. But God also speaks in whispers as He did to the Prophet Elijah when he huddled in a cave in fear.

"God said to Elijah, 'Go stand on the mountain before the Lord.' As God passed by a mighty wind shook the mountain so that the rocks broke around Elijah. But the Lord was not in the wind. And after the wind came an earthquake, but God was not in the earthquake. And after the earthquake came fire, but God was not in the fire. And after the fire the sound of a gentle blowing...and the Voice of God said to him, 'What are you doing here?'" (1Kings 19:9-13)

Moses' attention was drawn by a burning bush. King Hezekiah saw that shadow of the sun on the steps recede ten steps, and then God spoke to him. For Pharaoh it took ten miraculous plagues before God had his attention.There are so many more instances in which God called someone to attend to Him. Now those were some unique attention-getters! These were not distractions. They were

God speaking to someone whose life would turn on their response to that event .

Perhaps the greatest attention-getter recorded was the star and angelic hosts that attended the birth of the Messiah The shepherds could not miss the appearance of the angels! Even non-Hebrew wise men saw the attention-getter and came to pay homage to the New King. God announced the arrival of His Son in a miraculous way!

Do you pay attention to God's attention-getters? His whispers? These attention-getters may not be as dramatic aa an earthquake or a burning bush, but that does not mean they are less significant. Just paying attention is worthless unless we respond. God expects His alerts to beckon us to do or be or go or grow or repent. We must not suffer from spiritual deafness. We mustt strain to not miss a word of what God says to our hearts. Just remember, no cave is safe from God's words.

Consider: How do you hear God? Or do you hear Him at all? Sharpen your alertness to hear His Voice!

BAA! BAA! BLACK SHEEP

We all remember the nursery rhyme, "Baa, baa, black sheep! Have you any wool? Yes, sir, yes, sir, three bags full" We've all heard descriptions of sheep like dumb, silly, timid, followers, wanderers, etc. We are told that sheep, left to wander alone will get entangled in briars, wander away and be lost, fall and be unable to get up without help. They become prey for hungry animals. And we may recall the phrase, "He's the black sheep of the family".

Yet, we see scenes like the one witnessed while driving a country road. There was the herd of sheep, no human in sight. They were all moving along as the faithful. little dog herded them to new pastures. None wandered off. They all kept together as if they knew their canine shepherd. When laden with wool, the sheep-shearing time is a welcome relief. Docilely sitting, the clippers remove the weight of wool. Both black and white wool is a coveted commodity. The sheep has no idea that in the future his coat will be worn by someone human.

What we do know is that sheep need a shepherd, someone to watch after them and keep them safe. The scripture reminds us of that.as we read of the birth of the Messiah.

"There were some shepherds staying out in the fields and keeping watch over their flock by night." (Luke 2:8)

There are many verses in the Bible which speak of sheep, often referring to humans rather than our wooly friends. The Hebrews were an agrarian, nomadic people, often moving herds from pasture to pasture in search of food. These people were called sheep by Moses when he asked God to provide a leader who would replace him.

"May the Lord, the God of the spirits of all flesh, appoint a man over the congregation who will go out and come in before them, and who will lead them so they will not be like sheep which have no shepherd." (Numbers 27:16-17)

All through their history, the Hebrews tended to wander away from their Shepherd, God. They resorted to their own wisdom and fell into sin. The Prophet Isaiah, in speaking of the Suffering Servant who would one day come, he described their need.

"All of us, like sheep, have gone astray. Each of us has turned to his own way. And the Lord has caused all of our iniquity to fall on Him." (Isaiah 53:6)

Many years before Jesus came, the Psalmist David, a shepherd himself, penned these words. He understood that shepherd-sheep relationship which was explained by Jesus many years hence.

"The Lord is my Shepherd. I shall not want He makes me lie down in green pastures. He leads me beside quiet waters. He restores my soul. He guides me in the path of righteousness for His Name sake." (Psalm 23: 1-3)

Many years passed before this Shepherd came, but when He did, life took on a new dimension. The Apostle John recorded for us in John 10 Jesus' teaching about the relationship between sheep and their Shepherd.

- The Shepherd is the doorkeeper of the fold, the one who watches over the sheep by night.
- He knows each sheep by name.
- The sheep follow Him because they know their Shepherd's voice.
- The sheep will not follow a stranger.
- The Shepherd will give His life for His sheep.

Whether we admit it or not, each of us needs a shepherd, someone trustworthy to lead us through life, provide safety, and ease our fears. We are those sheep, and He is our Shepherd!

Question: Are you following the Good Shepherd, Jesus?

Bad News or Good News?

$\mathcal{W}$hy is it that so often what we hear is bad news? The media sources seldom present any good news except as a short blurb about some "good deed". On and on they go about the awful state of our country our world, tech giants and political entities. Daily someone is maligned, criticized, made fun of, or viciously attacked. Bad news is rampant!

Christianity and Christians in general are often the targets of such speech. Politicians delight in passing laws which penalize Christian business owners for their stance. Those with charitable efforts to help others are called "do-gooders" with an agenda. Children are forbidden to speak to classmates about Jesus. Neighbors shun "those Christian folks" as religious nuts.

All bad news! Negative thoughts and actions permeate society in general and Christians in particular. Why is that? There may be a myriad of reasons we are deemed ":bad news", but here are a few of the more obvious ones.

- The Christian standard of conduct seems out of reach for "ordinary people".
- There is too much dogmatism, never bending to accept a lesser "truth".
- Christians are pharisaical in our beliefs.
- We are all talk and no real action.
- We refuse to lower our standards to match the current societal trend.
- Hypocrisy among church member is common...

Any one of the above is cause for concern since the goal is to emulate Jesus in thought and deed. When right and wrong becomes subject to opinion rather than truth, there will always be "bad news" for true believers. As Christians we have an obligation to adhere to God's standard of excellence. At the same time, we cannot let our code of conduct build a wall between us and unbelievers. The more we focus on the "bad news" around us and to us, the less we can focus on what God has designed us to be.

Jesus was the ultimate bearer of Good New. For that very reason, He was persecuted When we understand that the "bad news" hurled at us is to be expected, we can better identify with Jesus. He has a clear message... The very first statement sets the standard for us.

"I say to you, 'Love your enemies and pray for those who persecute you so that you may be sons of your Father who is in heaven; for He causes His sun to rise on the evil and the good, and sends rain on the righteous and the unrighteous." (Matthew 5:44-45)

Jesus' words to His followers foretold what we today must understand as well.

"If the world hates you, know that it has hated Me before it hated you...If they persecuted Me, they will also persecute you...These things they will do to you because of Me because they do not know the One who sent Me."(John 15:18,20-21)

Perhaps the main reason we hear such "bad news" spoken about us is that we have failed to show God's great love for each of His creations. Are we showing God's love in the face of the abuse? Are we kind in our replies when confronted with scorn or verbal insults? It is never too late to start being the bearers of the Good News that God is God over everyone and desires all to become His children. Let us consider our own speech and actions and decide if they emulate our Savior in attitude, word and deed.

Question: Are you more often the source of bad news or good news?

Baffled!

*W*hat is most baffling to you? Something trivial like how the red sock got in with the white washer load? Or where you put your keys, phone, or the "to do" list? Perhaps we all are baffled as to how to fix a computer glitch or the answer to a difficult question. Such "mind muddlers" can cause us great angst, sleepless nights or extra work. We fret, puzzle, inquire, seek, determined to solve the "baffle". Where do we turn for a solution? A family member, friend, policeman, teacher, minister, neighbor? We all want to be rid of the "baffle"

There is one thing that tops the list of "bafflers". It is this: Why is there such a chasm between the awesome blessings and commands of God and one's indifference, stubbornness, or inertia over obeying Him?

God, at times, roars like a lion, hammers at us with His hand, whispers gently in our ears, restates His commands to ensure clarity. Yet we go on with life as if He has not spoken. Our habits remain the same. Our hearts remain set in stubborn refusal to obey or even to acknowledge that He has spoken. Why? The Prophet Isaiah says a similar thing of God.

"O Lord, Your hand is lifted up, and yet they do not see it." (Isaiah 26:11a)

The Prophet Jeremiah characterizes such people as foolish, senseless, sightless and deaf.

"Now hear this, O foolish and senseless people, who have eyes but do not see, who have ears but do not hear." (Jer.5:21)

It is a "baffler" which has been with mankind from the beginning. Adam and Eve ignored God's command and ate forbidden fruit. Moses, many years later, lamented over the wandering Israelites refusal to listen to their God .

"Yet to this day, in spite of God's provisions, you have unhearing ears and sightless eyes." (Deuteronomy 29:2-4)

The simple answer is stubbornness of heart. There are many words in the Bible for this: stubbornness: hardness, stiff-necked, brazen-faced, uncircumcised in the heart, lacking sensibility, etc. Whatever the term used, this is neglect of the commands of God, which are set aside or replaced by our intent to "do it my way". The result is a burden of guilt which permeates all of life. When we replace God's ways with our own, we sign our own sentence of guilt. The redeeming factor of this "baffler" is the grace and mercy of God which beckons onward and upward to obedience.

"The Lord's mercy never ceases. His compassions never fail. They are new every morning. Great is Your faithfulness. The Lord is my portion, says my soul. Therefore, I have hope in Him. The Lord is good to those who wait for Him, to the person who seeks Him." (Lamentations 3:23-25)

God's anger and disappointment does not obscure His redeeming love. His love for His people is eternal. His mercies never cease. Nor does His offering of a solution in spite of our disregard for His commands. Isaiah's declaration must be ours as well.

"Behold, God is my salvation; I will trust and not be afraid. For the Lord God is my strength and my song, and He has become my salvation." (Isaiah 12:2)

Question: Are you baffled by the human condition which defies God at every hand? Or is your bafflement with God that He seems slow to answer?

BE SURE TO WASH YOUR HANDS!

*W*ash your hands! How many times have we heard that in the last COVID year? Literally thousands! As virus rages across the world, the advice of medical professionals is that for your own safety do so every time you touch someone or something. At this point we either have gotten germs from not washing or have the cleanest hands ever. Mothers through the ages have admonished their children before eating, "Wash your hands!" Germs, dirt, paint jam all seem to end up on our hands.

Hand washing has long been a tradition in many countries and cultures. It has sometimes signified cleanliness of the whole person or the status of one's beliefs. Such was the case in Jesus' time. The religious leaders were adamant that hand washing should precede eating, not because hands were dirty, but to signify one's status as a righteous Jew. When they observed Jesus' disciples not following their rules, they confronted Jesus.

"Why do Your disciples break the tradition of the elders? For they do not wash their hands when they eat bread." (Matthew 15:2)

Note that they called the washing of hands a "tradition". Jesus called the religious leaders to task, pointing out that they were transgressing the commandment of God for the sake of their tradition. He called them hypocrites!

On another occasion, as Jesus was asked to have lunch with a Pharisee, His host was shocked that Jesus had not ceremonially washed before eating the meal. Jesus' reply was forthright.

"Now you Pharisees clean the outside of the cup and of the platter, but inside of you, you are full of robbery and wickedness. You foolish ones! Did not He who made the outside make the inside also?" (Luke 11:38-39)

Jesus knew the heart of man was filled with all manner of sinful things, any of which rendered them "unclean" in the eyes of God.

"It is not what enters into the mouth that defiles a man but what proceeds out of the mouth of man." (Matthew 15:11)

The most notable hand washing episode in the Bible took place when Jesus stood before Pilate, the Roman official. Having found Jesus to be innocent of any civil wrong, Pilate wished to be rid of the matter.

"When Pilate saw that he was accomplishing nothing, but rather a riot was starting, he took water and washed his hands in front of the crowd saying, 'I am innocent of this Man's blood. See to that yourselves,'" (Matthew 27:24)

Did that act of hand washing render Pilate innocent of Jesus blood? No! The symbolism is lost as we consider the spineless ruler's decision to take no affirmative action. The outcome for Jesus would have been the same because He was destined to bear our sins on the cross. But Pilate's act serves as a warning to us. He had to live with his cowardice the rest of his life. His warning is to clean up more than our hands if we wish to be clean before God.

"Create in me a clean heart, O God, and renew a steadfast spirit within me." (Psalm 51:10)

This prayer by King David was uttered after he had been confronted about his sin. He asked to be thoroughly washed, to be as white as snow

The same must be our prayer before Holy God as we seek to be clean within and without. We must come to God with holy hands, lifted up in praise to the One whose blood cleansed us from our sins.

Challenge: Remember to wash all of yourself both inside and out!

Been There, Done That, Bought the Tee Shirt

"So, what's new with you?", we ask a friend. We hear him reply, "Nothing, just the same old stuff." Implied in this is a sort of lethargy which has invaded the life of the friend. Life seems boring, lacking color, less challenging. The daily routine has become a rut that is slowly becoming a ditch of depression.

Blah, blah, blah! Life has gone flat. Seen it all. Done it all, or tried at least. So there is nothing new. This condition has been more prevalent with the passing years as we are constantly searching for some "kick start" to our lives. This is not a new phenomenon.

A king once said, "That which has been done is that which will be done. There is nothing new under the sun." (Ecclesiastes 1:9)

These words were uttered by a man who had everything a person could want. Yet his world had turned colorless. He had "been there, done that, bought the tee shirt", so to speak. This man's name was Solomon, son of David. So despondent was he that life had become colorless, gray, lacking in joy. He had invested his life in bigger houses, grander gardens, ambitious irrigation systems, many slaves, silver and gold, and not the least, many wives.

Even becoming a great king endowed by God with great wisdom so that people from all over the territory came for advice, he was not satisfied. There was an aching void refusing to be filled.

"Vanity, vanity, all is vanity! What advantage does a man have in all of his work which he does under the sun?... All things are wearisome." (Ecclesiastes 1:1:2-3,8a)

After rambling on for many chapters in pessimism and sadness, he again repeats the lament, "All is vanity". How sad! And yet this is a scene repeated throughout mankind as we are ever seeking for more, more, more. Never satisfied and always discontented, life seems drab. Been there, done that, so what else is there?

Where is the peace Solomon's father found? Where is the peace God promised to all who rest in Him?

"The steadfast of mind You will keep in perfect peace because he trusts in You. Trust in the Lord forever, for in God, the Lord, we have an everlasting Rock." (Isaiah 26:3-4)

Ah! There's the key! Resting in God and not our own accomplishments, we find peace.

King David declared, "Those who love Your Law have great peace, and nothing causes them to stumble." (Psalm 119:165)

Will we ever learn that lesson? It seems not as the world goes from one crisis to the next. Ill content is pervasive even among the Christian community of believers. We, too, get the "blahs". Consider the advice some New Testament writers shared. Their words may resonate within us and steady our hearts to find peace.

"Let the peace of Christ rule in your hearts, to which you were indeed called in one body; and be thankful" (Colossians 3:15)

"May the Lord of Peace Himself continually grant you peace in every circumstance." (2 Thessalonians 3:16)

"Grace and peace be multiplied to you in the knowledge of God and of Jesus, our Lord, seeing that His divine power has granted to us everything pertaining to life and godliness through the true knowledge of Him who called us by His own glory and excellence." (2 Peter 1:2-3)

Question: Is your world colorless these days due to what you are observing or experiencing? Get out your spiritual crayons and let God introduce you to His panorama of color.

Between the Cross and the Crown

Have you ever been on a trip and found yourself stuck short of your intended destination? Or have you begun a task only to find that you could not complete it? Or perhaps, you have followed a lead only to discover you lost the clue to the next step? These instances are more and more common occurrences in our scattered lives. The causes for these incomplete tasks leave us in between satisfaction and dismay. The reasons are plentiful: poor planning, insufficient information, lack of resources, too little time, failure to read the directions, heeding fleshly impulses, interruptions, too hard for you alone and a reluctance to ask for help. The list of reasons is quite lengthy.

On the spiritual level, this is a BIG PROBLEM. Somewhere between redeemed and blessed, we get lost, forget the directions, fail to heed Godly advice, let busyness overtake our time with God, ignore the warning impulses of the Holy Spirit. On and on the reasons go. Rocky roads and hard places cause us to want blessings without considering what God expects, yes, demands, of a life redeemed.

In an age of short cuts and quick fixes, impatience is rampant. We forget that the Christian life is a marathon, not a sprint. The journey itself is designed to teach us and lead us closer to the One who is the true leader, wise Counselor, Guide without equal. In between the cross and the crown is the daily discipleship of a pilgrim bent on a holy destination.

A good picture of this journey to maturity in Christ and the blessings of an ordered life is the gap between childhood and adulthood. It is called adolescence, a time of learning to be what we hope to become. As most have discovered, these years are filled with challenges, adventure, discovery, and even defeat and retreat. All the while, parental supervision is at hand to bolster the journey and offer guidance and wisdom. Each lesson learned, each obedience completed, each step taken leads closer to the goal of adulthood.

So, too, we must consider the journey of the children of Jacob as they left the arduous but relatively secure land of Egypt and embarked on a journey to freedom which God had promised. Their time of wandering in the wilderness was laced with challenges, hardships, tests, and failures. All along the way was the disciplining hand of God. Setbacks came as a result of unwillingness to obey God's leadership and wanting everything to be perfect as they defined it. Obedience yielded progress and rich blessings. Between their eventual destination of the Promised Land and their journey to achieve that goal, they needed maturity of faith in their God. He noted their failures and charted their progress in the development of their relationship with Him. Was it easy? No! Did they want to quit? Yes! They even wanted to return to their bondage in Egypt rather than endure the challenges set before them. How sad! (Read Exodus!)

Such is the gap in the life of a believer. Having redemption settled, we must begin the journey across the wilderness called life. We are tasked with listening to the instructions of God as He leads us to holiness. He will shower us with blessings and discipline us according to the stubborn willfulness of our hearts. Anything less than obedience may lead to being stranded along the roadside as we retrace our steps to our present state of affairs. Progress is delayed, and devoid of the peace that accompanies obedience to the King of Kings. Like the Hebrew wanderers, there is a delay in reaching the end of our journey where we will receive the crown of life promised to those who complete the trek across the wilderness. We journey with many other pilgrims whose aim is the same. We want to echo the Apostle Paul's statement.

"I have fought the good fight. I have finished the course. I have kept the faith. Therefore, there is laid up for me the crown of righteousness which the Lord, the righteous Judge, will award to me on that day, and not only to me but to all who have loved His appearing."((2 Timothy 4:7-8)

Question: Are you running well? How big is the gap between wholeness with God and where you are today?

BLESSED!

"I'm blessed up one side and down the other." This is the answer given by a friend when asked the question, "How are you?" There was no doubt in my mind that he meant it, but what does he mean by that response? What exactly is it to "be blessed"?

Blessed defined: means spiritually prosperous with joy and satisfaction in God's favor and grace regardless of outward condition or circumstances.

Matthew recorded Jesus' definition of those who are blessed. They are:

- Poor in spirit, that is, humble in their approach to life.
- Mourners, those who need comforting
- Meek, mild mannered and longsuffering
- Hungry and thirsty for righteousness
- Pure in heart
- Makers of peace, not just lovers of peace
- Persecuted for righteousness sake, that is, for the right reasons.
- Reviled and persecuted for the sake of our belief in Jesus

In each of these characteristics, there is an accompanying blessing, God's manner of noting and rewarding those who bear such Godly character.

It is quite a list, and one, which on a strictly human level, isn't so appealing to consider. Who of us wants to be persecuted or reviled? How many of us struggle with humility? How often do we think of ourselves as "purehearted"? How many times are our words a verbal war at someone or something? Do we hunger more for pleasure and ease than for God?

The Psalmist David, in the midst of a time of danger and distress, wrote words of admonition to all.

"O, taste and see that the Lord is good. How blessed is the man who takes refuge in Him!" (Psalm 34:8)

David's son. Solomon offered similar advice.

"Blessed is the man who finds wisdom and gains understanding." (Proverbs 3:13)

Surely we all seek to be blessed by God! But, if we define "blessed" as God does, what must we be asking for? May I suggest these?

- To wear humility as a comfortable garment, putting off my "self robe" in favor of God's garment of praise.
- To truly mourn and grieve over the sin that is rampant in my world and in my own heart. To grieve over the things which grieve the heart of God

- To hunger for the Word of God and thirst to hear Him speak into my life.
- To be able to "cut some slack" for those everyone, to be the face of mercy.
- To be washed in the blood of the Lamb of God so that no impure thought or motive remains
- To bring peace, diffuse contentions, be a calm voice in the midst of the self-motivated
- To endure persecution, verbal or otherwise, when I don't deserve it and to deflect it when I do deserve it.
- To take no offense when reviled or spoken evil of or falsely accused.

What is the reward for all of these trials of faith? Actually, the reward has already been given. We have been adopted into the Kingdom of God as heirs and joint-heirs with Jesus. Because of Jesus' sacrifice on our behalf, the riches of the Kingdom are at our disposal. Everything we need (not want) God has provided. We have protection from the "evil one". And we have the promise of eternity with Him. What a list of blessings!

Suggestion: Read Psalm 34:12-23 Meditate on its words.

BOUNDARIES: IT'S THE LAW!

*L*ife is filled with a variety of boundaries imposed by rules, regulations, laws, requirements. And yes, there are even moral boundaries though these seem to get moved at will. Boundaries are not mere suggestions. Pay your taxes. Abide by the Power of Attorney. Register to vote. Don't exceed the speed limit. Be licensed before you drive. Qualify to compete. To ignore any of these boundaries brings consequences. Even "bending the rules", sometimes called "situation ethics", is not without cost. Boundaries, AKA laws, were made for our safety and wellbeing, for record keeping, and sadly, sometimes to satisfy the whim of a legislator or boss. We cross boundaries at our own risk, and as we discover, ignorance is not an excuse. "I didn't know the rules! The sign was obscured. Others are doing it so why can't I? Who made this dumb rule anyway?" Does this sound familiar?

The policeman writing the speeding ticket doesn't care that we missed the sign. The judge imposing a sentence will not heed our pleas of innocence. If the IRS finds we cheated on our tax return they will not erase the penalty. If the medicine dose is "one pill per day", six are not better. If I step out of the boundaries while running with the football, the yards gained will not count.

Boundaries generally are not set to make us miserable or to unnecessarily confine us to an orderly behavior. They are not just suggestions. Enforcers of the law are not our enemies out to get us. There is not a category called "Punishment Police". Perhaps as we list all the categories of law makers, we place God on that list' Is that how we view God? Stern. Rigid, Vindictive. Eager to catch us in a transgression. Too lax on some and too hard on us. We need a serious attitude adjustment.

If then, God's laws are so important, why is it that we humans ignore them at will? God did make laws. They are called Commandments. These are not suggestions. Yet we blithely ignore them as if they are relegated to others or to another time. Or we arbitrarily choose which ones we will obey and which we will ignore. Often we fume at God because His boundaries "cramp our style". We whine that these laws are too strict. We may even view God as a happiness killer.

In Jesus' day, there were many laws to follow, most imposed by religious leaders in an effort to exert power over the people. The number of laws had become so cumbersome that people had lost sight of God's intent in giving them His rules to live by. For example, instead of honoring the Sabbath as a day of rest as God intended, there were now numerous laws as to how far one could walk, how much to lift, prohibition of healings, food preparation, etc. The penalty for breaking any of these laws could be as severe as ostracism from Temple worship.

Jesus is often seen challenging these man-made rules. He healed the sick even on the Sabbath. He allowed His disciples to glean grain to stave off hunger. He and His disciples did not follow the rules about ritual washing. Jesus knew that His Father's intent was not to impose unnecessary restrictions on His people, but to bring order, responsibility, and life to them.

Are we guilty of using Jesus as an example for permission to ignore the laws God has set forth? Perhaps we have decided that it is easier to ask for forgiveness than permission.

To ignore the laws of God is called sin, whether we do so on purpose or unintentionally. It is only by the grace of God in Jesus Christ that we are granted mercy and forgiveness. Often there is discipline involved as well. What is the penalty for remaining in the category of "law-breaking sinner without Jesus"?

- "The wages of sin is death, but the gift of God is eternal life through Jesys Christ our Lord." ((Romans 6:23)
- "Out of heaven God made you hear His voice that He might correct, discipline and admonish you." (Deuteronomy 4:36)
- "Such people who do not know God or ignore or refuse to obey the Gospel of the Lord Jesus Christ, these people will pay the penalty of everlasting ruin, eternal exclusion and banishment from the presence of the Lord." (2 Thessalonians 1:8-9)
- "For the Lord corrects and disciplines everyone He loves, and He punishes everyone He cherishes. You must submit to correction because God is dealing with you as His children." (Hebrews 12:6-7a)

- "For the time no discipline brings joy, but seems painful; but afterward it yields a peaceable fruit of righteousness to those who are trained by it." (Hebrews 12:11)

A final example is given by God to His chosen people to whom we find ourselves joined by our fellowship in Christ. Read Deuteronomy 28 to hear God explain the blessings of obedience and the penalties for disobedience. Who among us does not want to live in the blessings of God instead of the penalties of sin? We are blessed by our faithful adherence to God's boundaries. They are His Law!

Question: Are you a law abiding citizen of God's design? Which of God's laws is easiest for you to break?

CAMPING OUT

*C*amping out is such fun! Just the anticipation of a campfire, roasting s'mores, fresh air, and fun explorations. While
camping has in these days often turned to "glamping", an RV and all
the amenities, there is nothing to compare with the "back to nature"
adventure. This, of course, requires us to pitch a tent, large or small
to protect us from the rain, night visitors, etc. For the real diehard
campers who are minimalists, just a waterproof sheet will do, and
whatever fits in a sizeable backpack. Those folks take pride in living
off the nature around them and braving possible dangers as they
explore the beauty God has provided. Even these folks carry up-to-
date equipment to aid their outdoor time.

Tent camping is not a new idea at all. Every nomadic culture all
over the world constructs tents based on available materials and the
climate. Plains Indians used deer skins for their tents. Other tribal
groups used other animal skins. The early Hebrews, a very nomadic
people, used woven black goats' hair. It was dark inside, but there
were pinholes of light coming through the fibers. When the rains
came, the fibers shrank and sealed the tent, even the pinholes. When

one of the panels broke down, it was replaced with a new one, probably one a year.

These tents were not for "camping out". They were the family home, usually one of a small group of like tents for additional family and friends as they travelled together from place to place in search of food and water for their animals. When these ancient Hebrews looked up at the night sky and saw their tent, it was as if God had spread His tent over them to shelter and protect.

The earliest mention of Abraham, father of the Hebrews, as a tent dweller is mentioned in Genesis 13:3 as he and Sarai and Lot returned from Egypt.

"He went on his journey from the Negev, as far as Bethel, to the place where his tent had been at the beginning..." (Genesis 13:3)

The analogy of the tent permeated the religion of the Hebrews as they considered God's care for them.

"It is He (God) who sits above the circle of the earth...who stretches out the heavens like a curtain and spreads them out like a tent to dwell in." (Isaiah 40:22)

"Enlarge the place of your tent; stretch out the curtains of your dwellings; spare not. Lengthen the cords and strengthen your pegs. For you will spread abroad to the right and to the left. And your descendants will possess nations, and will resettle the desolate cities." (Isaiah 54:2-3)

This was a call to enlarge one's family, thus needing a larger tent. Just as the old ones died and new lives were added, so old tent panels were replaced with new ones. When King Hezekiah of Judah had faced illness and recovered, he wrote about it. Listen to his analogy of tent dwelling. It reflected the frailty of life.

"Like a shepherd's tent, my dwelling is pulled up and removed from me. As a weaver, I rolled up my life. He cuts me off from the loom. From day until night You (God) make an end of me." (Isaiah 38:12)

The idea of God spreading His protective "tent" over them was still very prevalent in New Testament times as well. In John's description of Jesus coming to earth to dwell among men, he described it as the Hebrew was written. Note that the word "dwelt" is replaced by the literal Hebrew phrase.

"And the Word became flesh and "spread His tent over us". And we saw His glory, glory as of the only begotten of the Father, full of grace and truth". (John 1:14)

In the same sense as the Hebrews of old, we are to be those who dwell in the shelter of God, His tent of protection and grace over us. Fortunately, we do not need to pack a back pack of provisions to camp out with Him since God has promised to supply everything we need according to the riches of His grace. As Christ dwells in our" earthly tents", we become rooted in Him. Let us echo the words of the Psalmist.

"You have been a refuge for me, a tower of strength against the enemy. Let me dwell in Your tent forever. Let me take refuge in the shelter of Your wings." (Psalm 61:3-4)

Question: Are you "camping out" with God as your true shelter and home?

CHALLENGES

*A*re you ready for a new challenge? Do I hear a groan followed by the statement, "My life has enough challenges already, thank you." Every day seems to bring a challenge of some sort. Lose those extra pounds. Conquer fear of public speaking. Be a better wife,,husband, friend or employee. Learn a new skill. Complete that novel. All of us see challenges and set goals to accomplish what looms as a real challenge to time, brainpower, skill, knowledge, heart. Sadly, so often these challenges remain unrealized or set aside due to obstacles which seem too much to tackle.

Have you ever felt like a quitter? Probably, if you set New Year's resolutions. How many of these go unrealized, if undertaken at all? Perhaps the overriding reason beyond our slothfulness is that we seek help in the wrong places.

This attitude of defeat permeates the Christin life as well. We feel as if we will never measure up to the standards God has set for us. There seem to be so many "rules and regulations" to follow. Sometimes we fail to understand the purpose behind the challenges we have read in scripture. The language befuddles us. Let's look at a few examples.

- Jesus said, "You are the salt of the earth; but if the salt has become tasteless, how can it be made salt again?" (Matthew 5:13)
- Jesus said, "You are the light of the world. A city set on a hill cannot be hidden. Nor does anyone light a lamp and put it under a basket, but on a lampstand, and it gives light to all who are in the house." (Matthew 5:14-15)
- The Apostle Peter said, If you have tasted the kindness of the Lord, He who came as a Living Stone rejected by men, you also are living stones being built up as a spiritual house for a holy priesthood to offer up spiritual sacrifices acceptable to God through Christ Jesus." (1 Peter 2:3-4)

In a few short verses we are called salt, light, and stones, and challenged to use these qualities for kingdom purposes. Often these are sometimes used to describe our disposition rather than being viewed as a Godly quality. Has anyone ever called your language too salty? Have you ever been described as stubborn as a rock? Have you ever hidden your light out of fear?

Yet our Bibles record these as challenges to live a life of usefulness to God and man. We are, in effect, told to influence our world! The best part of this challenge is that God equips us to do just that. He gifts us, leads us, encourages and admonishes us, shelters us under His wings to protect us spiritually.

Peter, in his letter to the persecuted and exiled believers, described them as "God's own possession" .He was reminding them of the One to whom they belong. (1 Peter 2:9)

Let's present a few challenges to consider as you examine you own status as one who belongs to God.

1. If you were salt and light to those around you, would they be drawn to you or repelled by your manner?
2. Are you willing to set self aside in order to serve, "season", or heal someone in Jesus' Name?
3. Is anything too great a sacrifice for you to pursue Jesus' command to be salt and light
4. Are you willing to set self aside in order to serve, "season", or heal someone in Jesus' Name?
5. Is anything too great a sacrifice for you to pursue Jesus' commands to be salt and light?

CHOSEN

I am chosen! What does that mean? As children on the playground, we longed to be chosen for a particular team, the winning one, of course. To not be chosen until the very last brought a feeling of shame as not being good enough. To be chosen was an honor, a privilege bestowed by the captain.

In choosing a life mate we carefully review our mental list of qualities we hope for. Handsome, smart, strong, loving, willing to work out differences, supportive, and foremost, loves God. In almost 100% of these instances our choices include qualifications, likes and dislikes, wishes and longings. This "must have" qualities are deemed vital to a sustained and healthy relationship.

But what about being chosen by God? Who gets chosen and why?

The Apostle Paul wrote these words to the believers in Ephesus some of whom were Hebrews and some Gentiles.

"Even as God chose us for Himself before the foundation of the world that we should be holy (set apart) in His sight, above reproach before Him in love. He foreordained (chose beforehand) us to be adopted as His own children through Jesus Christ in accordance with His will." (Ephesians 1:4-5)

We were chosen! Even before we were a twinkle in our mother's eye, God chose us! Even knowing our traits, our weaknesses, our abilities, He chose us! What an humbling thought!

What does this chosen status mean? It means that we don't have to qualify or earn God's grace.

"For by grace are you saved and that not of your own doing. It is the gift of God not as a result of works so that no one may boast." (Ephesians 2:8)

We aren't left behind because of some lack. He knew us and chose us anyway because He formed us to reflect His image. We were chosen on His own terms, not ours. That one thought should forever be the driving force to seek us to please Him, to love Him, to praise Him, to thank Him. And it should be the impetus for us to share this great news with others.

Verses 11 and 12 in Ephesians 1 continues this thought.

"We have obtained an inheritance, having been predestined, (chosen beforehand) according to His purpose, who works all things after the counsel of His will, to the end that we who were the first to hope in Christ, would be to the praise of His glory..."

It is a rich heritage filled with the abundant mercy and grace of God who sent His Son to provide for us all of the blessings, guidance, support, and strength needed to live out His choice of us.

On a spiritual level and in one's daily life, what does that look like? In other words, what are God's expectations? For starters, He looks for obedience to His laws. Then He stands ready to forgive when we repent after sin has marred our lives. He expects a willingness to submit to discipline when needed and without whining That is a big hurdle for us since no one really enjoys discipline when applied. To reject any of the above is in effect to say to God, "I do not wish to be chosen for Your team It is too hard. The expectations are too great. I am afraid of failure..."

God's chosen people, the Hebrews, did not value their chosen status. And they suffered the consequences of God's keen disapproval of their life choices. Repeatedly God brought hard discipline to them to remind them of their choices to reject Him for worldly ways. Jesus came to give them visible proof of God's intent, but they rejected Him. Even today, many Jews still deny the Messiah as the Promised One, chosen of God to provide their salvation.

We can opt out of the status of "chosen", rejecting the marvelous blessings God has for us, the richness of His grace and mercy, the resources He provides for us daily. Or we can celebrate that chosen status by putting our lives in His hands to do with as He wills. It is literally a choice of life or death. The choice is ours.

Question: Are you counted among those who have chosen to embrace God's choice of you? What difference has that made in your life?

Citizen of the Kingdom

What comes to mind when you think of a kingdom? A King or Queen? Royalty? Pomp and pageantry? Palaces and servants? Crowns and scepters? Absolute rule? As a parent I may help my little daughter dress up like a princess, complete with a pretty crown made from paper. She feels like a princess without really understanding what that really means. To her it is just make-believe fun! She has no duties and no thought of inheriting the title of "Queen".

Even today, we have such a limited concept of what a kingdom is. We sometimes see through the eyes of a royal event such as we witnessed with the funeral of Prince Phillip of England. It was complete with formal horns announcing the arrival of the procession attended by the Palace Guard, horns of certain sound, and the parade of the royal family behind the vehicle carrying the casket of the Prince. For us in America it was an amazing show, but for the English, it was what was expected of royalty.

The concept of kingdom is one of the most, if not the most, important, concept in the New Testament. In English it has to do with territory or rulership over an area of land. But in Hebrew thought it is God ruling in the lives of men and women. Those ruled by God are "in the Kingdom". This Kingdom is evidenced by signs and wonders, miracles and laws. Wherever God's power is demonstrated, there is His Kingdom.

In the same way, when people saw Jesus in action, they saw the Kingdom at work. This is what Jesus meant when He said, "Say to them, The Kingdom is near you." (Luke 10:9) These were words Jesus spoke as He sent His disciples out ahead of Him into the towns and villages He would later visit. He was not saying that His Kingdom was not something they could not see, but rather that it would be intimately near them, obvious to those with spiritual eyes to see.

Jesus was laying claim to His sovereignty as King of Kings. He had come to set prisoners free, one soul at a time. So dramatic was this action that on one occasion, Jesus was accused of using demonic powers. (Luke 11:15) Why did Jesus focus on proclaiming that the Kingdom of God had arrived on earth? He did so because everyone expected the Messiah to restore their kingdom that had been wrested away by Roman rule. They knew that God had promised many years ago to anoint a King from their people to reign over all the earth.

"The scepter shall not depart from Judah, nor the ruler's staff from between His feet until Shiloh comes; and to Him shall be the obedience of the peoples." (Genesis 49:10)

"For a child will be born to us, a Son will be given, and the government will rest upon His shoulders...There will be no end to the increase of His government or of peace on the throne of David and over His kingdom to establish it and uphold it with justice and righteousness from then and forevermore. The zeal of the Lord of hosts will accomplish this." (Isaiah 9:6-7)

Jesus Himself, teaching His disciples how to pray, offered the same promise.

"Thy Kingdom come, Thy will be done on earth as it is in heaven." (Matthew 6:10)

In fact, the Jews had been praying that in a similar way for years. Their prayer began,thus.

"Therefore do we wait for You. O Lord. Our God, soon to behold Your glory, when You will remove the abominations from the earth and idols shall be exterminated, when the world shall be regenerated by the Kingdom of the Almighty, and all humankind evoke Your Name."

Jesus told several parables about the Kingdom. These teachings slowly transformed the thinking of His followers' understanding of Kingdom. (See references below)

What does this mean for us? As Christians we are now a part of that Kingdom and as such are subject to its Supreme Ruler, God. We are held accountable to Him for our adherence to His laws. The

Psalmist said, "For the Kingdom is the Lord's and He rules over the nations." (Psalm 22:28)

Examples of Jesus Kingdom parables: Matthew 13; 18:1-6, 21-35; 22:1-14; 25:1-13

Challenge: Listen to Handel's Messiah. Then describe what God's kingdom will mean for us one day.

Defend Yourself!

"**O**n garde!" So says the sword bearer when facing his opponent. In laymen's terms this means. "get ready. I am coming for you!" The opponent hopes he has adequately prepared for the forthcoming thrusts of the challenger facing him... Suitable attire. Proper stance. Sharp weapon. Personal alertness to every movement of his opponent.

Often an opponent gives no warning of the attack. The playground bully just plows ahead whether his target is ready or not. A person bent on evil gives no warning that he means harm to you. Such times cause us to ask ourselves, "How should I prepare for such attacks?" Do I need to take karate lessons? Learn to kick box? Beef up my muscles? Do target practice? For those of us who are peace-loving pacifists, no answer seems appropriate or sufficient to defend ourselves from sudden, unwarranted attack.

Some would say, "The best defense is a good offense." This is very true in life and in the realm of the Spirit as well. The Apostle Peter offered a word of warning to the persecuted Christians in Asia Minor.

"Be sober of spirit. Be on the alert. Your adversary, the devil, prowls around like a roaring lion seeking someone to devour. But resist him. Be firm in your faith, knowing that the same experiences are happening to your brethren in other places as well." (! Peter 5:8-9)

Jesus warned His disciples to be aware of false prophets, people who speak lies masked as truth.

"Beware of the false prophets who come to you in sheep's clothing, but inwardly are ravening wolves. You will know them by their fruits." (Matthew 7:15-16)

In America we have been fairly safe from attack by unbelievers or antagonistic opponents of the faith, but such assaults are increasing at an alarming rate, causing us to wonder how to prepare ourselves. What must we do to prepare ourselves for the thrusts of an opponent?

- Be alert. We read in many places in the scripture about the watchfulness of God and the admonition to us to be on the alert. Nehemiah, supervisor of the rebuilding of the wall around Jerusalem, knew there was danger from those who opposed their efforts. He said, "So I stationed men in the lowest parts of the space behind the wall, the exposed places..." (Nehemiah 4:13)

  Jesus warned His followers. "Be on the alert, for you do not know which day your Lord is coming." (Matthew 24:42)

The Apostle Paul said, "Be on the alert. Stand firm in the faith, like men, be strong." (1 Corinthians 16:13)

- <u>Be prepared.</u> We are to arm ourselves well. Ephesians 6:11-18 gives a full description of the armor we will need as we prepare to do daily battle with our arch enemy, Satan.
- <u>Resist.</u> Picture a tug-of-war in which resistance is exerted by both teams. The stronger, more determined and persistent will emerge as the winner. James said, Submit therefore to God. Resist the devil and he will flee from you." (James 4:7)

So, Christian, ""En garde!"

"Let us run the race set before us, fixing our eyes on Jesus, the Author and Perfecter of our faith." Hebrews 12:1-2)

Question: Are you prepared to defend your faith in God?

Did I Hear You Right?

id I hear you right? That question is not about the degree of hearing but what the message meant. In other words, "What do you want to impart from what you just said?" That may be dependent on our attention to it or the language used. It may also be due to the extraordinary character of the message delivered.

For most of us as Christians the hardest thing is to be certain we have heard the Lord clearly. Since we must rely on words spoken to our spirits and not our ears, we waver as to the answer to our pleas. "Surely God didn't mean that." Have you ever had that thought? Or perhaps, we may wonder if God is speaking at all amidst the cacophony of worldly sounds. Fear may hold us back from receiving the truth. Usually, we want some proof that we have heard rightly.

There were numerous times in the scripture when this important question could have been or was asked of God. One of the most remarkable stories in the Old Testament is about a man who had just such a dilemma. Gideon was a man living in time when judges ruled Israel. He was laboring in the fields of his father, not a thought as to what was about to change his life forever. God addressed Gideon as a man of courage. Gideon's response was much like ours may be.

"Who me, Lord? I am a nobody, the least in my father's house" (Judges 6:15 paraphrased)

Even with God's reassurance, Gideon wanted proof. Had he heard God right? In spite of God's reassurance that He would be with him all the way, Gideon made a bold request, one we hesitate to make lest it proves futile.

"Please show me a sign that it is really You, God, who is talking to me." (Judges 6:17)

Caution! Don't pray such a prayer unless you want an answer. And consider that the answer may not be the one you expected. Gideon was given a task that he considered dangerous. He was to destroy the altars of the false gods in his neighborhood. Even with God's reassurance, Gideon was afraid to do this in the daylight hours. He waited until night to do as the Lord commanded, but in the end he did obey.

Verse 14 reveals an amazing change in Gideon brought on by God's Spirit. As the Midianites and Amalekites joined forces to retaliate against Gideon, the Spirit of the Lord clothed Gideon and took possession of him . You would think that would be enough, but no, Gideon wanted further proof of God's help.

The story of the wet and dry fleeces is the sign Gideon requested. For us, this seems strange and even dangerous. It seems more like a challenge of God's sincerity and reliability. Gideon himself might have had that thought because he asked God not to be mad at him. (Judges 6:36-40)

Chapter 7 records the story of the defeat of the enemies coming against Gideon, and of Gideon's victory. Because of this great victory the men of Israel wanted to make Gideon their ruler. They were crediting the wrong source for the victory! (There is a lesson here for us. Whom do we credit for the victories in our lives?

After the victory, the men of Israel wanted to make Gideon ruler over them to thank him for their safety. However, Gideon set them straight. He knew who had really won the victory.

"I will not rule over you; nor shall my son rule over you. The Lord shall rule over you." (Judges 8:22-23)

The postscript is this:

"The land had peace and rest for forty years in the days of Gideon." (Judgrs(8:28)

Read Judges 6-8. Then ask God to help you hear Him speak into your life what he has for you day by day, hour by hour, regardless of the situation. Then, with courage and the assurance of God, go forth to do battle with the challenges and opportunities presented daily. Be sure that God gets the credit for any and all success.

A challenge: As you read the Bible look for instances when someone might have asked either out loud or in their heart "Did I hear you right, Lord?"

Divide and Conquer
Unite and Reign

Long a strategy of conflicts and wars, "divide and conquer" has been an effective tool in the subduing of an opponent. Battles have been fought when an army of few went up against a much larger enemy. Often in the dividing, confusion reigned, adding to the opportunity for victory.

This concept has also been prevalent in the war of ideologies. and philosophies. Companies split apart, families break apart, institutions collapse, and all too sadly, churches are destroyed because of the divisions of things important and trivial. Color of the new carpet. Who will lead the choir. Which songs we will sing. Doctrinal divides. Often division survives, and the church becomes weaker and less effective. This is true in companies and families, clubs and institutions, politics and government. Each entity, intent on conquering a position, a rank, a country, etc. finds that often to divide does not mean to conquer.

Behind all of this urge to be right, be first, in the lead, best, chief of the clan is the great divider, Satan. His tactic is and always has been to divide and conquer. Biblical examples abound.

- Satan divided Adam and Eve from their relationship with God
- Sin divided Cain and Abel and Jacob and Esau.
- The desire to have one's own way caused the division of the kingdoms in Israel into Northern and Southern. Both were weakened by this.
- Division in beliefs caused a clash between Pharisees and Saducees.
- Division in the churches in the New Testament caused bitterness and mistrust.
- Division between Paul and Barnabas caused the breakup of their team.

In each of these instances, harm was done to one or both parties. On rare occasions God instructed His people to divide and conquer, promising victory. Joshua's instructions to the Hebrews as they went to conquer the city of Ai is an example. He divided the men, taking one group to draw the enemy out of the city, and the other to wait in ambush to take possession of the city left unprotected. (Joshua 8:1-8)

Even as Joshua faced his old age, he had these words of wisdom to share with the hardheaded Hebrews.

"If it is disagreeable in your sight to serve the Lord, choose for yourselves this day whom you will serve...but as for me and my house, we will serve the Lord." (Joshua 24:15)

Even a divided mind is the "devil's playground". Recorded in Matthew's gospel, Jesus addresses the issue of division.

"No one can serve two masters; for he will either hate the one and love the other, or he will be devoted to one and despise the other. You cannot serve both God and mammon (wealth)." (Matthew 6:24)

On another occasion Jesus spoke of the division which will occur when He returns in glory to reign over His Kingdom.

"All the nations will be gathered before Him; and He will separate them from one another as the shepherd separates the sheep and the goats. And He will put the sheep on His right, and the goats on the left. Then the King will say to those on the right, 'Come, you who are blessed of my Father. Inherit the kingdom prepared for you from the foundation of the world." (Matthew 25:31-34)

What is the massage for us? If we are to be "more than conquerors through Him who loved us" we must unite our hearts in love. Jesus prayed for His disciples that they would be 'perfected in unity as proof that He was sent from the Father." (John 17:23) We must lay aside our desire to win, be first, on top of the order. In its place we must be united in Christ for the sake of righteousness.

"Behold, how pleasant it is for brothers to dwell together in unity." (Psalm 133:1)

"Put on love which is the perfect bond of unity. Let the peace of Christ rule in your hearts to which you were indeed called in one body." (Colossians 3:14-15)

Question: Have you ever been a "divider" when you should have been a voice to unite? Was God pleased?

"DO-OVERS"

Our lives seem filled with endless opportunities to do over again something we have messed up. Crooked cuts of a saw. Too little seasoning in the soup. Failure on a test. Omitting a vital element in our job assignment. Missing the mark aimed for. Groaning, we exclaim, "I wish I had done this right the first time!" Thankfully, most of our mistakes requiring "do-overs" fix the problem without too much effort or delay. We can retake the test, add seasoning where needed, recut the piece of wood, rethink the job assignment, shoot another arrow at the mark. "Do-overs" are great!

In a "throw-away society" often we just pitch out the mistake and find a replacement. However, sometimes there is not the opportunity to do something over again with greater success. We may not be able to find another substitute for our mistake. Sometimes our mistakes and omissions are irreversible, much to our dismay.

Consider on a spiritual level the implications of needing a "do-over". Throughout the history of God's people, we read that sin captured their hearts and ultimately resulted in begging God for a "do-over".

Over and over again they ignored the manual of commands God had given them to live by. Even in the face of promised blessings, the Hebrews went their own way. Chance after chance! God warned, admonished. Yet they continued to bow down to false idols and adopt the ways of their pagan neighbors. We see the cycle of disobedience, disaster, repentance, then pleading with God, for mercy repeated and repeated. It is interesting to note that one must reach the end of the line, so to speak, before being willing to bend to God's commands. This sad pronouncement is made in the last verse of the book of Judges.

"In those days there was no king in Israel. Everyone did what was right in his own eyes." (Judges 21:25)

The consequences of refusing "do-overs" results in disaster. Jeremiah the Prophet recorded one of the saddest stories of this disobedience. He wrote to King Jehoiakim a reminder of God's Laws. He sent his representative, Baruch, with the message to the king in hopes that the king would heed the word of the Lord. Baruch dutifully, and probably with great trepidation, read all that Jeremiah had written to the king and his court. (Jeremiah 36:1-21)

What did the king do?

"When Jehudi had read only three or four columns, the king cut it with a knife and threw it into the fire that was in the brazier until all the scroll was consumed by fire." (Jeremiah 36:23)

He threw the scroll into the fire! He destroyed not only the scroll but sealed his own fate as well. The response of the Lord to such blatant refusal of a chance for a "do-over" was severe.

God instructed Jeremiah to write a second letter to the king containing God's response to such sinful refusal to listen. For King Jehoiakim, there would be exile and death for him and for his mother. No one of his line would ever rule Israel. Calamity would come upon all of his descendants. (Jeremiah 22:24-26)

To ignore God's commands or explain them away brings dire results. And the refusal to accept a chance to do over whatever has put us in peril is asking for God to pass His judgment on us. The missed opportunities to ask our merciful God for a "do-over" not only greatly impacts our own spiritual lives but also influences negatively those who observe us. To need a "do-over" for an everyday mistake is one thing. But to continue to ignore God's offers of a "do-over" (It is called repentance and forgiveness) is to be subject to God's judgment. What punishment awaits the stubborn refusals and what blessings await those who are willing to accept God's offer of a "do-over"!

Question: Do you need a "do-over" with God? What are you waiting for? Get started!

DOES THAT SOUND FAMILIAR?

*T*he most asked question is "Why?" Why did you do that? Why must I obey? Why is this thing broken? Why is there such a mess in here? Why did this happen to me? Why? Why? Why? Often the question is asked in anger, distress, frustration, or angst. Most of the time the answer we get is not that satisfying. It is usually begun with the word "because..." And most often the question or answer has resulted from something gone wrong or someone who has erred or displeased us.

It is an age-old question, one most of us have asked... Full of angst, the Psalmist had a "why" question for God.

"Why do You stand afar off, O Lord? Why do you hide Yourself in times of trouble?" (Psalm 10:1)

It appeared to the Psalmist that God was in hiding just at the time His presence was needed. This is not the singular time such a question was asked of God. Here are just a few examples from the Psalms.

"My God. My God, why have You forsaken me? Far from my deliverance are the words of my groaning." (Psalm 22:1)

"Why are the nations in an uproar?" (Psalm 2:1)

"I will say to God, my Rock, 'Why have You forgotten me?'" (Psalm 42:9)

"O God, why have You rejected us forever?" (Psalm 74:1)

Often following the poignant question, the Psalmist enumerates the things he sees as needing God's attention. Attention is called to the wicked who prey on the weak, greedy men who curse God, innocent victims, the oppression of God's people by an enemy. Sometimes the question is asked of a personal need. And often this plea was the last resort when oppressed or in trouble as if they said, "We've tried everything else. Let's ask God for help."

The most heart-rending question of all was Jesus' question as He hung on the cruel cross, experiencing agony and shame. You will recognize the quote as from the above Psalm 22.

"My God, My God, why have You forsaken me?" (Matthew 27:46)

God was silent as His Son, His Beloved Son, took on all the sins of the world. Jesus became sin that we might be forgiven of our sin. That separation was agony for Jesus who had never been separated from Father. And it was the agony of His Father as well.

Today we ask the "why" question in the same way the Psalmist asked. As we look on all of the brokenness of our world, all of the oppressed people, the forgotten ones, the wicked who seem to prosper when the rest of us struggle to make ends meet, etc. We look around and wonder where God is. Why has He not punished the wicked?. Why is this sickness here? Why is there such hatred among us? Why don't You do something? It seems that God is indifferent to such cries. But He is not! The Psalmist knew what we, too, must recognize. God sees the pain and suffering, and He sees the sin in human hearts. He was, is, and ever will be faithful. On that belief the Psalmist proclaims.

"The Lord is King forever...He has heard the cries of the humble of heart and will act to vindicate the oppressed." (Psalm 10:17-18)

Note that the Psalmist answered his own question as he recognized the presence of God was there all along. The familiar question "why?" does not escape His ears. His trust is in God even when he does not get an immediate answer from God.

It is right that we cry out about the evil in our day and to pray for God to intercede. It is also a time that, as we wait for God's justice, we present to the world a picture of righteousness from our own lives. The God who watches over us will sustain us through those tough questions. We must trust that one day "He will break the arm of the wicked". He indeed will answer our question.

Question: What is your biggest "why" question? What answer do you seek from God?

Do's and Don'ts Still Apply

When we were young children growing up there seemed to
be such a long list of "do's and don'ts" Most of those were
issued to help us successfully navigate the world without suffering
harm. Some were given to encourage growth in a particular area
of skills or activities. Don't forget to make your bed. Don't touch
the hot stove. Be sure to tie your shoes so you will not trip. Don't
run into the street before looking both ways. Each day the list grew.
When these commands were breeched, there followed an "I told you
so!", the reminder that we messed up or were disobedient.

Sometimes there was the vow by the youngster, "One day when I
am a parent, I won't be so strict with my children!" In truth, when
that "one day" comes, we begin to understand why our parents were
so careful to show us the way to live with the best results. The new
parent realizes that the "do's and don'ts" still apply, generation after
generation.

The same is true of the Word of God, our Heavenly Father's "do's
and don'ts". Many hundreds of years ago God gave His people, the
Hebrews, rules to live by. There were do's and don'ts about foods,

social contacts, families, judgments, neighbors, feasts and holy days, treatment of strangers, etc. All of these were not given to restrict the people, but to help them live fruitful and safe lives. What to us may seem harsh or restrictive was meant by God to keep them from harm and to live an orderly existence. As they prepared to enter the Land of Promise, Moses, their leader for all of the more than 40 wilderness years, spoke to the people about this issue of laws.

"Now this is the commandment, the statutes, and the judgments which the Lord your God has commanded me to teach you...so that you and your son and grandson might fear the Lord your God to keep all His statutes and His commands all the days of your life, and that your days may be prolonged. O Israel, you should listen and be careful to do it, that it may be well with you and that you may multiply greatly..." (Deuteronomy 6:1-2)

Moses' speech was long and specific. It concluded in Deuteronomy 11 by telling the Hebrews what would happen if they obeyed and what would happen to them if they were disobedient. Neither you nor I would care to experience the curses part, yet that is what eventually happened to the Hebrews as their disobedience multiplied more and more.

Today we are often prone to disregard all of the many 'do's and don'ts" God gave His people. "They no longer apply", we say. Perhaps the reason is that we try to take them out of the time in which they were written, when health practices, sanitation, and lawful behavior were lacking. But when we look through the lens of wisdom, we see that many of these "do's and don'ts" are indeed still true today. The sad truth is that even though they should still apply, we have refused to follow the wisdom God had in their use.

As examples, consider our abuse of women, the abortion of babes in the womb, the corruption of the law and judges who lord over us, the disregard of healthy eating habits, the lack of neighborliness and care of widows and orphans, the failure to worship our Creator. On and on the list may go as we consider how far we have come from what God intended as a holy way of life.

Jesus pointed to the Law of God as He taught His followers on the mountain. They needed to hear this because of the many changes which would come after Jesus was crucified and ascended to His Father.

"Do not think that I came to abolish the Law or the Prophets. I did not come to abolish the Law but to fulfill. For truly, I say to you, until heaven and earth pass away, not the smallest letter or stroke shall pass from this Law until all is accomplished." (Matthew 5:17-18)

The day will come when Jesus will return and all will be put right again. Until then, we are to heed the "do's and don'ts" God has scattered throughout His Word. When we fail to do so we cut off the oxygen which gives us direction for our lives. Before, you dismiss out of hand what God has said, let Him speak to your heart about you own obedience and what His "do's and don'ts" mean for us today.

Question: Are you a law-abiding citizen of the Kingdom of God?

EAT HEARTILY!

*H*ave a good appetite? Eat heartily! We love to eat, especially those delicious fatty, calorie-filled yummies. Who wouldn't love to hear those words! After all, we need nourishment. That, however, isn't a message for those of us who struggle with the bulging waistline and unwanted pounds of fat. Hmm! What are the qualifiers?

- Hold the mayo
- Try fat-free
- No sugar, please
- Lighter and less taste

Instead, daily we are encouraged to try this or that new food combination which is sure to satisfy our longings. Have you ever counted the calories in one of those super big, calorie-loaded hamburgers? Wow! However, it might surprise you to know that such hearty eating enhances good health and quality of life. By now you are thinking, "Bring I on! Let the eating begin!"

Actually, these thoughts must be applied spiritually. The benefits of such a diet are eternal. From the Garden of Eden where Adam and Eve had plenty of choices of food but chose the forbidden fruit to Revelation where we believers are invited to eat at a banquet with the King of Kings, spiritual food is a real and vital factor for everyone in order to maintain good spiritual health.

Our insatiable appetite for rich, tasty food is the subject of many stories in the Bible. The Israelites journeying through the wilderness, complained to their leaders about their hunger.

"Would that we had died in the land of Egypt where we sat by the pots of meat and filled up on bread! You have brought us into this wilderness to kill all of us with hunger!" (Exodus 16:2-3)

God heard their pleas and provided food for them, manna and quail enough for each day, no more and no less.

There are even good examples of healthy eating in the Bible. Consider the story of Daniel and his friends who were offered the tastiest meal their captors could supply. Knowing that partaking of the king's rich food and wine would defile him, Daniel sought permission to abstain. He and his friends ate a diet of vegetables and water for ten days. At the end of the time not only did they look healthier than the youths who had eaten the King's food, they had actually put on a few pounds! Even the King was impressed! (Daniel 1:8-20)

Jesus, fed the multitude with spiritual food, the words of life, and then fed the large crowd a physical meal with a little boy's lunch I don't think anyone there was calorie-conscious or dissatisfied with his meal. All were grateful for the food since there was no convenient McDonalds nearby. There were even left-overs! The One who is the Bread of Life had fed them! (Matthew 14:14-20; John 6:35)

The promise of eating and drinking at table with the Lord is a thought almost overwhelming to consider. Jesus Himself extended the invitation to all who remain true to Him to the end.

"You are those who have stood by Me in My trials; and just as My Father has granted Me a Kingdom, I grant you that you may eat and drink at My table in My Kingdom." (Luke 22:28-30)

A final reminder about food comes from the Apostle Paul.

"The Kingdom of God is not eating and drinking but righteousness, peace, and joy in the Holy Spirit." (Romans 14:17)

We are to eat heartily as unto the Lord, knowing that our bodies are temples made for Him. He is our source of spiritual food. (I Corinthians 3:16)

Challenge: Search the scriptures to see what else the writers had to say about food, the true food we need.

ENTERTAINING OR VITALLY IMPORTANT?

Why is the cinema more interesting or exciting than church? Why are the scenes more gripping or inspiring? Why do we spend more time staring at the television or I Pad or phone than we do in the reading of the Word of God or in the worship of our Creator? Why do we cheer and yell wildly at a football game, but sit in stony silence at the words from the pulpit? Church used to be the place we went to settle the questions of life and death. Has church changed from the place we find comfort and answers to the perplexities of life, or have we changed in our outlook? What has happened?

A look at the early church after Jesus' ascension may provide some answers. As often as the new believers gathered to partake of a meal together, that was not their focus. Their attention was riveted on what the Apostles were sharing about the Messiah. That message was straightforward and singular in intent. " Believe in Jesus, who He is and what He has done so that you may have life." Though we do not know in detail what those early days were like, we do know that the new believers hungered for the truth of God. They met in one accord. They shared what they had. Deacons ministered to the widows, orphans and strangers among them. They prayed together, seeking unity and a greater faith. It was a time of being able to share one's heart openly without being judged and to ask the hard questions without fear of ridicule. (Read Acts)

Does that look like the church of today? Not very often! We have sought to make church a feel-good social gathering where the problems that trouble us are hidden from any who might be critical. We have inserted entertainment in the place of deep delving into the Word of God. In our attempts to please the masses, we have offered a party or a picnic or blow-up kiddie toys instead of pleading for their souls.

We prefer order to the restless presence of our God. We opt for cozy and comfortable instead of facing the blunt, often disturbing truth of God's Word. When God's Spirit seeks to invade our presence, we try not to let Him get us too excited lest we embarrass ourselves. Often we try to explain away what we do not understand or think it was meant for "another time".

We talk too much and listen too little. Bouncing into the presence of Holy God, we present our list of requests which sometimes seem more like demands. We have not taken the time to ask God how we should pray or what we should pray for. And there is little time allotted to meditation or listening for God to speak. The descriptions above are meant in love to help us distinguish what is vitally important from what is contrived for comfort.

Where is our sense of expectancy? Do we sense that God is with us, among us to bless and instruct and comfort? Or do we go to church out of duty or habit rather than a sense of expectancy about what we may hear. Dealing with God can sometimes be "messy", not easily packaged. Hiding our blemishes, we are hiding from others but are not hidden from God... The person next to us may not notice our warts, but the God who made us sees all and loves us unconditionally.

Divisions among us prohibit the Spirit of God from working in our midst. Jesus' prayer was that we would be one as He and the Father are One. That oneness can only happen if we lay aside our wants and desires, and let God speak into our lives. The delight and wonder that ensues from hearing God speak and recognizing our place in His plan is a joy like no other. Then church gets really exciting! We delight in worship, and share freely with other believers. We are not alarmed to hear a cheer for God or a loud "Amen". Arms are raised in praise and thanksgiving to our God as we worship. God's ears are attuned to our praise. It pleases Him that His people hunger after Him.

All of this is not to say that church cannot be entertaining as long as what is being entertained are our hearts and souls as they soak up the Word of God. Let's give a shout out to God! "Father, You are awesome! You are faithful! You are caring! We love You!

Question: What is "church" like for you? Are you being fed from the Word of God and challenged to press on to a more consistent life in Him?

Equipped for the Times

*T*hese are perilous times in which we live. Danger lurks around every corner, and those who bring evil are clothed in masks of "right". On both sides of any issue are those who loudly proclaim their "truth", challenging us to believe. Threats of impending doom attend their words and actions as if we will be very sorry if we do not agree.

Who among us has not prayed for Divine protection and for wisdom to discern our enemies? Casting our trust on God who alone is able to keep us from falling, we nevertheless wonder if we have done all we can do to equip ourselves for the battles ahead.

What does a well equipped and prepared Christian look like? What characterizes those who will be "mighty men of valor", heroes of our times, stalwart bastions of faith in a faithless age? 1 Chronicles 12 records some important characteristics of such valiant soldiers of God. records that They were characterized as "a great army like unto the army of God". Why did the historian picture them in that way?

- They were trained for war, proficient in the use of the implements of war. In their case these might have been spears, shields, and arrows. Their determination was written on their faces. They were physically fit, fleet of foot, and with a proven record of bravery. They were sure of the righteousness of their cause.

- They were men who understood the times. They had knowledge of what Israel should do. How very important that is! This is an awareness of the hearts of mankind within the culture of their day. It enabled them to recognize the wiles of the enemy or the heart of an ally. Such discernment provided a vision of their course of action because they knew God's heart for His people. We would say today that they had a Christian world view.

- They served with an undivided heart. These were not fair weather soldiers who enlisted for good times and easy battles. They were committed for the long haul, confident of their leader, and prepared to pay the price of victory. There was no conflict of interest in them. They were not fence sitters or wishy-washy agents.

- They came with a perfect heart. That means they came with the sole predetermined purpose of making David the king. Theirs was a cause ordained of God. They were single minded in their mission.

What a list of characteristics! From it we must ask ourselves the following questions.

- Are we prepared to wage the kind of war the scripture describes, the one "not of flesh and blood, but against

rulers, against powers, against the world forces of darkness, the spiritual forces of wickedness in heavenly places"?
(Ephesians 6:12)

- Are we proficient in the use of the weapons at our disposal to
  combat such enemies of God? Are we wearing the armor of
  God and using as our defense the "breastplate of righteousness, shield of faith, helmet of salvation, and the sword of
  the Spirit which is the Word of God"? (Ephesians 6:13-17)

- Can we discern the times in which we live and recognize
  the intents of those who war against the purposes of God?
  Can we distinguish foes from allies? Will we join the "eat,
  drink, and be merry" crowd while the world ascribes to the
  notion that everything will be all right? Can we see the
  handwriting on the wall and realize that the time is short
  before the King of Kings comes again to judge the world
  and all its peoples?

- Is the face and heart we present to the world undivided,
  convinced of the truth of the Word of God? Are we able to
  articulate that truth with clarity?

- Are we settled as to the mission we have been given to disciple the world in the knowledge of Christ, or are we still
  unclear as to our individual responsibility is? We have been
  commanded to be lights in a dark world, cities set on a hill
  for all to see. We are the people of God who will give glory
  to His Name through our character and voices.

Admonition: These are weighty questions for you to consider!
God help you to look to Him who is able to keep you from falling,
and to be characterized as "mighty men and women of valor".

Examining the
Corners of One's Soul

*M*ost of us, if not all of us, at one time or another examine our bodies to detect flaws. We may find an unwanted pimple, a deeply embedded splinter, a roll of fatty tissue, a crooked nose, a gray hair! Such examination mat cause a variety of responses.

- Should I consult a doctor?
- Where are the tweezers to pull out the splinter?
- I need my nose straightened!
- Oh no! I'm getting old!
- Where did this extra fat come from?

We all want to be rid of the imperfections. We all seek wholeness of body by attending to every ache, pain, abnormality, flaw. The search for greater "perfection" is a strong force within us that causes us to go to great lengths to achieve "the perfect body", whatever that is.

In a far greater sense, we must examine our internal blemishes, the things which mar the soul. What is in us crying out to be tended? What lurks in the corners of our being, hiding from the healing light? What great potential is waiting for expression? There is within each of us a God-given desire for wholeness, cleansing, healing, an unblemished soul. The One who made us wills it so.

Why then do we resist the examination of our innermost being? Why do we resist probing the thorns or infections which often emerge to indicate lack of perfection? These are indicators of poor spiritual health. Is it fear which holds us back? Perhaps complacency or resignation to the status quo are the enemies of our souls. Have we bought into the Enemy's lie that we will never be any good, much less achieve perfection. He whispers condemnation over our desires, past failures, efforts to improve.

Do we dare lift off the covering of the corners of our soul to discover the truth and allow healing to begin? The Psalmist David thought himself to be a man of integrity and a strong trust in God. So he made a specific request of the Lord.

"Examine me, O Lord, and try me. Test my mind and my heart." (Psalm 26:3)

That is a bold request, to be sure! He asked God to see the most obscure corners of his soul and render His verdict. Can you even imagine the consequences of such an examination?

Many years later the Prophet Jeremiah spoke of just such an examination as he questioned God about His take on the injustices which Jeremiah thought needed God's judgment. Like David, Jeremiah presented himself as one whose life was in accord with what should be.

"You know me, O Lord. You see me and You examine the attitude of my heart .toward You". (Jeremiah 12:3)

God does indeed know us, every cell and drop of blood we possess, every hair on our head and freckle on our face, What will it require of us to probe the depths of who we ae in order to allow God to make us into who He wants us to be? It is the search of a lifetime done one day at a time with at the control. the guiding hand of our Father. In the discovery, we will find ourselves on the most awesome journey to wholeness. I dare you to lift the corners of your soul and let God take it from there o perfection.

"Test yourselves to see if you are in the faith. Examine yourselves! Or do you not recognize this about yourselves, that Jesus Christ is in you – unless indeed you fail the test." 2 Corinthians 13:5)

Challenge: Choose something about yourself in relationship with God which needs closer examination. Ask God to help you make that whole.

EXTENDING THE BOUNDARIES OF GOD'S GARDEN

A father and his young son were going to plant a garden, a first time for the boy. So Dad gave him some instructions to help him learn about plants and their growth.

"We must use only good seed if we want a healthy plant. This is how you plant them, just this deep." said Dad. "Space them apart a little so they will have room to grow. Then cover the little seed with a bit of dirt and gently water it. This will help the seeds to grow. Later we may add some nutrients to the soil and pull the weeds which seem to try to take over the little plants."

The boy nodded and carefully followed his father's instructions. A few days later, the little boy was again at the garden with Dad. His excitement at a discovery came bubbling out. "Oh, look, Dad! I see the plant peeking out of the ground! Soon we will have vegetables to eat!"

"Yes, my son, and perhaps next year we may have to enlarge our garden so we can have many more delicious things to eat." said Dad.

What an exciting thought! God gave His children the soil on which they could plant things which would sustain life.

"The Lord planted a garden toward the east in Eden, and there He placed the man He had formed. Out of the ground the Lord caused to grow every tree that is pleasing in the sight and good for food." (Genesis 2:8-9)

It was only after the sin of disobedience by Adam and Eve that the ground began to yield "thorns and thistles", weeds. Man would then have to do the planting, tending and harvesting with hard work. The lush garden was "out of bounds" for them. The authority God had given to them was damaged as well. In the place of peace, the seeds of sin had infested the hearts of those made in the image of God.

This agrarian scenario parallels our lives as the ones who are now sowers of truth, often by the sweat of exertion or sacrifice. We are those whose responsibility is to cultivate and produce "fruit". The chasm which divided man from Eden's close fellowship with God was too deep to cross on our own. Jesus bridged the chasm which divided us from Creator God and made it possible for sweet and fruitful fellowship to be restored.

Jesus told His disciples just that as He spoke to them of their responsibility to extend the boundaries of God's human garden.

"You did not choose Me, but I chose you and appointed you that you would go and bear fruit, and that your fruit would remain so that whatever you ask of the Father in My Name, He may give it to you." (John 15:16)

Jesus sent the Holy Spirit to help us plant well and harvest the fruits of the Spirit. The Apostle Paul tells us what the fruit looks like.

"The fruit of the Spirit is love, joy, peace, patience, kindness, goodness, faithfulness, gentleness, and self control." (Galatians 5:22-23)

Seed sowing is a cooperative effort. The Apostle Paul gave us an example.

"I planted. Apollo watered, but God gave the increase." (1 Corinthians 3:6)

What will we plant in our garden? Will our lives bear fruit according to the plan of God? Will the weeds of sin encroach and cause us to have bad fruit? As we seek to plant the message of God's love in others, let us do so using the gifts of the Spirit of God.

Question: Are you a sower? Is it good seed and able to produce good fruit?

EYEWITNESS

The trial court was set, the jury in place. The defense and prosecution had laid out their cases before the robed judge and the jury. A crowd had gathered to hear what would be the outcome of the trial., Among them several who would be called to testify under oath. Then, as anticipation built, the judge said, "Please call your first witness." From the first row a man stood and walked to the seat beside the judge's bench. He was nervous, but sure of what he had seen. He was an eyewitness to the tragedy under scrutiny. With his hand raised, he swore to tell only the truth as he had seen it. He could not testify to hearsay or rumor. Nor could he add to the facts.

This was not the time to call a "character witness". That is someone who is willing to state his perception of the character of the one on trial He had not seen the alleged crime. Nor had he even been a bystander after the fact. His job was to simply give a personal opinion, no more.

We all know what an eyewitness is. Perhaps we too have been among those who were called to testify to the truth of what we had actually seen or to testify to the character of a defendant. Both are important to a case, but the most credible is the eyewitness.

On a Friday night a religious council assembled to serve as jury for the defendant before them. They would render a verdict on a matter which, in their minds, had already rendered the prisoner guilty. They kept trying to obtain valid testimony from the crowd gathered. Many gave false testimony. Finally, some stood up to give what we may call "hearsay" evidence. They had heard Jesus vow to destroy their Temple and rebuild in three days without using human hands. Even that was so preposterous that the "jury" could not believe it. Finally they decided to ask the defendant to testify on His own behalf.

"Are you the Christ, the Son of the Blessed One?" (Mark 16:61)

The defendant answered simply, "I am". With those words He had sealed His own fate. He was judged to be worthy of death and condemned to die because He had spoken the truth. And Jesus was led away to be crucified.

On the first day of the week, very early in the morning, two women made their way to a tomb. They were carrying ointments with which to anoint the body which lay in a cave-like tomb. Who would help them roll the stone from the entrance, they wondered. As they approached they noticed that the stone had already been rolled asway! Then someone spoke.

"Do not be amazed. I know you are looking for Jesus, the Nazarene, who has been crucified. He is not here. See, here is the place they buried Him. But go, tell His disciples and Peter that He is going ahead of you into Galilee. There you will see Him as He told you." (Mark 16:1-7)

What is the amazing thing about that command? It is who the eyewitnesses would be. In those days women were never called to testify to anything as they had no status in the male dominated society. Yet, they were the very ones who would testify to the fact that the Messiah had indeed risen from the dead after being in the tomb three days. The women hurried back to report to the eleven disciples the miraculous thing they had witnessed.

The story doesn't end there, because the men did not believe the testimony of the women, thinking it to be nonsense. However, just to be sure Peter and John went to see for themselves. It was true! The eye witnesses were the first to know the truth of the claim the crowd had said. The temple of His body was slain and in three days His Father had raised Him from the grave, alive again! All four Gospels relate these events, so amazing is the account.

We cannot be eye witnesses to that event, but we can surely testify as character witnesses to what Jesus, our Savior has done in the lives of those who believe in Him. We can see the changes and relate the facts. Jesus is who He said He is and we are called to testify to that amazing fact!

Question: Will you testify on His behalf? Will people believe you on the basis of the life you live?

Follow the Money

So much of our lives these days seem to hinge on how much or how little money we have at our disposal. This is especially true if we live on a fixed income or retirement funds. Every penny counts, we say, thinking there surely must be a hole in our pockets which makes the money disappear all too quickly. How we use our resources often dictates our success or failure.

God made one requirement for our resources, one which we often conveniently ignore or forget. God asked that we bring to Him a tithe, a tenth of whatever our source of income is. It is not a gift we give to God. It is what rightly belongs to Him

"And all the tithe of the land, whether the seed of the land or the fruit of the tree is the Lord's. It is holy to the Lord." (Leviticus 27:30)

This command was given to an agrarian society, so the people would recognize this as the "all" of their income.

"You shall surely tithe all the produce from what you sow, which comes out of the field every year." (Deuteronomy 14:22)

Why did God require a tithe? Does He need it? No!

- It provided resources for the work of God through the tabernacle/Temple system of worship.
- A portion was set aside to care for widows orphans, and strangers.(Deuteronomy(14:29)
- It was to help people understand their utter dependence on the Lord. It was plain He expected the "first fruits". That is the tithe paid before the bills were paid and income enjoyed. An example of the dependence on God is shown in the giving of the manna in the wilderness. Just enough for each day was given, no more and no less. God was their Supplier.
- The end result was a huge blessing because of the obedience in giving.
  "Bring all the tithes into the storehouse that there may be food in My house, and prove Me now says the Lord of Hosts, if I will not open the windows of heaven for you and pour out a blessing that there will not be room to receive it. (Malachi 3:10)

Proof that this requirement was carried out year after and into the time of Christ is found in Matthew 23:23 and Luke 18:12. Jesus Himself cautioned His followers to give to Caesar what was rightly his and to God what was His.

"Render to Caesar the things that are Caesar's and to God the things that are God's" (Matthew 22:15-21)

Clearly Jesus requires a dedication of life, not just money or resources. But the tithe was still important to obedience.

The church today embraces the rule of the tithe, though the majority of believers ignore the "rule of the tenth". Statistics show that the average church member in 2005 gave only 2.5% of his income to the church. As salaries have increased, giving has decreased. Although the American Christian church controls about half of the global Christian wealth, 98% of our church income stays here within our church and communities. When God instituted the tithe I am certain He had in mind a better use of resources than that. God doesn't ask us to do the impossible. That's His job. We are to give of ourselves as God directs us through open doors of opportunity.

He does expect us to share the treasure we have so that the greatness of God may be seen through us. Paul's admonition should ring in our ears.

"Let each one give as he has decided in his heart, not reluctantly or sorrowfully or under compulsion, for God loves a cheerful giver" (2 Corinthians 9:7)

Question: What do you give to God?

For One Sin

SIN! Such an awful word! All that it signifies, great and small, makes us aware of its wrongness, perversity, immorality, rebellion, filth. We know ourselves to be sinners, doers of sinful acts, thoughts, and emotions. Sin seems to cling to us against our every effort to rid ourselves of it. Yet, as often as we sin, we also try to excuse ourselves. After all, we say, "It wasn't such a bad sin. So many do much worse things, And besides, God will forgive me."

Where did that attitude come from? For starters, lets consider the one who would have us believe that God is a liar from whom we should separate ourselves. His name is Satan, the great deceiver. Then, there is the fact that every sin we commit is committed against God, the very One who created us to bear His image. God hates sin! Every sin! All sin, big or small, if such categories exist. Yes, God is forgiving. He has provided a way for us to be cleansed of all our sins. The blood of His Son, Jesus, on the cross assured us that we may live knowing that we have been redeemed from the curse of sin.

Is any sin without consequences? No, sin always has consequences though at the time we may not see any. The results of sin may play out over a lifetime. We often fail to consider that, clinging to the thought that it was only a "little sin". Can any sin be labeled "small"?

Ask Adam and Eve. For one sin, one bite of disobedience, they were cast out of the Garden of Eden. Their close, intimate fellowship with their Creator was severed. The fellowship they had enjoyed as they walked and talked together was gone. Forever mankind lay under the penalty of death. (Genesis 3)

Ask Moses, God's chosen man to lead His people to the Promised Land... For one sin, striking the rock to bring forth water as if he was the provider of water and not God, Moses was excluded from entering that land. Just one sin! (Numbers 20:8-12)

Ask Ananias and Sapphira. For one sin, deceitfully lying about their gift to the believers in the early church, they paid with their lives. (Acts 5:1-10)

Ask Miriam, Moses' sister. She traded her timbrel and praise to God for a tongue of complaint against God's appointed leader, Moses. She became instantly leprous. (Exodus 15:20-21; Numbers 12:1-10)

We belong to the Holy God who loves the sinner while hating the sin. Throughout the Bible we find clear evidence of God wooing His people to live a righteous life of obedience to His precepts. Each sin matters because it separates us from intimacy with God. Against the hope that God will be forgiving and merciful, we sin, calling it mistakes, human weakness, youthful ignorance, or Satan's enticement. We all remember the little phrase from a TV character who said,

"The devil made me do it." God created us to be sinless, free from the bondage of failure. He wants close fellowship with us.

The Apostle Peter reminded us.

"As obedient children, do not remain in the former lusts which were yours in ignorance, but, like the Holy One who called you, be holy also in all your behavior because it is written 'You shall be holy, for I am holy." (1 Peter 1:14-16; Leviticus 11:44)

What does "be holy" mean? It literally means to be set apart for a specific function. As Christians we are set apart to live for God and show the world Who He really is. It is to live a life defined by our obedience to God and our love for Him exhibited through our actions, words, and thoughts.

Let us make Paul's prayer in his letter to the believers in Thessalonica our prayer.

"Now may the God of peace sanctify you entirely; and may your spirit, soul, and body be preserved complete, without blame, at the coming of our Lord Jesus Christ." (1 Thessalonians 5:23)

Question: What makes you recognize sin when you see it in yourself or others? Is action required on your part to try to correct the problem?

FORMULA FOR SUCCESS

*A*ll companies and businesses, great and small, want to have a formula for success. Individuals also yearn for this. Everyone who has a formula savors it and protects it. SUCCESS! It is a word which holds many meanings and elicits just as many emotions. In it is the idea of doing one's best, striving earnestly, and working tirelessly. For as many facets to success that there may be, there are just as many formulas for achieving it. Corporate leaders plan long hours. Churches pray earnestly. Individuals dream big dreams. And always there is the seeking for a better way to achieve that goal of success.

There is one timeless formula that is failproof and eternal. Born of the will of God, its success is assured. It is so simple in its conception as to be overlooked by Christians. Today's church leaders and members often look for a grander plan, one wrought by committee and requiring participation by many members. What is the simple plan? It is God's plan.

Luke, the physician, a keen observer of cause and effect, noted this plan as he wrote the book of Acts. The first things he noticed are found in Acts 2:42-47.

- The believers continually devoted themselves to the apostles' teaching, to fellowship, and to prayer.
- They shared what they had with one another.
- They were of one mind.
- As they ate together, they experienced joy and sincerity of heart.
- They continually praised God.

As they did these simple but necessary things, the church began to grow with new believers. Luke further observed that they were "going on in the fear of the Lord and in the comfort of the Holy Spirit". (Acts 9:31) This simple but powerful formula ensured that the church, the body of believers would increase and grow stronger. It would be "successful" in spiritual terms. Three things are worth noting

- There was a "going on". This phrase denotes continuous action, not a sometime or once for all effort. Nor was there a "good for today but a better way tomorrow" attitude that is so prevalent today.
- The phrase "in the fear of the Lord" did not mean they were scared to death. It meant that the focus was on the Lord, not on the plans of men. It was all about what God had done through His Son, Jesus, and continues to do. They learned what their responsibility in that plan was and how to live it out. New believers watched the apostles because they knew

they had seen firsthand the Gospel being born. They had followed Messiah as He taught them His Father's plan. And they were in awe of all that God was doing in their midst.

- They lived "in the comfort of the Holy Spirit". The One whom Jesus had promised to send had indeed come onto the scene to translate into the hearts and minds of each believer the eternal plans and purposes of Father God. In their world that was hemmed in by captivity. pagan culture, and danger to their new faith in Messiah, this message brought comfort and peace. In Luke's description of their lives one word leaps out at us. It is the word <u>continually</u>, the constant keeping on of their belief in Messiah.

These three things were a formula for growth of the individual as well as the church. For as long as this formula was followed in their lives, the church thrived. Take heed, believers! This same formula for "success" applies today. We desperately need to apply it to our lives and in our churches Our God has the perfect formula for kingdom success and for our personal walk of faith in fellowship with other believers.

Admonition: Listen carefully, Church! Are you continually doing the things the early church did to strengthen their faith?

Fractured World, Fractured People

*W*ars between countries. Wars within countries. Riots in the streets. Fractured relationships within companies, among people and organizations. Marriage breakups. Church splits, Political acrimony among leaders. Personal health issues. Climate and environmental disasters. We live in a fractured world among fractured people. We are submerged in a society filled with lies and subterfuge, deceit and broken promises. We feel bombarded by issues too complex for us to solve. Wholeness is a rare quality amidst all of the chasms we face.

All our efforts to find a cure, a peaceful solution, a healthy relationship leave us stressed and exhausted. The more we review the options, the less we see hope for the state of our world and its people. The pain of our fractured world penetrates our very souls. Our cries of frustration and anguish ring loudly in our lives.

Such feelings are not new just in our day. Many years ago, at a time of great personal and spiritual anguish, the Prophet Jeremiah penned these words.

"My soul, my soul, I am in anguish! Oh, my heart, my heart is pounding within me! I cannot be silent, because you have heard, oh my soul, the sound of the trumpet, the alarm of war. Disaster upon disaster is proclaimed, for the whole land is devastated... for my people are foolish; they know me not. They are stupid children and have no understanding. They are shrewd to do evil, but to do good, they do not know." (Jeremiah 4:19-22)

God's people in the land of Judah were facing disastrous devastation by their enemies and captivity in a foreign land. We can hear the anguish and despair of Jeremiah's soul echoed in our own hearts as we see how that unfolds in their lives. It is this very despair and longing for help which will bring them back to their God, the only One who has a remedy. It is true for us as well. Words from the Psalmist who had seen more than enough of warfare and conflict in his own time, may offer to us the comfort and reassurance we need.

"I will lift up my eyes to the mountains. Where does my help come from? My help comes from the Lord who made heaven and earth. He will not allow your foot to slip; He who keeps you will not slumber...The Lord will guard your going out and your coming in from this time forth and forever more." (Psalm 121:1-2,5,8)

Isaiah spoke of the way to peace as well.

"Thou will keep you in perfect peace whose mind is stayed on You because he trusts in You, God. Trust in the Lord forever, for in God, the Lord, we have an everlasting Rock." (Isaiah 26:3-4)

Is it as simple as that? Or is it that easy? Can a fractured heart, a fractured relationship, or a fractured people be healed by a steadfastness of mind that remains focused on the ultimate Peacemaker?

The Word of God says a resounding "YES!"

How, you ask, does one set one's mind steadfastly on God? As a place to begin, open His Word, the Bible, and let Him speak to you through His recorded proclamations. Pray those words over your own life. Let them sink into your soul. Then speak those words to other fractured souls, to other fractured relationships. Let the peace you have found echo to others. Believe what the Psalmist proclaimed. God will guide your going and coming as you do so. We may not be able to mend our fractured world, but we surely can touch one life at a time to bring ripples of peace on troubled waters.

"And the peace of God which surpasses all understanding, will guard your hearts and your minds in Christ Jesus." (Philippians 4:7)

Question: What is the source of the anguish in your heart over some fracture? Have you visited the Source for healing?

Fragile Faith

A group of young teens at a Christian camp had just heard a teaching on faith. All agreed that it was an essential element to growth in the Lord. Since they had not met the other campers before coming to camp, each one shared his individual journey into belief in Jesus as Savior. Some were fairly new believers, and others had made that commitment as young children. After the teaching, the leader announced that they were now ready to test what they had just confessed.

Going outside, they were separated into pairs. Then the leader gave the instructions.

"Position yourselves back to front about a person's length apart. The one with back turned will be the "Faller" and the one facing the "Faller's' back will be the Catcher". When I give the signal, the "Faller", with eyes closed, will fall backward toward the "Catcher". Do you have faith that he will catch you when you fall? Ready! Go!"

Not one "faller" moved! Surely that was not the command! What if I am dropped? I may be hurt! I don't know him well enough to know if he will be able to catch me!

You can guess what the response from the leader was. "Where is your faith?

Such an important question! It is one we each must answer as it concerns our own walk of faith. Lest we think we are unique in our times of fragile faith, remember the Hebrews on their trek through the wilderness to the Land of Promise. So significant was their lapse in faith, that it is recorded in both Exodus 32 and Deuteronomy 9.

Moses, their leader, had gone up the mountain to meet with God. There God would share with Moses the laws and regulations which would help to mold His people into a strong nation. Moses remained on Mt Sinai for 40 days as he listened and wrote on stone tablets what God had said. As Moses descended, he heard a celebration going on. People were eating and drinking and playing in front of a golden idol. Aaron, Moses' brother and second in command, had caved in to the demands of the faithless Hebrews and had made an idol of gold.

"Now when the people saw that Moses delayed to come down from the mountain, the people gathered around Aaron and said, 'Come, make us a god who will go before us; As for Moses, who brought us up from the land of Egypt, we do not know what has become of him." (Exodus 32:1)

This was not the first time, nor the last, that the fragile faith of the Hebrews had shown itself. They had whined often over what they perceived as a lack on God's part to care for them.

- "Is it because there were no graves in Egypt that you brought us out here to die in the wilderness?" (Exodus 14:11)
- The people grumbled, 'What shall we drink?'" (Exodus 15:24)
- "Would that we had died by the hand of the Lord in the land of Egypt when we had plenty to eat and bread to the full. You have brought us out into this wilderness to kill the whole assembly with hunger.'" (Exodus 16:3)
- "Why have you brought us up from Egypt to kill us and our children and livestock with thirst?" (Exodus 17:3)
- "Why is the Lord bringing us into this land to fall by the sword?" (Numbers 14:3)

The Hebrews railed and whined at Moses but they really were placing their faith in the wrong place. They were really lacking trust in their God. Moses was just the one God chose to be His voice. Apparently through the 400 years of their exile, the faith of the Hebrews had become stunted. So when God offered them opportunity to leave, there was so little built up faith to rely on. They had to learn how to trust.

Faith is a fragile quality, especially in newer believers but sadly, in all of us. At the first sign of trouble, we are brought to the realization that we lack faith in God to be the answer. Maybe not the answer we want, but the answer He has in mind for our good.

The cost of faithlessness for the Hebrews was serious. Forty years of wandering around in the wilderness! Let it not be so for us. Let us put our faith in God who holds the master plan for each of our lives and loves us through it all.

Question: On a scale of 1-100 where is your faith in God?

Freedom Isn't Free

We all want free stuff. Look at all the ads which promise a product sample "free". Just sign up and we will send it to you. Then they ask for your credit card number, e mail, address, age, sex, everything but your shoe size. So, it really isn't free, is it?. Join the gym because membership is free–except if you want to use the pool. Then it will cost you. This subscription is free, but we will nag you frequently to increase your subscription. Use this new diet fad. It is guaranteed to help you lose tons of weight and "free" you from all of those fad diets. No exercise is required. Just eat this way. Does all of this sound familiar?

Who has not thought about freedom these days as so many of our freedoms have been taken away. Every day external forces hack away at our freedom to do or be, come or go, wear or not wear. Even the Constitutional foundations of our government are weakened by the cacophony of dissenting voices. Being politically correct, whatever that is on any given day, has replaced the freedom of speech and thought. Little by little the noose of bondage is being tightened around the fabric of our lives.

Even as we pray for people in other countries whose freedoms, and very lives, are threatened daily by persecution and death, our own countrymen and women are waging verbal and political war against Christian ethics and morals. Censorship of speech is rampant, especially if you are not one of the "in crowd".

No longer can we pray in schools. Merry Christmas has been replaced with Seasons Greetings. Manger scenes depicting Jesus' birth have all but disappeared from view. Media "celebs" poke ridicule at straight folks who live pure lives, and they encourage us to "loosen up". Not sure what that looks like in their minds, but it sounds dangerous to the soul.

Today in America we are less free than in 1776 when our founding fathers declared freedom from the tyranny of Mother England. What does this mean for us as Christians? Are we to join the militant throng seeking to force an opinion or way of life on us? Must we sit silently by for fear of consequences to job, schooling, person? As we watch true freedom eroding daily, how shall we consider the cost of remaining free?

We, like the early Christians, are facing an enemy which seeks to denigrate our personal choice to believe the Word of God. Violence did not ensure their freedom even as it does not ensure ours. Freedom is costly. True freedom is only found in Christ as He invades our hearts with truth. The issue of freedom is far larger than the loss of a few man-made rules.

Jesus, from the outset of His public ministry, faced ridicule, scorn, unbelief, and persecution. Cold, unbelieving religious leaders consistently found reasons to challenge His status and teachings. In spite of the challenges He faced, Jesus never remained silent or compromised His message. He spoke what He heard His Father tell Him, and He admonished His followers to remain free.

"You shall know the truth, and the truth shall make you free." (John 8:32)

The Psalmist, David, wrote eloquently of his praise for God who delivers freedom to the oppressed and those in bondage of any kind. The entire Psalm talks of the responses of God to the forces set against God's appointed king. It opens fitly with praise.

"I love You, O Lord, my strength. The Lord is my Rock and my Fortress, my Deliverer, my Rock in whom I take refuge. My Shield and the Horn of my salvation, my Stronghold." (Psalm 18:1-2)

Let us stand in the strength of the Lord in this day in which we face the threat to our freedoms. We must remember that our true freedom cost the Son of God His life so we could remain free. Yes, true freedom is costly, but it is free in Christ.

Question: How free are you? What is the greatest threat to your freedom, and how will you address that?

From Despair to Salvation

*H*ave you ever found yourself in a situation from which there seems to be no solution? In such times a myriad of emotions assault us. Fear. Anger. Angst. Helplessness. Not knowing where to turn for help, we may fall into despair and depression. Our physical and emotional health takes a nose dive into hopelessness. Often, to abate the feelings, we may seek relief in harmful ways. Self abuse. Drugs. Suicidal thoughts. Retaliation against the perceived cause.

Almost as an afterthought, we rail against God for the problem. Why God? Where ae You when I need You? Though this may seem like a turning to God, in effect it looks as if we are scolding God for His lack of assistance. Instead, we should give thanks to God for the deliverance He will provide in His time and even in a form we had not expected.

Such was King David's situation as he faced death. Psalm 30 ranges from praise to pride and back to praise. The title of the psalm could have been "The Helplessness of Man Without God". David had said that in his prosperity he felt invincible. Blinded by his own success and pleased with the prosperity that ensued, he believed his good fortune would last forever. Then a crisis occurred as circumstances changed. While we are not told exactly what the situation was, we do know that it awakened David's awareness of his sin of pride. He felt the withdrawal of God's help as he recognized his sin, and, ever the psalmist, David let out his heart in song.

David began to understand that God hates a prideful and arrogant heart because these characteristics serve to alienate us from our true Source of strength. So deep was David's repentance that he shared his understanding with the whole congregation, giving God the credit due Him.

"I will extol You, O Lord, for You have lifted me up and have not let my enemies rejoice over me. O Lord, my God, I cried to You for help and You healed me...You have turned my mourning into dancing. You have loosened my sackcloth and girded me with gladness that my soul may sing praises to You and not be silent. O Lord, I will give thanks to You forever." (Psalm 30:1-2, 11-12)

Praise emanated from a grateful heart and a desire to make right the relationship between David and his God. The additional benefit came in the sharing of what David had learned and his willingness to be vulnerable before others in order to bring glory to God.

Many years before, Moses, in preparing the Hebrews to enter their land of promise, reminded them of their need for humility before God.

"You shall remember all the ways which the Lord has led you in the wilderness these forty years that He might humble you, testing you to know what was in your heart whether you would keep His commandments or not. He humbled you and let you be hungry and fed you with manna which you did not know, nor did your fathers know, that He might make you understand that man does not live by bread alone; but man lives by everything that proceeds out of the mouth of the Lord." (Deuteronomy 8:2-3)

Why did Moses remind these people of their ungrateful behavior as they travelled northward? He did so because he knew their tendency to forget their Source, the God who had provided all they needed all those weary miles.

"Otherwise you may say in your heart, 'My power and the strength of my hand has made me this wealth.' But you shall remember the Lord your God, for it is He who is giving you the power to make wealth..." (Deuteronomy 8: 2-3,17-18)

Pride is often the root of our feelings of despair because we have failed at something we took pride in. When we exult in our accomplishments without acknowledging God's hand we set ourselves on Pride Road and lose our way to the One who led us to success. We are saved from despair not by our own efforts but by God's grace. It is to Him we must turn when despair hits us and we feel at a loss. He is ever the faithful God.

"Pride goes before destruction and a haughty spirit before a fall." (Proverbs 16:18)

Question: Have you ever felt deep despair? To whom did you turn for relief?

Getting Back to Plan A

*H*ow often have we set out with a plan, either consciously planned or at least habitually done, only to find we cannot execute it as expected. Our Plan A hasn't worked out, perhaps due to insufficient planning, unexpected glitches, etc. On to Plan B we go. It was not what we wanted to happen, only a less than wanted substitute. Plan B. What exactly do we expect as an outcome if we deviate from the first plan? This is a vital question especially when it regards some serious issue. Sadly, so often we find ourselves living in a Plan B world. There may a variety of reasons for that, but the primary cause is failure to prepare sufficiently in order to see our plan A come to fruition.

As Christians committed to following Jesus Christ and His way of life, de we realize that we have available a preplanned Plan A? Is the plan clearly etched into our souls and minds so that each moment of each day is lived by Plan A? The bigger question is: How many of us even know what God's Plan A is for us?

We know that from the beginning of creation God had a Plan A for Adam and Eve. It was this.

Live in the world I have created for you. Tend to it and its creatures.
Be fruitful and multiply as you care for each other. All things are
here for your use except the fruit of one tree. That is off limits for
you. I will come and fellowship with you.

Seems simple enough. Right? God had no intention of abandoning
his Plan A. We all know how that went down. Eve and Adam went
to their Plan B. They lost close fellowship with their Creator, were
tossed out of Eden, and,worst of all, they passed on to us the effects
of their disobedience. All of this catastrophe occurred because they
did not recognize that there was no Plan B in the mind of God. He
expected execution of Plan A, His very best plan.

God has never abandoned His Plan A, the desire for all mankind
to be in fellowship with Him as children of the One God and heirs
with His Son for eternity. Jesus, teaching His disciples to pray in
the prayer model we call the Lord's Prayer, asked them to pray this.

"Your Kingdom come, Your will be done on earth as it is in heaven."
(Matthew 6:10)

Jesus, the Son of God, came as man to point all of mankind to the
Father and to center us on His Plan A for living both in the present
and in eternity.

So what does that mean for us beyond that initial acceptance into
the Kingdom of God? Jesus outlined it simply. This is Plan A for
the believers in Jesus' day and for us today.

"Go! Make disciples of all nations. Baptize them in the Name of the Father, Son and Holy Spirit. Teach them to observe (keep as rules of life) all I have commanded you. I am going to the Father to make that come to pass, but I will always be with you in Spirit. (Matthew 28:19-20)

That Plan A was given to a very diverse group of people, unique in personality, gifting, and temperament. Jesus did not say that all must do it exactly alike or in just one way. But He did and does expect the plan to be carried out as He commanded. That Plan A has never changed.

Each of us today is different, too. We have different personalities, giftings and temperaments. If we are living our lives in Plan B, we have abandoned God's plan as surely as did Adam and Eve. We, too, will reap the consequences. Our imperative is to ask God how He wants us to execute Jesus' command for us individually, and then to adhere to His Plan A for us. The execution of Plan A may look a little different for each of us, but the bottom line, the Plan A, is the same. Let us abandon our Plan B and strive to live out God's will on earth. Let us be Plan A people!

Question: What is your "Plan A"? Is it God's plan for you?

GIFT WRAPPED

What a delight to receive a package all wrapped up for a special occasion! Christmas. Birthday Anniversary Mother's Day or Father's Day. Even more delightful is the unexpected gift on no special occasion at all. Carefully wrapped in colorful paper, and embellished with ribbons and trinkets, these gifts bring serendipitous joy. It is fun to speculate about the contents much like children on Christmas morning. Anticipation builds.

Feeling blessed, we offer thanks to the donor, even if the color or size is not quite right. We would never say, "What a cheap gift!." After all, the thoughtfulness of the giver is what matters. Nor would we exclaim, "I don't want this at all!" It would be very rude and thankless, even insulting to the kindness of the person who gave us the gift.

The very nature of gift giving speaks of gratitude. In fact, sometimes we go beyond the usual "thank you". We may try to return the favor by doing something special for the giver. Out of gratitude we become givers ourselves, spreading the happiness and delight.

What a lesson here! The most generous Giver of all is our God. He is forever giving out gifts to His children. His loving heart overflows with opportunities to gift us. A beautiful sunrise. A refreshing rain for the parched earth, The sweet song of a bird proclaiming his presence in the treetop. The peace of twilight after a hard day's labor. The answer to a puzzling question. The prompting of a friend to call to say "I miss you and love you." God's unnoticed gifts are numerous, unending, and so often taken for granted or not noticed at all.

How often do we pause to thank Him for these simple, yet life enriching gifts? Would we ever say, "I don't want that" or "I don't like that!"? Thank you is such a simple thing to say.

The greatest gift ever given to us was the costliest gift ever given. It was the gift of His Son. Jesus came gift wrapped we are told.

"When the days were accomplished for her (Mary) to give birth, she gave birth to her first born Son; and she wrapped Him in swaddling cloths and laid Him in a manger, because there was no room for them in the Inn." Luke 2:6-7)

The giving of this precious Gift had been promised centuries before by God through the Prophet Isaiah.

"Therefore, the Lord Himself will give you a sign. Behold, a virgin will be with child and bear a Son; and she will call His Name Immanuel, meaning God with us. (Isaiah 7:14)

"For a child will be born to us, a Son will be given to us. And the government will rest upon His shoulders. And His Name shall be called Wonderful Counselor, Mighty God, Eternal Father, Prince of Peace. There will be no end to the increase of His government or of peace. On the throne of David and over his kingdom to establish it and uphold it with justice and righteousness from then on and forever more. The zeal of the Lord of Hosts will accomplish this." (Isaiah 9:6-7)

The Apostle Paul wrote in his letter to the Romans about this precious gift.

'The wages of sin is death, but the free gift of God is eternal life in Christ Jesus, our Lord." (Romans 6:23)

James, pastor of the Jerusalem church and brother of Jesus, proclaimed this.

"Every good thing given and every perfect gift is from above, coming down from the Father of Lights with Whom there is no variation or shadow." (James 1:17)

When Jesus ascended back to His Father, He sent us the gift of the Holy Spirit who would teach us all things.

"But when He, the Spirit of Truth, comes He will guide you into all truth." (John 16:13a)

And so we are richly gifted! Let us give thanks to God!

Question: What would you say is the most precious gift you have ever received? Why?

GOD BLESS YOU!

"God bless you!", we say when someone sneezes. The origin of that phrase is lost to most of us. However, originally it was the idea that the saying would ward off any bad results from the sneeze. It was sort of a good luck charm. Another old saying is "Bless your heart!" as if to console or thank someone for a good deed or offer a compliment. What do we mean when we say such things? Do we ever stop to think what the real meaning might be? Just what does "blessing" mean?

The dictionary defines <u>blessing</u> as approval, encouragement or something conducive to happiness or welfare. It is also used to refer to the prayer offered before a meal. Are those what the word really means?

The Bible defines blessings using three words.

The first is *ashre, Hebrew* meaning a sense of happiness and wholeness that comes from living in good relationship with God. Psalm 128:1-2.

"How blessed is everyone who fears the Lord, who walks in His ways. When you shall eat the fruit of your hands, you will be happy and it will be well with you." (Psalm 128:1-2)

Second, *barak, Hebrew* meaning what God shares with us in the abundant life we receive at salvation. The blessings of the Lord are connected to our relationship in God as His abundant blessings are given to us.

"Behold, shall the man be blessed who fears the Lord. The Lord bless you from Zion, and may you see the prosperity of Jerusalem all the days of your life." (Psalm 128:4-5)

Third, *Makarios,* a Greek word meaning fortunate, well off or happy. Jesus' sermon on the mount reflects this.in Matthew 5.

From beginning to end the Bible recounts the blessings of God. In Genesis 1:28 God blessed Adam and Eve as He said to them, "Be fruitful and multiply and fill the earth and subdue it..."

As God chose Abraham to be the father of the Hebrew nation, God blessed him.

"And I will make you a great nation, and I will bless you and make your name great; and you will be a blessing. And I will bless those who bless you..." (Genesis 12:2-3)

Each of the twelve tribes received a special blessing unique to their future life. (Genesis 49)

King David, even in the trials and perils of his life was showered with blessings from God. His gratitude was poured out in the many psalms of praise he wrote.

And so, throughout the Bible, blessings continued, concluding in Revelation where God gives seven blessings. (Revelation 1:3; 14:13; 16:15; 19:9; 20:6; 22:7,14) Each of these has to do with the lives of those who are faithful to the end.

Though difficulties in life come and go, the power of God to bless remains and multiplies as we live according to God's laws. We are recipients of the bounty in many ways, day by day, sometimes totally unaware of each blessing. It is up to us to be mindful of these and to thank Him as we lift up our praises to Him. He is the One who blesses us abundantly; and we are those who pass on those blessings to others.

"It is good to give thanks to the Lord and to sing praises to Your Name, O Most High; to declare Your loving kindness in the morning and Your faithfulness by night...For you, O Lord, have made me glad by what You have done (Your blessings). I will sing for joy at the works of Your hands." (Psalm 92:1-2,4)

Consider: Today is a great day to begin to make a list of the bounteous blessings God has given you!

God My Exceeding Joy

*J*oy is defined in numerous ways: To experience great pleasure or delight; a state of happiness; the emotion evoked by well-being, success, or good fortune; Joy is a feeling, but it is more than that, deeper than just being happy that we didn't goof up or pleasure that we were successful in some endeavor.

What brings you joy? The gathering of family after a long absence? Southern fried chicken and all the "fixins"? The warmth of the sun after a cool, rainy day? The birth of your first child? Fellowship with a dear friend? Getting through the grueling pace of college with a diploma in hand? Your team winning the Super Bowl? So many things make us happy, but that kind of joy is fleeting.

The writer of Psalm 43, in the throes of distress and a plea for deliverance proclaimed this.

"God is my exceeding joy." (Psalm 43:4)

Deep within the depths of his troubled soul he knew that whatever happened, God would be there with him. The hope he had in

God was the factor that enabled him to have great joy in the midst of trouble. After laying out his anguish before God, he was confident that the key to the heart of God was to take joy in his Creator, Sustainer, Protector.

Many years later Nehemiah, a man of faith and a wall builder, with the remnant of Israel had labored against great odds to restore the walls of Jerusalem. The people had heard the precious words of God's law read to them by Ezra, the priest; and they wept at all they had missed for so long. Nehemiah sought to comfort them and point them to their God.

"Do not be grieved, for the joy of the Lord is your strength." (Nehemiah 8:10)

And years after that event the Apostle Paul penned words to the persecuted believers in Philippi.

"Rejoice in the Lord always, and again I say, rejoice!" (Philippians 4:4)

The wonder of this statement is that when Paul wrote this letter, he was in prison in Rome. In fact, Paul had written encouragement to the believers in Rome even before he was in prison. He knew they needed courage in their walk with the Messiah.

"The kingdom of God is not eating and drinking, but righteousness, peace, and joy in the Holy Spirit." (Romans 14:17)

Can it be that each of these men of faith had discovered the key to a victorious life? So it appears. Each of them had faced seemingly insurmountable challenges and hardships in their daily lives. Enemies abounded. Word was physically hard. Conflicts even among the people occurred. Whether harassed by enemies, having to supervise recalcitrant workers, facing physical perils, or remaining true to the task at hand, they all took opportunity to find and express joy in the Lord.

Were they happy to be oppressed, persecuted, harassed? No! No one is! But joyful in spite of it all? Yes! The reason for this is that happiness may come from the externals, but true joy comes from the Lord.

We know that one of the fruits which result from our walk with God is joy, joy so pervasive that even on our hardest or darkest days, we may find joy in the One who holds our lives in His hands. We can join with the Psalmist to say, "God is my exceeding joy."

Challenge: Seek to find joy in every day. Record your discoveries.

God's Billboards

When travelling down any of our country's interstate highways, we can hardly miss the huge billboards that decorate the roadsides. Designed to catch our attention, they suggest we need gas, a motel, restaurant, newest and best of something we just must have. Occasionally an information billboard warns us of road construction, a traffic snarl indicating delay, a detour. On and on the seemingly endless graffiti assaults our eyes and begs for our attention. Occasionally a sign may elicit a giggle, but more often a groan. Will they never stop cluttering the scenery with such things?

One day a Christian had an idea. Why not erect billboards with messages from God? You have probably seen these. They are phrased to catch our attention with a short, succinct message. These are couched in scripture and designed to provoke thought about God. It was a novel idea and a refreshing change from the constant advertisements.

Billboards have been used for as long as there have been roadways. Some are quite unique and do entice us to pause at a store, restaurant or roadside attraction. If you travelled down Route 66 you understand this because some of the signs are still there even past the time or the place they advertised. Do we still notice them or ignore them as so much clutter? Sometimes the constant sign parade causes us to be blinded to any of their messages.

Think about this. How many billboards does God put in front of us, asking us to read and heed. Do we ignore these? Is there any reaction? Do we notice them at all? You may say, "I never saw a billboard erected by God. He doesn't do that." Hmmm! Think a minute. A billboard, by purpose, is something which call us to notice and react.

Throughout history God has put His messages of love and grace, correction and mercy, admonition and command before us. Each of these "billboards" is there to cause us to react in some way which will draw us closer to Him. They may be an assignment as a servant of God, a change of direction, a repentance needed, thanks to be offered, a new knowledge of the One who made us.

Sadly, our responses to God's messages are much like our responses to the highway billboards. A scowl of displeasure. Failure to heed the warning. A chuckle at the phrasing. No attention at all to the message as we go our own way. Like Elijah, prophet of God, often these "billboards" are not blatant shouts but whispers. As Elijah was hiding in a cave to escape Queen Jezebel who sought his life, God sent more than one billboard. There was a violent wind, an earthquake, and a fire all sent to capture Elijah's attention.

"After the fire a gentle blowing...and a Voice came to him and said, 'What are you doing here, Elijah?'" (1 Kings 19:12-13)

When the mountain shook Elijah perhaps remembered the "billboard" God had used to call attention to His power and majesty as He lad His people out of Egypt.

"Moses brought the people out of the camp to meet God, and they stood at the foot of the mountain. Now Mount Sinai was all smoke because the Lord descended upon it in fire...and the whole mountain quaked violently." (Exodus 19:17-18)

Perhaps the most startling of God's messages was the "billboard" He sent at the birth of His Son. He sent the hosts of heaven to sing and a star so directional that it led the way to the place where Jesus lay. Even the magi from the east saw and heeded the sign. (Luke 2:1-15; Matthew 2:1-2)

Whether a star in the sky, a storm at sea, the miracle of feeding the 5000, each was God's message to teach and strengthen the faith of believers. His billboards are important, too important to ignore!

Question: Are you watching for God's "billboards" and heeding the messages? Or are you riding down the road of life heedless of His attempts to draw you to Himself?

GOOD GRIEF

*W*e have all heard Charlie Brown's response to a troubling situation with "Good grief!". Used as an expression of exasperation, it seems devoid of any real angst. However, the word "grief" usually elicits thoughts of loss, sorrow, and heartfelt pain. Often the emotion come unbidden or sudden, triggered by a memory. But most often it is felt in the wake of a recent loss of a loved one, a treasured friend, a prized possession, one's vitality or health, one's physical abilities to function as usual. The tears which come often and unbidden in unexpected moments are a cleansing of the soul to the one who grieves.It is a process as old as creation in processing loss and coming to the place of acceptance and peace.

In Jewish culture a period of deep grief focuses on the loss. If someone has died, burial takes place quickly based on the command of God in Deuteronomy 21:23 not to let the body remain all night. There is a custom called "keriah", the tearing of the clothes which is an acknowledgement of God's sovereignty They say, "God has given. God has taken away. Blessed be the Name of the Lord."

Following the burial, a week of mourning, called "sitting shivah", is observed. It is a period of restraint from normal activities to actually grieve the loss. Instead of denying the aching grief or burying it inside, grief is welcomed as a healing process. The Psalmist wrote God's response.

"You have seen my grief. You put my tears in a bottle." (Psalm 56:8)

To examine grief from a Biblical point of view, we find grief apparent not only at the loss of a loved one but in many other situations. The Apostle Paul, wrote to the Corinthian church about spiritual grief.

"I am rejoicing not that you were grieved, but that your grief led to repentance. For you were grieved as God willed... For Godly grief leads to repentance without cause to regret and leading to salvation, but worldly grief leas to death." 2 Corinthians 7:9-10)

Important truths are found here.

- Godly repentance ensues from grief over the sin that ensnares us. A word spoken in anger, a habit not easily broken, an act of unkindness, the betrayal of a trust, a refusal to live by the commands of God are examples of the grief we may experience when confronted by the reality of our behavior.
- To rejoice over someone's grief must lead to an eternal positive. Though Paul did not wish his readers to grieve, he used it as an opportunity to point out that their repentance from sin and a turning to a new life in Christ yields eternal results.
- If grief alone is the end, we grieve on. Such grief must lead to repentance before God and a change of life. God has

promised to remove our sins from us "as far as the east is from the west." That is an infinite distance!

- We must distinguish worldly grief from Godly grief. Grief over some material loss or regret over being caught in the act of some sinful thing, while real, is not the most important grief we feel. It is wrapped in guilt which is hard to distinguish from real guilt.

King David faced a time of sin which led him to a period of loss and of great grief over his choice to sin. He poured out his confession before God

"Be gracious to me. O God, according to Your loving kindness. According to the greatness of Your compassion, blot out my transgressions. Wash me thoroughly from my iniquity and cleanse me from my sin. ...Against, You and You only, have I sinned and done evil in Your sight" Create in me a clean heart, O God, and renew a righteous spirit within me...Restore to me the joy of Your salvation and sustain me with a willing spirit..." (Psalm 51)

This is a picture of searing grief and sincere repentance. It was David's plea to be returned to right relationship with his God.

Noted Bible scholar, A.W. Tozer, said, "Human feelings can never be completely stifled. If they are forbidden their normal course, like a river, they will cut another channel through life, and flow out to curse and ruin and destroy."

Understanding that God is with us in our grief is vital. Because of that we can approach God in our time of grief with assurance that

He sees our tears and hears our hearts, and that He stands willing to help us heal. The Psalmist spoke a truth for us to embrace in our grief.

"Weeping may last for the night, but joy comes in the morning." (Psalm 30:5b)

Question: Have you ever grieved over your own sin? What did you do to complete the grieving process?

GRADED BY GOD

(Part One)

With the opening of school many children return to the place where they are daily graded by their teachers. Based on performance, achievements, effort or attitudes, the teacher assigns a grade to each pupil. This leads to a recognition in the student as to whether he or she has measured up to expectations. There is a knowing within the student about what will bring the highest grade or extra star. Some hope for leniency. Others cross their fingers in uncertainty. And a few are just sure they have gotten the desired A grade. But all are subject to the same standard consistent with certain requirements. I, for one am glad those nervous days are over for me! Which of us enjoys the pressure of trying to measure up?

There is another type of grading of externals, the grading of land in preparation to build. For hours we hear the roar of machinery pushing and digging, hauling and leveling to assure a solid foundation upon which to build.

Often we are graded either verbally or subconsciously by someone who wants to approve or disapprove of something we said or did. Often this grading is hurtful as our words or deeds are misunderstood. And perhaps we did not pass inspection as if we are in the army. There are all kinds of grades administered throughout life.

There is one grading which is of the utmost concern but is often ignored by Christians. God has promised that one day we will be graded, and rewarded by Him according to our daily lives here on earth. He has a report card awaiting us.

The writer of Hebrews gives an admonition about the preparation we must do before the time of judgment or grading which will come to all of us.

"Therefore, leaving the elementary teaching about the Christ, let us press on to maturity...For God is not unjust so as to forget your work and the love you have shown toward His Name in ministering to the saints." (Hebrews 6:1, 10)

Even as students are expected to increase in ability and knowledge as the years pass, we are encouraged to do likewise as believers in Christ. We must not "repeat a grade" because we have failed to progress in the faith. Often opportunities and crises are upon us before we have had time to practice... Yet we are still charged with the responsibility to perform. The good news is that we are promised that God takes note of our growth.

We encourage students to overcome their tendencies to slack off in their work or offer excuses for failure. No, the dog did not eat your homework! As Christians we to are commended for being over-comers. There are some wonderful promises in Revelation 2 and 3 made to those who do overcome whatever trials were present in life.

- The right to eat from the Tree of Life
- No second death
- A new name written on a white stone
- Authority over nations
- Clothed in white
- Name written in the Book of Life
- Will become a pillar in the Temple of God forever

That is an awesome list of rewards when our lives are examined by God.

Lest we forget, Jesus laid out for us the Master Plan for life in the Kingdom of God. He didn't say it would be an easy test. He did promise to provide the Spirit of God as our teacher and guide. The question is, "Will you be pleased with the grade you get?" All of us want to hear these words, "Well done, good and faithful servant" Let that be our focus as we await our grade.

Question: Are you an "A" student or just squeaking by?

GRADED BY GOD

(Part Two)

*H*ow can I get a passing grade? It is a common thought voiced or silently held by any student, especially when struggling to master the material. It is also a human trait in all of us when we meet a hard obstacle to overcome. What is required in order to make this right? Do I try harder? Study more? Seek help? Struggle and fret, determined not to seek help? Adopt the attitude of failure? "Life is hard, not for the weak", so they say.

Someone once wrote a short answer to this which is funny, but true. Consider this as a formula to go by.

Life is easier than you think. All you have to do is:

- Accept the impossible
- Do without the indispensable
- Bear the intolerable and
- Be able to smile at anything

May I offer another alternative to this? Be vine-ripened.

Jesus said, "I am the True Vine and My Father is the Vinedresser. Every branch that does not bear fruit, He takes away; and every branch that bears fruit, He prunes so that it may bear more fruit. ... Abide in Me and I in you. As the branch cannot bear fruit of itself unless it abides in the vine, so neither can you unless you abide in Me. I am the Vine and you are the branches. He who abides in Me and I in him will bear much fruit, for apart from Me you can do nothing." (John 15:1-5)

At the end of this discourse Jesus added a very important statement.

"My Father is glorified by this that you bear much fruit and so prove to be My disciples." (John 15:8)

The list of qualities we are vine-ripened by is lengthy. To cite a few, consider these.

- Endurance through trials
- Handling praise with humility
- Proper use of the gifts of the Spirit
- Use of the weapons of righteousness
- Purity of speech, thoughts and actions
- Sincere love of the brethren and compassion for strangers
- A giving, sacrificial heart
- Daily communion with the Father

The Apostle Paul's report card as he saw it is a list of difficult things he endured with faith in order to be the recipient of the "well done" from God when he stands before the only One whose grade really counts.

""Give no cause for offense in anything, but in everything, commending ourselves as servants of God in much endurance..."

From there Paul went on for a long time citing all of the challenges upon which we will be graded by God as He sees our hearts for Him. (2 Corinthians 6:3-10)

Question: Again, I ask you (and myself), "What grade will you receive when you come before Holy God to account for your life here on earth?"

Great Expectations

*E*xpect (defined): look forward to, anticipate, consider probable or certain, hope for with a degree of certainty

What do you expect? Anticipate? Consider within the realm of certainty? We all have expectations. Some are based on desire, some on hope. All expectations are in the future, not just now, not today or tomorrow perhaps. Some expectations are performance based; some are circumstantial; some are based on past events. We expect rain based on the sky conditions. We expect a raise based on merit. We expect an "A'" based on the amount of study. We expect!

The Bible is full of expectations especially regarding the Messiah. God's people looked forward to the day when a deliverer would come, their king, their savior. These expectations were based on the sure promises of God.

"For unto us a child will be born, a son will be given. The government will rest upon His shoulders. And His Name will be called Wonderful Counselor, Mighty God, Eternal Father, Prince of Peace." (Isaiah 9:6)

Many years later John the Baptist heralded the Messiah's coming as he preached to crowds in the wilderness. One day Jesus came to be baptized by John. As Jesus came up out of the water a miraculous affirmation of Who He was echoed from heaven.

"and behold the heavens opened and he (John) saw the Spirit of God descending like a dove and lighting on Him (Jesus) And behold, a voice from heaven said, 'This is My Beloved Son in whom I am well pleased.'" (Matthew 3:13-17)

Jesus Himself said that the people of His generation expected a sign of His status as Messiah come from God. (Luke 11:29) The expectations of most of the Hebrews was of someone who would come to rescue them from their Roman oppressors and set to right their understanding of God's promises of a kingdom.

One day as Jesus taught the multitudes and fed the multitude with a boy's small lunch, the people searched for Jesus, expecting more. Jesus pointed out their wrong expectations based purely on physical wants.

He said, "Don't waste your expectations on things that perish. Seek instead that food which endures to eternal life." (John 6:26-27)

These few examples make us keenly aware that expectations seem to be the norm for us humans. So here is the important question. What are your expectations? Are they based on physical wants, perceived needs, future events, all of which are subject to human intervention? Or are your expectations based on the goodness of God's abundant love for His creation fulfilled in His Son? He is the bread giver, the water of life, the supplier of all of our needs. This is our Great Expectation!

It is based securely on truth. Therefore we can more than hope. We can expect God's mercy and grace to flow freely into our expectations and make them a reality. I expect that! Do you?

Challenge: Take a few moments to think of what your expectations of God are. Do they line up with what God has promised?

HERE COMES THE JUDGE

*A*ccording to Webster, a judge is one who weighs the evidence to give an informed opinion. He is a person of wisdom and able to discern the truth. Then he decides the outcome after all evidence is considered. In many cases it means to govern or rule. Having heard stories of good and bad judges, if we find ourselves in a courtroom, we hope that the judge will be fair and merciful as we plead our case. Though we know there is a panel of jurists, He alone seems to hold our fate in his hands. Will he be kind, patient, compassionate? Will I be able to say that I had a fair trial?

When asked to characterize God we enumerate his attributes: love, faithful, patient, merciful, compassionate, just, almighty, omnipresent, etc. But seldom do we include as a characteristic of God: the title of Judge. Somehow that doesn't fit our picture of a loving and merciful God. Yet, from the beginning of Genesis and ending with Revelation, God is seen over and over again as Judge, the One who weighs the evidence.

Weighing the evidence, God judged Adam and Eve guilty of rebellion against His command. He sentenced them to banishment from the idyllic Eden to struggle in life thereafter. (Genesis 3)

Abraham, Father of the Hebrews, called God "Judge of all the earth". (Genesis 18:25)

The Psalmist calls God "a righteous Judge" (Psalm 7:11)

Isaiah said, "The Lord is our Judge, our Lawgiver, our King" (Isaiah 33:22)

The writer of Hebrews called God, "the Judge of all" (Hebrews12; 23)

When Jesus came, He proclaimed His authority to judge as given to Him by Father God. He spoke of condemnation for those who refuse to accept Him as Messiah.

"Not even the Father judges anyone, but has given all judgment to the Son so that they will honor the Son as they honor the Father. ...He who hears My word and believes Him who sent Me has eternal life and does not come into judgment but has passed out of death into life." (John 5:22-27)

The Apostle Peter understood this attribute of Jesus well since he had stood before Jesus as guilty, yet forgiven. When he wrote to the churches in Asia Minor he was clear about the penalty for rejection of the Truth.

"They will have to give an account to Him Who is ready to judge and pass sentence on the living and the dead." (1 Peter 4:5)

Why then do we recoil at the thought of God as Judge? Would a God Who did not care about right and wrong be just? To do so would be indifference to sin. The question then is not "Does God judge?" We know He does. The question becomes, "Will we trust God's judgment on us when we sin?"

The Bible is certainly replete with instances when God passed judgment, but then extended mercy and grace. Judgment must be viewed in that light. Where there is judgment on God's part, there is also justice and opportunity to receive mercy, forgiveness, and a fresh start. Shall we cite a few examples?

- Out of Egyptian bondage, wilderness wandering and sin, forgiveness and opportunity for a new beginning.
- The period of the Judges of Israel and the Kings when repeated judgments by God caused repentance and a new cycle of life.
- Return from Babylonian exile and opportunity to make right the rebellion of past days.
- Redemption of Paul, persecutor of believers, on the Damascus Road
- And of course, Simon Peter's denials and repentance that resulted in forgiveness and restoration

God is indeed Judge of all the Earth! That includes you and me.

"Let us then come boldly to the Throne of Grace that we may receive mercy and find grace to help when we need it." (Hebrews 4:16)

Consider: Picture yourself in the courtroom of heaven with your attorney, Jesus, at hand. How will you plead?

HISTORY REPEATED

*H*istory repeats itself, so the saying goes. A look at history of countries and peoples confirms it in so many ways. We are, it seems doomed to repeat our mistakes and failures as well as those made by the generations before us. Failing to learn from the mistakes others have made and the foolishness of reckless leaders, we go merrily on the same path to ruin. Particularly is this true in the arena of politics.

In the early days of the American Revolution with the army in disarray and the Congress faced with such monumental issues that it rendered them uncertain and hesitant, John Adams wrote to his wife.

"Unfaithfulness in public stations is deeply criminal. But there is no encouragement to be faithful. Neither profit nor honor nor applause is acquired by faithlessness. There is too much corruption even in this infant age of our Republic. Virtue is not in fashion. Vice is not infamous."

When asked if he thought America would succeed in the struggle, Adams replied.

"Yes, if we fear God and repent of our sins."

This sounds familiar today as unfaithfulness among our public officials is rampant. Virtue is not only not in fashion. It is a non-issue, having been replaced by a "whatever mentality". Are we doomed to repeat the failure of the past? Will we be able to right the ship of state as those first Americans did? They achieved a moral victory, and our country was born. Are we too far gone to turn back? I wonder.

The history of God's chosen people, Israel, is rife with instances of the repetition of unfaithfulness. Their cycle of disobedience was followed at last by a cry to God for mercy as they repented before Him, only to begin the cycle again. History repeated!

Psalm 78 bears witness to this cycle of faithlessness. As the Psalm goes on, the faithfulness of God is contrasted to Israel's lack of faith. The words "yet and but" leap out at us as this tragedy unfolds. In spite of God's warnings, the nation proceeded to live in hurtful, ungodly ways. The fear of God was replaced by complacency toward His laws and commands. God had a conversation with His prophet, Jeremiah which opens the mourning heart of God for His people.

"The Lord said to me in the days of King Josiah, 'Have you seen what faithless Israel did? She repeatedly played the harlot. I thought that after she had done all these things, she would return to Me, but she did not return. ...Yet in spite of all of this, her treacherous sister, Judah, did not return to Me with all of her hear but rather in deception.' declared the Lord." (Jeremiah 3:6-10)

If we are to survive as a nation, we must fall on our knees and beg God for mercy. The words that Jesus spoke about Israel in those days ring loudly in our ears.

"You unbelieving and perverted generation, how long shall I be with you? How long shall I put up with you? (Matthew 17:17)

Can you hear Him saying those words over our country just now? John tells us what to do.

"If we confess our sins, He is faithful and just to forgive our sins and cleans us from all unrighteousness." (! John 1:9)

It is not too late for us to return to righteousness before we repeat history to our demise. God is merciful when we repent and return to Him. As John Adams said, "Fear God and repent."

Question: What do you think would change the course of our increasingly pagan culture?

HOME IMPROVEMENT

*H*ave you ever bought a house that was a "fixer-upper"? We did, though we did not know it at the time. It wasn't long before we discovered that the roof leaked; so the roof had to be replaced and the ceiling in the den repaired. The ceiling light fixture was attached with tape instead of screws. Whoever painted cabinets was not a skilled painter or at least a careless one. Landscaping on the yard was never a priority for previous owners. Time has passed and still the home improvement continues. There seems to be no end to the projects!

Thankfully family members are skilled enough to fix most of the glitches. Some of us can sand and paint. All of us can garden. One of us has enough electrical know-how to repair the faulty switches. Sometimes the challenge is too great. Many days we wish for more skills in order to reduce the financial strain of hiring a skilled repairman.

When consulting an expert for advice as to how to proceed we have many questions. What material should be used? Where can I find this or that part needed? How long will it take to do the job? Must

I remove the old material before proceeding or can I just cover it up? "How much will it cost? The most important question is "Are you really an expert at what I need done"

Life is like that. Improvements are constantly needed somewhere, especially in us. We are in need of "home improvement". We gaze in the mirror and wish to be slimmer, more buff, less freckled. We yearn to be more talented as a musician, more patient as a parent, more caring as a friend, more skilled in our jobs. We need improvement! And some of us need an entire "makeover".

For a Christian the desire of our hearts should be "home-improvement" on the inside. As with physical issues, the effort is often hard and continual. It requires consistency and that four letter word, WORK!

In this effort to improve, we do actually have an Expert Source. God is our trustworthy Source of materials and answers as well as guidance. Not only does He offer advice and counsel, He also supplies the materials needed at no cost to us.

Scripture has something to say about building or rebuilding. Consider these.

- Everyone who comes to Me (Jesus speaking) and hears My words and acts on them is like a man building a house who dug deep and laid the foundation on a rock. When the floods came and the torrents burst against that house, it was not shaken because it had been well built." (Luke 6:47-48)

- In My Father's house are many dwelling places. I am going to prepare a place for you...and I will return and receive you that where I am there you may be also." (John 142-3)
- "Unless the Lord build the house, they labor in vain who build it." (Psalm 127:1)
- You, as living stones are being built as a spiritual house for a holy priesthood to offer spiritual sacrifices acceptable to God." (Hebrews 2:5)

What can we take away from these scriptures that will help us build or rebuild our lives so that internal "home improvement" will not be necessary so often?

- We first of all, must be certain to build on a firm foundation. Isaiah's words were a prophecy of the One to come who would be for us the foundation of our faith

"Behold, I (God) am laying in Zion a Cornerstone, a tested stone, a costly Cornerstone for the foundation. He who believes in Him shall not be moved." (Isaiah 28:16)

- We must rely on the Master Builder to help each of us build a house worthy of the salvation we have in Christ. Jesus paid the price for us so that we would have access to all we need in building our lives.
- As members of the Body of Christ, the church, we must recognize that God is building a people of praise to Him. We are living stones.

- And last, we must remember that our earthly houses, both dwellings and bodies, cannot compare to the place Jesus is preparing for us in heaven.

We must call on God to help us build and restore our lives to mirror what He has created us to be.

Question: What does your "house" look like to God? What improvements are needed?

How Do You
View the World?

Dorothy viewed the world through rose colored glasses. She saw everything in a good light. We see our world through sunglasses to avoid the glare of the sun and keep out some light. Jewelers view their work through magnified lenses to see the fine details of their work. We often see our world through critical lenses. In that we would not be the first to have critical sight or insight.

The words of the prophet Habakkuk written so many years ago may well echo the cry of believers today. He saw the perversion of truth, violence in the streets, and disregard for human life. Strife and contention, malice and hatred seemed to be the "order of the day". In just such a time as this Habakkuk cried out to God.

"How long, O Lord, will I cry for help before You listen? How many times do I have to yell 'Help!" before You come to the rescue? Why do You force me to look at evil and stare trouble in the face every day?

Anarchy and violence break out, quarrels and fights all over the place .Law and order fall to pieces. Justice is a joke. The wicked have the righteous hamstrung and stand justice on its head." (Habakkuk 1: 2-4 Msg)

Listen to God's answer. It was not what Habakkuk was expecting,, to be sure.

"LOOK! Look around at all the godless nations. Look long and hard. Brace yourself for a shock because something is about to take place.You are going to find it hard to believe." (Habakkuk 1:5 Msg)

They were shocked! They were captured, exiled, and their sacred Temple was destroyed. Life as it had been was no mor, all because of their blatant disregard for the laws of God. (2 Kings 17:6)

Does this sound familiar? Violence and disregard for personal property. Quarrels and hateful words spewed out at anyone who is deemed different. Law and order disregarded. Justice for victims missing and the perpetrators of chaos excused. Spiritual apathy and disregard for laws, both civil and Biblical, Such are the days in which we live. Sin has invaded the very roots of our culture.

In our distress over what we see and hear, we have lost sight of God. We try to find solutions in the wrong places, and to no avail, we depend on our leaders to solve the rampant problems. Yet we cannot find the answers we need. Evil and disorder persist. We are powerless to make a change! We, like Habakkuk, cry out, "Help, God! Why must we live in such a broken and sinful world?"

Our view is blurred by the conditions around us. We need to view the world through the eyes of God. As in Habakkuk's day, He sees and knows the sin-drenched world we live in.

God alone holds the key to the world's problems. He is the Author of peace. He not only sees our distress. He also is at work. We must view the world through the eyes of faith because God never ceases to work on behalf of His creation. He, too, mourns the condition of mankind, those He created to reflect His image. He continually seeks to draw us back to Him.

We can only pray that the shock of the disobedient and sinful Hebrews will not come upon us. Change is coming. The scripture tells us so. Jesus spoke of the "last days",

"Many will come in My Name, saying 'I am the Christ', and will mislead many. ...Nation will rise up against nation and kingdom against kingdom. In various places there will be famines and earthquakes... Then they will deliver you to tribulation, and will kill you. And you will be hated by all nations because of My Name." (Matthew 24:5-9)

Our responsibility is to keep our eyes on God as He leads us day by day to flesh out His will and to be the peacemakers Jesus spoke of. Let us be light in this fractured world.

Question: Does your view of the world make you a part of the problem or part of the remedy?

How Many Times Must I Tell You?

$\mathcal{A}$ mother, in a tone of exasperation said to her child, "How many times do I have to tell you..." You fill in the blanks. Over and over, we admonish our children about something, wearily wondering if or when they will understand and obey. Sometimes these are trivial matters, but often these can be life altering truths. Perhaps you had a teacher who said that same thing in exasperation over your question. Some of us seem to need reinforced repetition over things we need to remember, especially as we grow old and memory becomes cloudy.

We don't know if Jesus was ever exasperated with His disciples over their failure to understand something, but we surely would understand it if He was. Using the Gospel according to Mark as a source we find Jesus at least four times explaining to His disciples that He would suffer and die and would rise again from the dead. (Mark 9:9; 9:31-32; 10:33-34;14; 8,28)

In each instance Jesus clearly told His followers what to expect. Their lack of understanding, or belief that such was even a remote possibility, was remarkable. They avoided thinking that anything bad could or would happen to their Master. We can almost hear Jesus saying, "How many times do I have to tell you?"

At one point the disciples, understanding the meaning of Jesus' parable about the vineyard and vine grower and the demise of the son, said "May it never be!" So convinced were they that they would always have Him, that they could not hear the truth. (Luke 20:9-18)

Even in the days of preparation for the last Passover meal Jesus would share with His disciples, their lack of understanding prevailed as Jesus was anointed for His burial. Having seen the woman pour costly perfume on Jesus, the disciples were indignant and said, "Why this waste? This perfume might have been sold and the money given to the poor."

Jesus' reply was clear.

"Why do you bother this woman? She has done a good deed to Me. You will always have the poor with you, but you do not always have Me. When she poured this perfume on Me, she did it to prepare for My burial." (Mark 14:3-8))

Surely the disciples in their teaching at the synagogue schools had heard the words of the Prophet Isaiah who foretold of the Messiah's death.

"He was oppressed and afflicted, yet He remained silent. Like a lamb led to slaughter is silent, so Messiah did not open His mouth. By oppression and judgment He was taken away...cut off from the land of the living... But the Lord was pleased to crush Him as He rendered Himself as a guilt offering..." (Isaiah 53:7-11)

Perhaps this was such a hard word that Jesus' followers couldn't wrap their minds around it. Remember, these were people who hoped the Messiah would change their circumstances and rescue them from the harsh hand of Rome. They could not understand that Jesus' sacrifice would not only change their lives, but would change the world eternally.

What of us? Do we read and reread the Word and yet fail to grasp the truth it has for our lives, our future? How many times in His Word does God tell us of His plan? The Good News is that Jesus promised the Holy Spirit to be our teacher, our guide to the truths of God. (John 16:13)

He is the One who is given to help us understand the hard- to-understand things God has planned for His creation. He is the One who helps us clear the cobwebs of doubt and uncertainty from our souls. He it is who will guide us into all truth (John 16:14-15) And I believe God is willing, as Jesus did, to repeat His message until we understand it.

Thanks be to God for such a Teacher! Let us listen well and heed what we hear!

Question: Is there something in your life that God has told you again and again, yet you either do not understand or fail to obey?

How Will You Say Goodbye?

$\mathcal{I}$t's time to leave. How will you say goodbye? See You later! So long Adios. Adieu. Sayonara. Is there a handshake, a hug, a smile, any words other than the greeting? Was the departure hard or easy? Will we see the one we are leaving again soon or perhaps not for a very long time? Much depends on our relationship with the one we are leaving. Close relationships bring much deeper responses, whereas casual acquaintances are easier. Perhaps it is a final goodbye of one we care deeply about. What then will we say? Will we miss an opportunity to say those last words, and then experience regrets at our silence?

The Apostle Peter, in writing his second letter to the Christians in Asia Minor felt the need to tell them a final goodbye. Peter had a sense of timing about his life that caused him to share these words.

> "I think it right as long as I am in "this tabernacle" (body) to stir up your memories since I know that laying aside this body of mine will come speedily as our Lord Jesus has made clear to me." (2 Peter 1:13-14)

We do not know for certain how Peter knew this. Had he been told by his captors? Was he ill? Certainly he was advanced in years. Or perhaps Peter was remembering Jesus last admonition to him on the seashore.

> "I assure you most solemnly that when you were young you dressed yourself and walked about wherever you wanted to go. But when you grow old, you will stretch out your hands and someone else will clothe you and carry you where you do not want to go." Jesus said this to indicate by what kind of death Peter would glorify God. And after this Jesus said, "Follow Me!" (John 21:18-19)

Peter had for many years obeyed the command of Jesus to follow Him. His life after that first encounter had been one of service and leadership in the body of believers and a testimony to what God had wrought in his own life. Peter wanted these people to whom he had ministered in person on many occasions to know for certain Who they trusted in and to Whom their allegiance belonged.

The word "know" or "knowledge" occurs more than 15 times in this short letter. Peter knew the power of worldly influences that would threaten to erode their faith, the false teachings and teachers which would creep in unawares to corrupt the truth of the Gospel. Much was at stake since the years since Jesus' ascension occurred. Peter yearned to have the purity of Jesus' message and sacrifice remain whole and uncorrupted. You can hear the sense of urgency in his words.

"I will diligently endeavor to see to it even after my departure that you may be able to call to mind the things I have taught you. For we were not following the cleverly devised stories when we made known to you the power and coming of our Lord Jesus Christ, the Messiah. We were eye witnesses of His authority...We actually heard the voice of God when we were with Jesus on the mountain." (2 Peter 1:15-18)

What about us? What will we leave as our last words when death approaches? Will we "tie up loose ends", so to speak? That is, do we owe forgiveness to someone or need to ask for that for ourselves. Are there words of encouragement and admonition we must impart? Let us follow Peter's example and make sure we have expressed our faith to family and friends so that they will be strengthened. Let us give them Peter's last recorded words.

"Grow in grace and knowledge of our Lord and Savior Jesus Christ. To Him be honor and glory now and forever! Amen! (2Peter 3:18)

Encouragement: Do not wait to say what is on your heart. No one has the promise of tomorrow.

I Doubt It!

"Seeing is believing", so the saying goes. We need proof, so we doubt. If someone points out a bird's nest way up in the tree, and we can't see it, we doubt it is there. If we are looking for a lost item we say, "I doubt I will ever find it!" A friend recommends a specific drug that may help you conquer your allergies, but you doubt it will work for you.

We always want proof! Show me! Convince me! We are a generation of doubters, resisting what we do not see and dismissing the evidence offered as that which we have not personally seen. What is unseen is scary, especially if we view it as life-threatening or life-altering. This has been brought home to us in recent days as we have confronted "the virus" named COVID. It has been very difficult to decide what or who to believe and easy to doubt the information we receive.

This syndrome of resistance is the basis for our unbelief, especially as it pertains to Christianity. We can't see God, so we choose to live in doubt, AKA unbelief. Failing to see the myriad of ways in which

God reveals Himself to His creation each day, we wear blinders called "doubt".

Let's use a good Biblical example of what that doubt looks like as we see the life of Thomas, one of the twelve chosen by Jesus to be His disciples. Thomas had lived with Jesus for three years, followed Him along the dusty roads, slept under the stars with Him, heard Him teach and perform countless miracles. He believed that Jesus was the Promised Messiah. Yet he doubted.

When Jesus appeared to His disciples after His resurrection, Thomas, for some reason, was absent. Later the disciples told him they had seen Jesus. But Thomas doubted. He wanted proof!

He said to them, "Unless I see in His hands the imprint of the nails and put my finger in the place of the nails, and put my hand in His side (the place where Jesus had been pierced as proof He had died), I will not believe!" (John 20:24-25)

The next time the disciples were gathered together, Thomas was present. Jesus came and stood in their midst. He singled out Thomas, I am sure, much to Thomas' embarrassment.

"Reach here with your finger and see My hands, and reach here your hand and put it into My side. Do not be unbelieving but believing." (John 20:27)

Thomas' response was so plaintive that we can almost feel his painful dismay.

"My Lord and my God!"

Jesus' response spoke to Thomas' reluctance to believe without doubt.

"Because you have seen Me, you believed? Blessed are they who did not see Me and yet believed." (John 20:28-29)

Have you ever been a "Doubting Thomas"? Here we are several centuries later, and still there is doubting. Many still want proof, tangible, visible proof. We want to know that God loves us, that He cares when we hurt, that He has a plan for each life, and that the future planned by Him will come to pass as He has said.

Why can't we just believe? It is because our faith is weak, as was Thomas', or because we have no faith at all. Ouch! It hurts to admit that! But let's confess and move out of the circle of doubters.

"Now faith is the assurance of things hoped for, the evidence/conviction of things not seen." (Hebrews 11:1)

Question: Have you been a doubter that God really Cares about your troubles?

I HOPE SO!

"*I* hope so!" That is what we say when the outcome is in doubt. We hope it doesn't rain on our picnic. I hope to get that raise. We hope the diagnosis isn't dire. Whether trivial or important, hope is what we express. It is a fragile, intangible, abstract term based often on the emotion of the minute, and probably hinges on a wish rather than any certainty. The dictionary defines it in a number of ways: patient waiting, expectation, shelter, refuge, trust.

In the Hebrew language because all words are viewed as concrete, the word we call" hope" is usually translated as "trust". It in no sense means to casually wonder if something will happen. It is to know that it will occur in the timing of God. In other words, we do not hope God will, we know in trust that He will.

The Apostle Paul wrote to the church at Corinth several times. His concern for them was evident. In the second letter Paul asserts that God is the Father of mercies and the God of all comfort. Based on that declaration Paul, burdened by the distress these believers were enduring, assured his readers of his hope in God.

"He on whom we have set our hope/trust." (2 Corinthians 1:10)

Paul's trust in his God as the One who keeps on His promises was relayed to those whose faith was fragile. He exuded a confidence they needed to hear. Later on in this letter Paul gave thanks to God in the midst of his own trials.

"But thanks be to God who always leads us in triumph in Christ and manifests through us the sweet aroma of the knowledge of Him in every place." (2 Corinthians 2:14)

Many years before Paul wrote these words of hope/trust, the Psalmist David poured out his distress to God. It is evident that he felt despair, a sense of calamity all around him, a personal anguish of soul and body. As he lamented his plight before God, David said something remarkable.

"For I hope in You, O Lord; You will answer, O Lord, my God." (Psalm 38:15)

In spite of his dire circumstances, David knew that God was the One in whom he must put his trust. This same belief was expressed often in the psalms he wrote. His was a patience birthed in evidence of the mighty acts of God.

"And now, O Lord, for what do I wait? My hope is in You." (Psalm 39:7)

Biblical hope is based on trust in the "now and not yet" of God's design. Often in scripture we find that waiting is the key which anchors the hope on God. The Prophet Isaiah was able to marry those two terms as he encouraged God's people to keep on hoping/trusting in God.

"It will be said of that day, 'This is our God for whom we have waited in hope that He might save us.'" (Isaiah 25:9)

"We have waited for You eagerly. Your Name, even Your memory is the desire of our souls." (Isaiah 26:8)'

"O Lord, be gracious to us. We have waited for You." (Isaiah 33:2)

How does hope work? It works only if we commit to believe every day in every circumstance that God is who He says He is, and will do what He says He will do. When we believe this, our expectation becomes tangible, not just a flimsy "hope it will happen". It is like having a never-ending warranty. Who would refuse that?

The old hymn says it well. "My hope is built on nothing less than Jesu's blood and righteousness."

Question: What do you hope for? Do you trust God to do it?

I PROMISE

*P*romises! Promises! I grew up in a time when a person's word was his bond, his promise to do as he had sworn to do. Marriage vows were sacred and divorce rare. The men who had been called to preach the Truth of the Word of God, did so. Even children promised with the entwining of pinkie fingers, made a promise to be kept. Not so any more. Treaties are broken before the ink is dry. Marriage is discarded at will. Men who fill the pulpits take issue of the inerrancy of the Bible. Few can truly be called trusted to keep their promises.

However, there is One whose very Name speaks faithfulness to His Promises. Almighty God! The Bible says,

"God is not a man that He should lie, nor a son of man that He should repent of breaking His word. Has He not said, and will He not do it? Or has He spoken, and will He not make it good?" (Numbers 23:19)

God is the ultimate Promise Keeper, the always faithful One. He keeps His promises to bless and to curse. From God's promise to

Adam and Eve in the Garden of Eden at the dawn of creation to His promises to Abraham, Hebrew patriarch, to His oppressed people in exile, right through to the promise of His Son, Jesus our Messiah and to us today as His children, God has been faithfully executing His promises.

It is one thing to accept the truth that God is faithful to His Word, and quite another to act upon that truth as a way of life. Just how much do we rely on the promises of God? We must be able to say with the writer of Hebrews,

"Let us hold fast the confession of our hope without wavering, for He who promised is faithful." (Hebrews 10:23)

For all of us there are times in our lives when it is a struggle to believe in the faithful promises of God. Tears of sorrow at a great loss, failed cherished plans, the clamor and demands of the world threatening to overwhelm us. A friend may betray our trust. The dark clouds of unbelief seem to cloud our faith. The Prophet Isaiah has a word of encouragement for us.

"Who is among you that fears the Lord...that walks in darkness and has no light? Let him trust in the Name of the Lord and rely on his God." (Isaiah 50:10)

Isaiah knew that dark times test our resolve to believe in our trustworthy God. He had seen firsthand the sin of the Hebrews as they forgot all God had done for them, all the promises He had kept through many years and even when they had succumbed to the sin of worshipping other gods. As he wrote what God spoke to his heart, Isaiah knew of darker days to come which would sorely test their fragile faith. And Isaiah also knew that God would remain the Promise Keeper.

Many years later, the Apostle Paul, in absolute confidence, wrote the Christians in the church fellowship of Corinth that same word of confidence as encouragement.

He said at the beginning of his letter, "God is faithful by whom you are called into the fellowship of His Son". (1 Corinthians 1:9)

And to the church at Thessalonica, Paul wrote, "Faithful is He who called you who also will do it." (I Thessalonians 5:24)

Paul was certain that the security of the believers was based not on their own ability to persevere, but on the God who keeps His promises. What was true then is true now for us. When troubles come, and they will, we are challenged to turn from inner groans to upward prayers to the God who listens and is faithful to walk with us through whatever besets us. Let us embrace Peter's words as our trust in the word of ourfaithful Creator in doing what is right." (1 Peter 4:19)

Question: How good are you at keeping your promises to God? Are the promises you make ones God wants to hear or are they more of a bargain?

I'M JUST SO ANGRY!

*H*ave you ever said, "I'm so mad I could ..." ? (You fill in the blanks) We exhibit anger over a wide variety of issues, situations, and people. Often the result of our anger is harm to someone or something. Probably most of us have seen uncontrolled anger come to a harmful conclusion and leave a lasting scar.

Is anger ever an appropriate response? Is it always a sin to get angry over something? A look at what the Bible has to say will be helpful in answering these questions. Let's begin with the Apostle Paul who, of all of the early believers, had reasons to be angry over something done to him. Writing to the Christians in Ephesus, he spoke of some things that characterize a true believer in Jesus. One of these was anger.

"Be angry, yet do not sin. Do not let the sun go down in your anger," (Ephesians 4:26)

Was Paul giving us permission to be angry? If so, over what? And when is anger an appropriate response? Remember that Paul knew of the trials and even persecution that faced those who had sought exile in Asia Minor. They saw and felt injustice daily.

John, one of Jesus' closest disciples, recorded an even in the life of Jesus in which we see an example of appropriate anger. Jesus had just come to Jerusalem to participate in the events of Passover. He entered the Temple and saw a scene which caused Him to take action. As you read this account, think of your own church and try to picture a similar scene of desecration.

"He found in the Temple those who were selling oxen and sheep and doves, and money changers seated at their tables. And He made a scourge of cords and drove them all out of the Temple along with the sheep and the oxen. He poured out the coins of the money changers and overturned their tables. To those who were selling doves He said, 'Take these things away. Stop making My Father's House a place of business.'"

His disciples remembered that it was written (by the Psalmist David, "Zeal for Your house consumes Me." (John 3:13-17: Psalm 69:9)

Another psalmist addressed God's response to the repeated sins of His chosen people. God is angered over sin and unbelief!

"When your fathers tested Me, they tried Me even though they had seen My works...Therefore, I spoke to them in My anger, 'Truly they shall not enter My rest.'" (Psalm 95:9-11)

The desecration of His Father's House caused anger to well up and overflow in Jesus' heart. The scene warranted such a response!

Knowing that Jesus never sinned, we must conclude that there are instances which cause anger of the right kind and an appropriate response.

It is impossible for Christians to remain unaffected by what we observe as injustice and outright sin. We must not remain indifferent to the sin we see every day unless we are emotionally dead. A heart of love breaks over human sin and suffering, and anger arises over the injustices which occur. We must never use anger as a tool of harm or hurt, but instead seek to put to right the injustice we view. Nor should we use anger as a reaction when we are the objects of someone's persecution or condemnation of us.

Here too, Jesus is our example. The scripture records that in Jesus' darkest hour of persecution and accusation, He did not respond in anger. Often He remained silent before His accusers even as the Prophet Isaiah had prophesied. So many years before. (Isaiah 53:7) We cannot say this was easy for our Master, nor can we even imagine the false accusations hurled at Him. Yet, anger was not His response. Let us measure our anger in such a way as to honor His examples.

Question: Have you ever experienced what we may call righteous anger? What was your response?

I'm So Tired!

Sweat drenched, breathing heavily, body taxed to the max, mind muddled, we face the tasks of life! Weariness seeps unwanted into every corner of our lives. Long hours. Long days. Some are spent in physical labor, some in mind-challenging duties, some in emotionally draining encounters. All leave us just plain tired!

We voice the frustration. "I wish I had more energy! I'm so weak! I tire so easily!" We often trudge through challenges of our own making. Our moans and groans are heard by family and friends, co-workers and passersby. And they are heard by God! We yearn for a refreshing cool drink of water. A long nap. A comfortable chair. A quiet refuge. Relief, sometimes in the form of unhealthy substances.

Is there no rest for the weary? Where can we find solace for the aches and pains of soul and body? Never more than when we are physically, mentally or emotionally spent do we need the One who can truly refresh us and infuse into us new life.

The prophet Isaiah heard God say, this.

"Have you not heard, the Everlasting God, the Lord, the Creator of the ends of the earth, does not grow faint. Nor does He grow weary. His understanding is inscrutable... He gives strength to the weary, and to him who lacks might, He increases power. Though youths grow weary and tired and vigorous young men stumble badly, yet those who wait on the Lord will gain new strength. They will mount up with wings like eagles. They will run and not get tired. They will walk and not become weary." (Isaiah 40:28-31)

What an amazing promise! Those words are a clear reminder that in our weakness and weariness, God is our Source. We have available to us God-infused energy. He never tires of coming to the aid of His children. His help is available 24/7/365 to provide in us what we need. His gifts of renewal are far superior to a nap, a cozy chair, or even a drink of water. It is God who is our strength!

We can observe what causes physical exhaustion. But what causes spiritual tiredness? What does that look like in the life of a believer? Let's use the word lethargy. How is that defined in spiritual terms? Webster's Dictionary defines it as "stresses, listlessness, or indifference resulting from fatigue induced by an external source or internal medication., or extreme sluggishness." Though on the surface those terms do not seem spiritual, a closed look may reveal that the underlying cause for this weariness of spirit and soul may reveal an absence from periods of refreshing with the Lord.

Luke, the physician and writer of the book of Acts of the Apostles, knew much about fatigue. He recognized its cure as well. He heard Peter address this very issue.

"Therefore, repent and return (to the Lord) so that your sins may be wiped away in order that times of refreshing may come from the presence of the Lord." (Acts 3:19)

Think of the picture David painted for us in Psalm 23, the Shepherd's Psalm, We can picture David lying in the grass beside a quiet stream with his sheep nearby. It is the scene of the refreshing which comes in the presence of the Lord.

"He makes me lie down in green pastures. He leads me beside quiet waters, He restores my soul." (Psalm 23:2-3a)

We feel the weariness leave David as he rests in the Lord. There is no greater need in the harried and rushed world in which we live than the restoration of our souls. We all seek for the "quiet waters" and "lush, green grasses" of rest. That requires us to stop! Stop our frantic pace and busier than need be lives and pause in the presence of God to soak up His rest.

"Jesus said, 'Come unto Me all you who are weary and heavy laden and I will give you rest. Take MY yoke upon you and learn from Me, for I am gentle and humble in heart, and I will give you rest." (Matthew 11:28-29)

Question: Are you in need of the rest of God? What will help you achieve that?

Important Recall

S o often now we receive a notice by mail or TV of a recall
of something we have previously purchased. From cars to
appliances and electronic devices to furniture or drugs, we are told
that some error in use may result in harm to us. We are admonished
to return the article ASAP for adjustment or repair. We hasten to
reply, knowing that we are among the throng who will seek satisfaction. There may be a refund to you or perhaps a replacement with
the "new and improved" version.

Human error is common. After all, "to err is human" as the saying
goes. No one is fail-proof. It is when there is a malfunction causing
danger or inconvenience that we moan the loudest. "What a piece
of junk!" "I can't believe that passed all the tests of reliability!" Why,
then, do we rail at imperfection leading to recall?

Such recalls, while annoying and inconvenient, are minor glitches
in life compared to the most important recall of all.

The Creator of all human beings has issued a mass recall of every
"unit" originally perfect made, regardless of the year or model. This is

due to a fatal defect in the central organ, the heart. This malfunction often reproduces the same defect in all subsequent human hearts. This defect has a name, SIN. The primary evidence of malfunction is absence of moral judgment and performance.

Continuing to operate this human "unit" without correction renders the Maker's warranty invalid, and it exposes the human "unit" to all manner of dangers. While the Maker is not in any way at fault for this malfunction, He nevertheless yearns for each "unit" to be restored to the condition for which it was created.

What does the perfect human "unit" look like? Picture Jesus, God's Son. The model of His life exactly mirrored that of His Father in attribute and conduct., even to His dependence on the counsel of His Father.

"Jesus said to them, "The Son can do nothing of Himself unless it is something He sees the Father doing. For, whatever the Father does, these things the Son also does in like manner. For the Father loves the Son and shows Him all things that He Himself is doing. (John 5:19-20)

Warning!!! Continuing to operate without correction will result eventually in danger to the human soul. The human "unit" will be impounded until judgment has been rendered.

What are some evidences of this malfunction? It may include loss of direction, amnesia as to origin, lack of peace and joy, selfish or violent behavior, depression or confusion in the mental component, foul vocal emissions, aberrant behavior, stubborn refusal to admit to the truth. Each human "unit" possesses a combination of these malfunctions as well as numerous others unlisted.

For free emergency service, kneel and contact this recall station. The number is P R A Y E R. The area code is J E S U S. Prompt assistance will be provided. The cost of such service has been paid by the Son of God.

While every recall is subject to the same overhaul, each human "unit" is unique in its flaws. This requires a time of examination to determine what must be restored to its intended, planned purpose. Then place the call to the Maker who stands ready to receive, forgive and restore.

"May the Lord Jesus equip you in every good thing to do His will, working in that which is pleasing in His sight, through Jesus Christ, to whom be glory forever and ever. Amen" (Hebrews 13:21)

Consider: Check yourself for possible need for repair or replacement of any spiritual "component"!

IN THE MEANTIME

*W*aiting! Seemingly interminable waiting! We hate to wait! Impatient to get on with whatever we want to be about next, we pace inwardly and groan outwardly. Waiting to go. Waiting for "fast food" at a slow restaurant. Waiting to see the doctor. Waiting for a much anticipated event. Waiting for the stoplight to turn green. Just waiting. In the meantime, we honk our horns impatiently, alter our words, complain about poor service and destroy our peace. We waste the period called "in the meantime" by unproductive habits and fits of temper.

In truth, much of life happens "in the meantime". Have you noticed? In between events, errands, tasks, responsibilities, there is "the meantime", that span of minutes, hours, days, or weeks we lose through wasted emotion, agitation, impatience and neglect. So, what are we to make of this "in the meantime" period? What should we do so that these precious times are not wasted?

The Apostle Peter was caught in just such a dilemma. We know that Peter was a man who liked action right now. Jesus, his Master had said to wait in Jerusalem. Wait!

"Gathering them all together (the eleven disciples), He commanded them not to leave Jerusalem but to wait for what the Father had promised which, He said, ' You heard from Me; for John baptized with water, but you will be baptized with the Holy Spirit not many days from now.'" (Acts 1:4-5)

Can you sense their wonder and anticipation at the wait? Jesus had promised that something very life changing was going to happen to them; but "in the meantime" they must wait. What were their expectations? They went to a familiar place, the upper room where they were staying. We do not know if it is the same place Jesus had His last meal with them, but perhaps it was because of the memories it evoked. How did they wait?

"These, all with one mind, were continually devoting themselves to prayer, along with Mary, the mother of Jesus and His brothers." (Acts 1:14)

They prayed! Continually, that is repeatedly. The result of this "in the meantime" period prepared their hearts for what was to come, the arrival of the Holy Spirit to indwell them.

Needless to say, what happened exceeded all prior expectations. As the Day of Pentecost dawned, the Spirit of God descended on the open hearts of Peter and the others who had waited with him. Just as Jesus had promised, the Power to be all they were called to be filled them to overflowing. The missionary arm of the church was born, all because they waited with prepared hearts. Their "meantime" was not wasted on fretting or agitating.

Peter was prepared to take the next steps in the new life ahead of him due to the period of waiting on God. He was now prepared to understand the things Jesus had been teaching him. The Teacher had come to continue implanting in Peter and the rest of the believers God's truth of their inheritance in Christ.

Have you ever considered what might have been the result if Peter had used the wait to fret and agitate instead of kneeling in prayer? Would he have missed the greatest blessing of God? Would he have been prepared to carry out Jesus' directive to spread the Good News to the world? Would he have been the strong rock that Jesus named him or just plain Simon, the fisherman?

What about you? How do you use your "in the meantime"? Do you agitate, fret, wriggle and squirm impatiently? Or can those times be used to pray through something God has laid on your heart? The possibilities are endless if we are willing to lay down our impatience and listen to what our Master has to say. In the meantime, pray!

Challenge: Choose a "meantime" to seek God, listen for His instructions, and receive His blessing.

INTIMACY

*I*ntimacy. The word brings a feeling of warmth, security, even belonging. We humans all desire intimacy and feel incomplete without some degree of it. Picture the intimacy of a baby cuddled securely in mother's arm or the sharing heart to heart with a treasured friend. Think of the intimacy of a child seated on Father's lap secure in his strength and protected by his arms... We even see glimpses of the need for intimacy in animals as the huddle together. Without words spoken there is within us a longing for the closeness of soul to soul. There is an ache within when such intimacy is lost or injured even briefly. And there is heartfelt joy when intimacy is restored.

Scripture provides a clear picture of the most important intimacy we may ever have, intimacy with God. The Apostle Paul wrote to the church at Philippi about his own desire for intimacy with his Savior.

"I count all things as loss in view of the surpassing value of knowing Christ Jesus, my Lord...that I may know Him, and the power of His resurrection, and the fellowship of His sufferings, being conformed to His death." (Philippians 3:8-10)

Paul desired nothing more than intimacy with his Lord. To him life held no greater pleasure. He wanted to feel Father's arms embracing him in his darkest dangers, to hear Father say, "well done, my child", to listen as God revealed some truth about Himself. In all things Paul desired to please the One with whom he shared such intimacy.

It is God who knows us intimately, every cell, every wart, every thought. He knows our weaknesses and our bent to sin. In spite of any negatives we may have, He loves us eternally. We are His, and His door to intimacy is always open. The scriptures tell us of God's intimacy with us even before we were ever born. The psalmist proclaims this truth as he tells us that God knew him even before he was born. Isaiah echoed that same thought of intimacy as he heard God support him.

"You have been borne by me from birth and have been carried from the womb. Even to your old age I will be the same..." (Isaiah 46:3b-4a)

Such is the nature of our God! He desires intimacy with us from the womb to the tomb and beyond. Such was Job's confession. (Job 10:19)

How does such intimacy happen? What engenders the desire for such a deep relationship? Let's consider some keys which may promote greater intimacy with God.

- Bring to the times of quietness with God a heart uncluttered by the things which press in on us to make us hurry through the sharing.

- Hold with care and consideration all that we read in the Word, and hear God speak to us through it.
- Question without fear the things we do not understand, and ask for insight from the Spirit of God.
- Accept the discipline God applies as correction is needed by us, remembering it is not sent to punish but to remove the barriers to fellowship with Him.
- Praise and thank God for who He is as well as what He does in and through us.
- Listen intently for instructions as to what He would have us do in any situation or opportunity before us.

Intimacy with God is costly. The price is the "loss of all things" as Paul put it. Our willingness to lay aside all of our wants and refocus on relationship with Father God is a lifetime of sweet relationship like no other. Here is the admonition of James.

"Draw near to God and He will draw near to you." (James 4:8)

Consider: Read Philippians 3:7, Paul's testimony from a Roman prison. Meditate on what that might mean for you.

Into the Storm

(Part One)

*A*ll eight passengers, nestled securely in comfortable seats in the private plane, watched dreamily as the fluffy clouds around them floated by. Occasionally the bright rays of the sun added glistening highlights to the clouds. The pilot, a seasoned veteran, chatted with everyone as he focused on the radar screen in front of him. As minutes passes, the radar screen's colors changed from a calm green to reds and yellows. As the passengers looked out the windows, they noticed that the fluffy clouds had been replaced with darker clouds and the wind seemed to buffet the plane a bit. The pilot said, "Looks like we are headed into some stormy weather ahead." The radar screen, now mostly reds seemed to say, "Danger ahead! Take evasive action!" White knuckles replaced calm demeanor as all of the passengers sensed the danger and anxiously asked, " Where can we go to escape? Lower? Higher? Could we fly around the storm? Are we going to crash? The pilot seemed calm even as he tried to maneuver the plane around the blackest clouds.

Finally the pilot announced, "We are going to have to fly through the storm as quickly as possible so we can reach calmer air. Buckle your seat belts!" A few terrifying minutes passed when the small plane was pushed to and fro by the winds as if to tear it apart. Seeing the terror on the faces around her, one passenger said calmly, "Our pilot knows what to do. We will be all right!" Then as suddenly as the storm had engulfed the plane, the sunlight peered through, and the dark clouds were gone. The skillful pilot had brought his passengers safely through the storm.

Being in the midst of a storm, whether literally or figuratively, is often quite scary. The unknown ahead seems formidable. Our resources to weather the storm seem inadequate. Anxiety and fear are never far away, it seems. Life has storms!

Some are circumstantial and unavoidable. Some may be of our own making. Often we sail through life unaware that our "radar screen" has issued a warning. When it comes, we are left startled and anxious or just plain scared.

Mark's Gospel tells us of a storm which suddenly engulfed the boat in which Jesus and His disciples traveled across the Sea of Galilee.

"When evening came, Jesus said to them, "Let's go over to the other side." Leaving the crowd, they took Jesus with them into the boat... And there arose a fierce storm, and the waves were breaking over the boat so much that it was filling with water. Jesus was sleeping serenely in the stern. They shook Him and said, "Master, do You not care that we are perishing! (Mark 4:35-38)

These seasoned fishermen had seen storms on the sea before and knew of the violence that accompanied them. Perhaps they had battled the winds before and the fears that beset them. Now all their focus was on the terror that filled their hearts.

"Jesus got up and, in rebuke, said to the wind, 'Hush! Be still!' And the wind died down and the sea became perfectly calm. He said to them "Why are you afraid? How is it that you have no faith?" (Mark 4:39-40)

In their moments of fear, the disciples had forgotten that Jesus had told them to cross the sea. They could only see the danger. Would God let His Son drown? Really? That never entered their minds, so focused were they on their own safety. Were they hoping for a miracle? Yes!

Jesus sharp assessment of their level of faith caused them to fear on a different level.

They said to one another, "Who is this that even the winds and sea obey Him?" (V41)

Let's ask a few questions.

- Did God send the storm?
- If so, was it to teach a lesson to the fledgling believers?
- What did He want them to learn as they battled the storm?

Consider: Are you battling a storm just now? Is Jesus "in the boat" with you? Does that calm your fears?

INTO THE STORM

(Part Two)

*L*ife is often a stormy mess. All kinds of storms buffet us, Storms that just batter us. Storms that rearrange the landscape of our lives. Storms that drench our efforts. Storms that cause a change of direction. Storms that teach. Storms in our marriage, our finances, our health.

What do you do when you see a storm approaching? What is important when the storm does come? Our responses are vital. Do we quickly call the doctor? Make a plan of action? Try to deny the storm ahead? Send for the fireman? Deny the outcome? Question God?

That last response is often the most common one. Like Jesus' disciples, we whine, "God, don't you see the storm I am in? Don't You care? Do something!" This response is an accusation hurled at the One who loves us most. He sees the dangers ahead and He sees our level of faith. Jeremiah reminds us that God makes the storm clouds! (Jeremiah 10:1). The God who forms the clouds is prepared to help us battle the storm if we are assessing the danger wisely.

Luke the Physician recorded Jesus addressing this issue.

"Jesus said to the crowds, 'When you see a cloud rising in the west, immediately you say that a shower is coming and so it turns out. And when you see a south wind blowing you say it will be a hot day, and so it is. You are hypocrites! You know how to analyze the earth and sky; but why do you not analyze this present time?" (Luke 12:54-56)

Our first response should be to bring the storm to God however brief or panicked our prayer may be. Sometimes we must also admit to God that the storm we are in is of our own making. Confessions like that are not easy to admit, but necessary. You see, God expects us to have made preparations that will help us when the storm arrives, and it will. What should we have done in preparation for the certainty of storms?

- Immerse ourselves daily in the Word of God. Listen to what He tells us through the lives of Bible characters.
- Ask God to explain what we do not understand.
- Believe that what He says He will do, He will do.
- Trust God to be our strong tower as the storm rages around us.
- Know of a surety that God is the Storm Maker, Storm Tracker and the Storm Stiller.

We can be in no safer place than in a storm of God's making. His piloting is flawless. Whether He takes us through the storm or around the storm, He is there.

Often we miss the warning signs. The Pharisees and Sadducees came to test Jesus. They asked Him to show a sign from heaven. Jesus gave this reply, a lesson on weather reporting.

"When it is evening, you say, 'It will be fair weather because the sky is red'. And in the morning you say, 'There will be a storm today for the sky is red and threatening.' Do you know how to discern the appearance of the sky but cannot discern the signs of the times?" (Matthew 16:1-3)

We too must discern the approach of a storm whether in our world or in our lives., and bring our fears to God.

"I know You, God, have been a defense for the helpless, a defense for the needy in distress, a refuge from the storm, a shade from the heat." (Isaiah 25:4)

The Lord answered me and set me in a safe place. The Lord is for me. I will not fear. What can man do to me? ... It is better to take refuge in the Lord than to trust in man." (Psalm 118:5-6,8)

Challenge: Read Jeremiah 10:6-18 to understand who commands the weather.

IS IT FREE?

*W*ho doesn't like free stuff? We all do! The truth is that there is usually a string attached that denotes the real cost somewhere, sometime. It may be hidden or delayed, but rest assured, it is there, the real cost.

A good example is the BOGO deals at grocery stores. "If you will shop at this store. You will get such a deal." Have you ever checked the cost of just one item at the everyday price? Many times it is lower than the sale. BOGO stands for "Buy one. Get One", but it isn't followed by the letter "F" for free.

Have you ever received a letter in the mail or a phone call inviting you to a free meal? Caveat: "And, by the way, we want you to buy one of these swell time shares." What isn't said is that you will have to listen to a lengthy sales pitch about how lucky you are to get in on this great deal.

Or what about the "free" hearing test. Do you really think they care about your hearing? No, they want to sell you their latest and greatest product. That may be repeated time and time again with any number of "can't live without" products.

The Hebrews were offered freedom from their bondage in Egypt. God promised to lead them to the land He had promised. But their freedom cost them greatly when they refused to trust God's promises to them. The generation which left Egypt all died without ever entering the Promised Land. Their faithlessness was costly indeed.

Surely all the men who have seen My glory and the signs which I performed in Egypt and in the wilderness, yet have put Me to the test these ten times, and have not listened to My Voice, shall by no means see the land which I swore to their fathers. Nor shall any of those who spurned Me see it." (Numbers 13:14-24)

We live in the" land of the free and home of the brave". But our freedom wasn't free. It came at great cost of lives and effort as men fought to be free of the shackles of English rule. The freedoms our ancestors longed for are found in our Declaration of Independence and Constitution. Our freedom today still comes with a cost as we strive to maintain our individual freedoms, the freedom to come and go as we please or to buy and sell anytime and place.

Some of us are even chained by ideas of what is popular at the time. We feel deprived if we cannot have the desires of our hearts. We rant about the encroachment of our freedom as politicians seek to impose new regulations "for our welfare", they say. Personal freedom is fragile.

Is anything free? Well, my salvation is free. I don't have to bargain for it or do things to earn it. I don't have to bargain, that I will if God will. Salvation is a gift." Yes, it is a gift because the Bible tells us that Jesus purchased it with His blood.

"The wages (cost) of sin is death, but the gift of God is eternal life in Christ Jesus, our Lord" (Romans 6:23)

Our precious free gift came at an awful cost. It cost our Savior scorn, beating, ridicule, agonizing crucifixion on a cruel cross, and temporary separation from His Father. It cost God separation from His Only Son, the very first and only separation. Consider the agony of soul and spirit involved is such a cost that we might be free.

What is our cost for that gift? The cost is ourselves offered to God as His faithful believers. The benefits are too numerous to count. We must echo the confession of the Apostle Paul.

"I am crucified with Christ, and it is no longer I who live but Christ lives in me; and the life which I now live in the flesh, I live by faith in the Son of God who loved me and gave Himself up for me." (Galatians 2:20)

Question: Are you free? If not, what enslaves you?

It Is Finished!

*H*aving labored long and hard on a project, it feels so good to be able to say, "It is finished! The labor was worth it. I am glad I committed to do the task to the very end." So often in life that is not true. We begin a project, task, or assignment and at some point lay it aside incomplete. Good intentions went away as frustration or weariness or perhaps just disinterest slid into place.

Sometimes a task or project is assigned by someone else, a boss, teacher, or parent for whom we must perform well. That is added pressure, and failure seems larger when that is so. The cost of failure to finish may be loss of employment, a failing grade, or the disappointment in the eyes of the parent who had high expectations of us.

Attitude is so important! Approaching any task with a foot-dragging reluctance assures an uncertain outcome. However, when we tackle an assigned task with a positive gladness of heart and a determination to see it to completion, we are much more likely to finish well. In some ways this positive approach makes the task seem easier, too.

The most difficult assignment ever given to man was the one given to Jesus by His Father, God. Put simply, the assignment was "Go, be Yourself, die". Unlike us, Jesus knew the final outcome of His assignment. It was death on a cruel cross as He took upon Himself the sins of all mankind. Not once do we read that Jesus gave up in frustration, though He had many challenges to do so. Never once do we see Him close the door of opportunity to succeed in His assignment. In fact, Jesus was firm in His resolve.

Jesus said, "When you lift up the Son of man, then you will know that I am He. I do nothing on My own initiative, but I speak the things My Father taught Me" (John 8:28)

In spite of long, weary hours, constant harassment by unbelievers, confusion by His disciples, and rejection by the very ones for whom He came, Jesus continued to be obedient and focused on His responsibility. We may all shudder to think of what our lives might be like had Jesus failed to finish the task God gave Him.

So well did He persevere that He was able to say,

"I glorified You on earth, having completed the work You gave Me to do" (John 17:4)

Jesus knew He had completed His assignment well. With His last breath, He said, "It is finished."

I think the Apostle Paul had this in mind when he was approaching death. He wrote encouragement to his young protégé, Timothy to remind him to finish the task before him.

"I have finished the course. I have kept the faith. Therefore, laid up for me in heaven is a crown of righteousness which the Lord, the Righteous Judge, will award to me on that day, and not only me but also to all who have loved His appearing." (2 Timothy 4:7-8)

The Apostle Peter describes this crown as "an unfading crown of glory" 1(Peter 5:4)

What must we do? What is our assigned task awaiting our completion? The Psalmist David answered this way.

'I will bless the Lord at all times. His praise shall continually be in my mouth. My soul will make its boast in the Lord...O, magnify the Lord with me and let us exalt His Name together." (Psalm 34:1-3)

Let us be among those who finish well!

Question: Is it your desire to finish well the tasks God has assigned you?

It's About Time

*T*ime! We never seem to have enough of it. Time dictates our lives whether we acknowledge it or not. Awaiting time to pass, we fret. Wishing time to last longer, we pine. Lost time we mourn. Hurrying to be somewhere we race as if time could change. Time with friends or family seems to pass too quickly. Time can be a friend or enemy as we all are bound by time.

We even coin funny phrases about time. Here are a few to ponder.

- Time flies when you're having fun
- Time marches on
- Time bomb
- Time warp
- In the meantime
- Time honored tradition
- It's Howdy Doody time!:

But what if time didn't exist? No clocks ticking off the seconds. No digital devices or alarms to remind us to get up, go, stay, hurry.

Imagine timelessness if you can. There was such a time. The Apostle wrote about it.

"In the beginning (meaning before there was time) was the Word and the Word was with God, and the Word was God.: (John 1:1}

So, time began with God. God even said of Himself, "Even from eternity, I am He." (Isaiah 43:13) Hard to grasp and harder to understand! No time constraints. Just eternity. The stress of hurry, nonexistent. The burden of deadlines, erased. The fret over what tomorrow might bring, gone. No one was there to measure time. In the Old Testament there is no general word for time; nor are there specific words for the categories of past, present and future There was only the distance or duration in which something occurs.

Though we cannot comprehend such a thought as absence of time, there are truths to consider. First and foremost, is the eternal, always existing Triune God. Nothing and no one else is timeless. All of creation stirred as time began at God's command.

The Psalmist expressed time this way.

"For a thousand years in Thy sight are like yesterday when it is past or as a watch in the night." (Psalm 90:4)

God offeres eternity to mankind. He gave us time to love, to heal, to produce, to grieve, to dance, to speak or be silent. At the appointed time God sent His Son to draw us back to the eternity we were made for. Jesus is the Way to eternity with God. God is even now waiting for all who will believe.

Though we await eternity with God, life here on earth is lived in the meantime. So important is this "meantime" that Jesus gave us instructions as to what we must be about.

"Go therefore and make disciples of all nations, baptizing them in the Name of the Father, Son and Holy Spirit. Teach them to observe all that I have commanded you, and I will be with you always, even to the end of the age (time)." (Matthew 28:19-20)

In the meantime we have time to be God's hands and feet, His Voice to a world desperately in need of truth, His light to penetrate the darkness that seeks to invade us, His assurance of rest for the weary. His offer of freedom to those in chains. Time is in His hands. Yes, we have time! Eternity awaits us.

"Teach us to number our days so that we may present to You a heart of wisdom...Confirm the works of our hands" (Psalm 90:12, 17)

Challenge: Search the scriptures to find the many occasions on which time is a factor. You will be amazed!

KINDLING FIRES

The branches, twigs, and leaves were all piled up, ready for a campfire! Roasted marshmallows! Hot dogs on a spit!! S'mores! The excited family waited for Dad to light the flame. Finally the tiny fire showed some sparks, but it didn't catch the pile on fire. In his impatience to get on with the kindling of the fire, Dad failed to take proper precautions. As he poured gasoline on the tiny flame, the fire roared to life, As it did Dad was severely burned on both legs! A trip to the ER, and later the hospital burn unit, turned into a weeks long healing process with skin grafting on his legs.

The lesson learned was a painful one. It is important to be safe when kindling a fire. Do not use gasoline as a fire starter! The lessons about fire are taught to our children at an early age so they will escape injury. We want them to understand the harm that may occur when care is not taken around open flames.

In the scripture an analogy is made using fire as a flame from our mouth. Passages emphasize the harm of a careless tongue. James tried to give that warning to the believers who were scattered throughout Asia Minor.

"The tongue is a fire, the very world of iniquity. It is set among our members as that which defiles the entire body and sets on fire the course of our lives. And is set on fire by hell...No one can tame the tongue. It is a restless evil and full of deadly poison. With it we bless our Lord and Father, and with it we curse men who have been made in the likeness of God. From the same mouth come both blessing and cursing. My friends, it ought not to be that way." (James 3:6-10)

We are not told exactly why James felt that he must offer this analogy, but we do know that he was not the first in scripture to do so. King Solomon knew the power of the tongue to kindle good and bad fires.

"There is one who speaks rashly like the thrusts of a sword, but the tongue of a wise man brings healing. Truthful lips will be established forever, but a lying tongue is only for a moment." (.Proverbs 12:18-19)

God Himself likened the tongue to a deadly arrow as He spoke of His wayward people.

"Their tongue is a deadly arrow. It speaks deceit. With the mouth one speaks peace to his neighbor, but inwardly he sits in ambush for him." (Jeremiah 9:8)

What are we to learn about the damage or good our tongues utter? In the times in which we live we hear violent words shouted, harsh and unfair accusations hurled carelessly about, lies spread. Throughout out towns and cities, communities and schools, businesses and some-times even churches, fires are kindled in the name of freedom and rights. Those fires spread, engulfing areas and damaging the peace.

We, as Christians are called to utter wise, healing words which kindle peace and harmony. We must refrain from using our words to stir up strife and unrest. We must not trade insults, but give a blessing instead. Listen to Solomon as he admonished his son.

"My son, listen to my words. Keep them in your heart. For they are life to those who find them and health to all their body. Watch over your heart with diligence, for from it flow the springs of life. Put away from you a deceitful mouth and put devious speech far from you." (Proverbs 4:20-23 paraphrased)

Challenge: Check your words! Are they life-giving or soul damaging?

KNOW YOUR SOURCE

*W*here does your peace come from? Your strength? Your wisdom? Your love? To whom do you look for these and other needs? It is a vital question for all of us, especially for those who claim Jesus as Savior and God as their Source.

Peter declared his Source. Shortly after the miraculous event on the Day of Pentecost when the Spirit of God descended and filled the disciples with power, Peter and John went to the Temple to pray. What happened there was proof of Peter's transformation from blustery fisherman to spokesman for God. A lame man who regularly begged for alms at the Temple, saw the two disciples and asked for a gift.

Requesting the man's attention, Peter declared, "I have neither silver nor gold, but I have something far better. In the Name of Jesus Christ of Nazareth, walk!" Then, taking the man's hand, Peter raised him to his feet. At once the man felt strength return to his feet and legs. Joyously the man began leaping and walking and praising God. Into the Temple he went, a place he had not been able to enter before. People, seeing him, recognized him as the beggar at the gate of the Temple, and they were awestruck! On Solomon's Porch they crowded around the disciples and the newly healed man with wonder and excitement.

Sensing a moment of opportunity to give credit to Whom it was due, said, "Men of Israel, why are you so surprised? Why are you staring at us as if we had power of ourselves to make this man walk?"

If you ever doubted Peter's change, listen to the clarity with which he brought the onlookers to the feet of the cross.

""The God of Abraham, Isaac, and Jacob, our forefathers, has done this through His Son, the very One Whom you denied and rejected. You disowned the Just and Blameless One and demanded He be crucified. You killed the very Source of Life Whom God has now raised from the dead. We are witnesses to the fact! It is through faith in His Name that this man you see before you now walks in perfect health. I know you acted in ignorance as did your rulers. Now, realizing this, repent that your sins may be erased and forgiveness may come to you from the Lord." (Acts 3:1-26)

Peter went on to explain the Old Testament scriptures to them in clarity. Wait! Is this that uneducated fisherman speaking? Oh, yes! Peter had drunk from the well of forgiveness, received the Holy Spirit to indwell him, and was now seeing the truths his Master had taught come to light. It should be noted that Peter's new outlook came with a cost. While Peter was still talking, the religious leaders arrested them and tossed Peter and John into prison! But that is not the end of the story.

Peter had another golden opportunity to testify about his Savior. He got right to the point, the Holy Spirit being his strength.

"If we are being put on trial here because a good deed to restore a cripple to health, know this! It was by the power and authority of the Name of Jesus Whom you had crucified. God has raised Him from the dead and has set Him as the Cornerstone of faith. There is salvation in no other."

Wow! What courage! Very unlike the cowering denials of a few weeks ago. Even the religious leader realized the impact of the miracle. If anyone doubts the power of transformation when a life is given over fully to God, remember Peter!

Question: What is your main source when troubled?

Let There Be Light!

Can you imagine living in a dark, colorless world devoid of light? No golden sunsets. No delicate pink roses or purple irises. No brilliant autumn leaves. No azure blue oceans and lakes. Just colorless landscapes made so by the absence of light. Even the thought of such a condition evokes mental pictures of despondency and despair. Darkness! For without light there is no color. Contained in light rays are the colors of the rainbow. We see objects by the light reflected on them. The magic of a prism held in the light is delightful to behold.

It is not by chance that God's first creation was light, because without it all else would have been colorless. In essence, God thrust Himself, the Light of the World, into His creation. The Apostle John wrote this.

"God is Light and in Him is no darkness at all." (1 John 1:5)

Shedding His Light on creation offered to Adam and Eve, and to us, a myriad of colors and hues too numerous to count. God said,

"Let there be light and there was light." In contrast, our lives lived without the Light of God, are dark.

The results of darkened lives are well recorded in the Bible and in many other books as well. Throughout the ages men living in darkness have brought shame, disgrace, and destruction upon themselves and others. Their light-deprived lives are stark examples of the failure of God's creation to live up to its potential as refractors of Light to dispel the darkness.

Yet in every age there have been those who walk in the Light. Through them we see color. The same Light who was with God in the beginning, the One who walked the earth as the Light of Life, is now the One who indwells His people so that we may be light. It is He who gives color to our lives. We live in the Light, unlike those who have refused the Light in favor of darkness. His Light shines through us.

Jesus said, "You are the light of the world. A city set on a hill cannot be hidden. Nor does anyone light a lamp and put it under a basket, but on a lampstand; and it gives light to all who are in the house. Let your light shine so that they may see your good works and glorify your Father which is in heaven," (Matthew 5:14-16)

We bear this Light because on the darkest day in history, Jesus, our Light, was crucified. In Matthew 27 we are told that as the sin of mankind was laid on Jesus, there was darkness on earth from the sixth to the ninth hour, in the middle of the day. It was as if God had withdrawn all of His Light from the earth.

Can you imagine the terror and despair that must have engulfed those who were suddenly thrown into stark darkness at midday? .But the darkness of that period of hours brought salvation given by the Light who can never be extinguished. Jesus had told His followers that very thing months before as He gave the Light of life to a woman accused of sin.

"I am the Light of the world. He who follows Me will not walk in darkness but will have the Light of life." (John 8:12)

The first to see the Light after His crucifixion were the women who visited to the tom where Jesus had been buried. Scripture records that "His appearance was like lightning, and His clothing as white as snow." He was revealed as the Light of the World. (Matthew 28: 3)

Paul saw this Light on the road to Damascus.

"I saw a Light from heaven brighter than the sun blazing around me." (Acts 26:13)

The Light shed such light on Paul's life that he was transformed from Saul, the Pharisee who persecuted believers, to Paul the powerful apostle of Christ whose message and letters still today give us hope.

One day when Jesus returns to reign over all, even the rays of the sun will not be necessary. His Light will be sufficient.

"The city has no need of the sun or of the moon to shine on it, for the glory of the Lord has illumined it, and its lamp is the Lamb." (Revelation 21:23)

Come Lord Jesus! Bring Light to our darkened world!

Question: Will you join me in prayer that all of us as believers may be light bearers?

LIFE IS RELATIONSHIPS

Our lives are built upon relationship with others: family, friends, doctors, teachers, business associates, etc. Some of these relationships may be classified as casual or infrequent. Others are necessary for the health and wellbeing of one's life. Some few are deeper, more intimate, more permanent. These are usually built upon effort and sharing of ourselves through time. Maybe, just maybe, one of these relationships is so impactful as to be a life changer.

One relationship that most assuredly fits into that category is our intimate relationship with God. It is this vital relationship which is truly a life-alterer. As we consider the ramifications of such intimacy, let's take a look at the lives of the twelve apostles chosen by Jesus. What were their relationships like? What were the elements which drew them closer and closer to the Master? What freedom did that afford them as day by day they became friends? Looking at these things may provide for us a window into our own relationships or lack thereof.

Using the Apostle John's record in chapters 13-16 as a window into their relationship, we can begin to see some interesting areas to consider in our own relationship with God. The events in these chapters occurred during the last few days of Jesus' time on earth. By this time the twelve had lived with Jesus, walked the dusty roads of Palestine, and broken bread together often. They had watched as Jesus healed the sick, cast out demons, mended broken lives. They had seen Him walk on water and calm a raging storm with a word. They had watched Him forgive and restore dignity to many. Each of these things was a learning experience and a peek into who Jesus really was.

Coming from diverse backgrounds and having differing personalities, each disciple crafted his own relationship with Jesus., John, the tender-hearted. Peter the brash and impulsive. Thomas the questioner. Judas the mask wearer. They had experienced fatigue, confusion, doubt, apprehension, fear, surprise, and awe, all components of their relationship with the One they called "Master".

The lessons they learned, sometimes after great struggle, were often difficult to grasp. Certainly these lessons were far from their original expectations of what the Messiah would be and what their friendship with Him would mean in the future. In straightforward terms, their relationships required WORK!

One very interesting facet of the disciples' relationship with Jesus was the freedom Jesus offered them to question Him on a wide variety of topics. Consider a few.

- "Lord, where are You going and why can we not come with You?" This was Peter's question after Jesus had said He would be going where they could not come. Can you sense Peter's dismay as he considered separation from his Master? (John 13:6)
- Lord, we do not know where You are going, so how can we know the way?" Thomas' question reveals confusion and dismay. (John 14:5)
- "Lord, what has happened that You are going to disclose Yourself to us and not to the world?" Judas (not Iscariot) was confused and failed to see what relationship with God is all about. (John 14:22)

The disciples were not the only ones who were questioners. Jesus Himself was often the questioner.

- "Do you know what I have done to you?" This Jesus asked the twelve after He had washed their feet. (John 13:12)
- Will you lay down your life for Me?" This is the question Jesus asked Peter when he questioned Jesus' leaving. (John 13:38)
- "Have I been so long with you, and yet you have not come to know Me, Phillip? He who has seen Me has seen the Father." Jesus' sadness is evident as he responded to Phillip's request to see the Father. (John 14:9-10)

What freedom they enjoyed to be able to lay out their questions before Jesus! We see the evolution of a relationship built on long hours of association with Jesus. So, what can we learn about our own relationship with God from this? Certainly we experience some of the same questions, confusion, wonderment, and, yes, doubt. We can expect to work at it daily, along dusty roads and weary nights. We can expect God to be there with open arms, ready to calm our fears, comfort our souls and, field all our questions with grace. These encounters are all about building a solid and eternal relationship with our God. Are you ready?

Challenge: Think about your closest relationship. Who is it with and why?

LISTENING SKILLS

*L*isten! Did you hear that noise? Listen to me. I have something important to tell you. Listen before you speak. Did you listen to the news last night? Oh No! I should have listened! I did not listen to the instructions my teacher gave.

Listening, really hearing, is so very important. Our ears were provided for a reason. As we listen we may escape danger, learn a needed fact, enjoy a favorite piece of music, avoid a wreck, attend to a cry od distress, relieve the fears of a friend, detect a leak in the plumbing, move to safety when a storm threatens. There are so many reasons why it is important to listen, to hear the sounds around us. To be hard of hearing or deaf provides much more opportunity to miss the vital messages of life and to leave ourselves open to danger.

Listening is not a passive skill. It elicits a response of some kind: pleasure, dismay, fear, warmth, confusion, acceptance, action, and sometimes anger. Some of us listen well. Some of us listen to several things at once and so, miss the message. Some of us talk when we should be listening.

The problem of listening is universal. All people everywhere have the same problems listening, unless the effort is urged on us by an outside force. Can you hear the Sergeant t hollering, "Listen up, you boneheads!"

Early in the life of the Hebrew nation God issued a warning about listening.

"See, I am setting before you today a blessing and a curse: the blessing if you listen to the commandments of the Lord your God, which I am commanding you today, and a curse if you do not listen to the commandments of the Lord your God." (Deuteronomy 11:26-28)

The God who listens had heard their cries in bondage and had led them out of Egypt. His people, however, proved to be poor listeners as they repeatedly walked away from the blessings of God and entered into sin. They had forgotten what happened to Pharaoh when he refused to listen to Moses as he delivered God's warnings. They had not learned that listening required a positive response in order to reap the blessings of God. As many times as they promised to heed God, that many times and more they forgot what they had heard and promised to obey.

Many years later Jesus issued this truth.

"Truly I say to you that he who hears My word and believes Him who sent Me, has eternal life, and does not come into judgment, but has passed out of death into life." (John 5:24)

As if to encourage the disciples' hearing as they were with Jesus on the Mount of Transfiguration, God spoke.

"This is My Beloved Son, My Chosen One. Listen to Him!" (Luke 9:35)

Again, we must be reminded that listening will elicit some kind of response. The hope is that hearing Father God speak so clearly, their faith would be strengthened. It was Jesus' hope as well as he gave a lesson in sheep herding.

"My sheep hear My voice, and I know them, and they follow Me." (John 10:27)

Note the progression of hearing. The response is to follow that Voice. This same statement applies to those who have heard the Voice of Truth and have joined the flock to follow our Shepherd. He knows His sheep.

A final admonition is repeated by God seven times in Chapters 2-3 of Revelation.

"He who has ears let him hear what the Spirit says to the churches"

That's us. We are the Church, those who will listen to the words of God and follow.

Question: Have you had your spiritual hearing checked lately? If not, do so now!

LONELINESS

 $\mathcal{W}$ e are social beings, a fact that cannot be refuted. We have seen or read of the detrimental effects of isolation, living cut off from human contact. Mental health is impaired. Intellect is stunted. Communication is unintelligible. These days we live in an electronic age when we keep in contact without real contact. Surrounded by cell phones, I Pads, and TV, we seek to ward off loneliness without physical human contact. Yet these very devices serve to increase our isolation. In recent days this feeling of loneliness has been accentuated by a virulent virus which has kept us homebound or quarantined. Depression has overtaken many.

Gone are the days when we meander through the woods with a buddy or sip a glass of tea on the front porch with a friend. Those are times which recharge our emotional batteries Instead we text, a poor substitute for a time of face to face sharing with someone.

Being alone is not the same thing as being lonely. The fear of being alone causes great discomfort, a sense of incompleteness. Loneliness is called a health robber, and at times this is so. However, occasional alone time can bring a strengthening of oneself. It can sharpen our focus and increase the appetite for fellowship. It can bring balance to the harried pace at which we live, a time of recharging our emotional and physical batteries.

The very best aloneness of all is that time spent with the One who made us for fellowship. In the quiet solitude the voice of God speaks to our weary and harried hearts. He speaks comfort and reassurance. The truth is that we are never alone, never lonely if we spend time with our best companion and truest friend, God. He needs no artificial devices to communicate with us; nor do we need them to communicate with Him.

.Consider these tidbits from scripture.

- "He (God) makes me lie down in green pastures..." (Psalm 23:2) Can you picture David, the shepherd boy, alone in the fields with the sheep, yet at peace on the grass? It is because he knows the Great Shepherd.
- "Pray on behalf of all men...so that we may lead a quiet and tranquil life." (1 Timothy 2:1-2) Paul knew that the world in which young Timothy lived with unrest and often a disconnectedness from former friends. So, he suggested prayer as a way to restore a sense of peace within.
- "Your adornment must not be merely external...but let it be the hidden person of the heart with the imperishable quality of a gentle and quiet spirit which is precious in the sight of God." (1 Peter 3:3-4) Peter is addressing women in this passage. There is something very needful in the life of a woman which can bring calm to a relationship.

This companionship with God is so necessary that when it is missing, we suffer. From the very beginning God desired fellowship with His created people. His perfect fellowship with Adam and Eve was broken, not by God, but by their disobedience. Having sinned against God, they hid themselves.

"They heard the sound of the Lord walking in the garden in the cool of the day, and the man and his wife hid themselves from the presence of the Lord. The Lord God called to man and said, 'Where are you?' He said 'I heard You walking in the garden and I was afraid because I was naked; so I hid.'" (Genesis 3:8-10)

They were truly alone for the first time. Fellowship with God had been severed. The One who could give them peace and comfort was distanced from them. They were alone!

What do we do to hide ourselves from God- as if we could ever really do that? In our loneliness is He the One we seek? Are you feeling lonely now? Look to God! Engage in fellowship with Him.

Challenge: Consider what is most needed in your life to combat loneliness. Seek to remedy that, beginning with a time with God.

LONGSUFFERING

$\mathcal{L}$ongsuffering. A quaint word, you might say, or at least infrequently used. In using the term we do not mean, "I have suffered so long with this or that malady." The synonym for longsuffering is <u>patience</u>. That word is also in short supply among mankind. By abundant example is the honking of the horn of the impatient motorist behind you who is wanting to hurry down the road, considering you too slow to move. Another common sign of our lack of patience is the fretting we do when experiencing an seemingly interminable wait for a busy doctor to see us. And then there is the distinct lack of patience we exhibit toward any and every person who crosses against the grain.

Consider these as Biblical examples of impatience from the Apostle Peter. Impatient and impulsive Peter. Unwilling to wait for the boat to reach the shore, Peter disrobed and jumped into the water. Soaking wet, he greeted Jesus, Hmmm! Wet, impatient Peter!. Then there was the time when Peter, impatient to get on with the mission of the Messiah, offered to go with Jesus only to have his offer denied. Or this time when Peter took matters in his own hands, and in an effort to defend Jesus, he drew his sword and lopped off the ear of one of the representatives of the High Priest.

Yes, we are deficient in patience and lacking in good human examples to emulate. There is One whose patience is perfectly exhibited time and time again as He deals with His impatient creatures. Here are a few instances in which we are awed by the patience of our God.

- "The Lord is slow to anger." That means He patiently endures our less-than-holy behavior. (Nahum 1:3)
- "The Lord is full of compassion, slow to anger." He sees our dilemma and is patient with us as we set aright the issue at hand. (Psalm 145:8)
- "The Lord God, compassionate and gracious, slow to anger and abundant in loving kindness and truth." This is God defining Himself. (Exodus 34:6)
- "You are a God of forgiveness, gracious and compassionate, slow to anger and abundant in loving kindness," (Nehemiah 9:17)

In each of these Old Testament passages the Hebrew word longsuffering is translated as "slow to anger", a way of saying "patient". God's patience causes Him to bear great insult without swinging immediately into action to avenge Himself or punish the wrongdoer. His patient restraint on behalf of man is evident in the question asked by the Apostle Paul in his letter to the Romans. Paul also answers this question.

"What if God, willing to show His wrath and make His power known, endured with much patience the wickedness of men destined for destruction?" He did so to make known the riches of His glory which He prepared beforehand for glory, even us" ((Romans 9:22-24a)

In light of God's great patience toward us we must consider developing greater patience toward others, regardless of their ill behavior. Yes, the scripture does say that tribulation works to build patience! This then develops character which in turn brings forth hope.

"We exult in our tribulations, knowing that tribulation brings about perseverance, and perseverance, proven character, and proven character, hope (Romans 5:3-4)

I am reminded of a friend who, realizing the need for more patience, prayed earnestly for patience. Then, as he related, "All that could go wrong did go wrong." Does that mean we should not pray for more patience in order to avoid increased troubles? No! We know that trials and problems will occur throughout life in this fallen world, but those are not a "get-out-of-jail-free card" to excuse our impatience. Through tribulations we build character and exercise our faith. And when we regress into impatience, we practice repentance – again and again! Thank God, He is patient with us still!

Question: Where are you on the "perseverance in longsuffering" spectrum? Are you making progress in that area?

MARKERS

*H*ow many times in life do we use markers, not the kind we color with, but as a reminder of something? We mark our place in a book we are reading. Mark our to-do list with a check-mark to signify "done". Mark a dot where we need to hang a picture. Mark our calendars to remind us of appointments or special events like birthdays. Mark an anniversary with a special gift. Grandparents leave markers of their lives for their grand children to remember them by.

Road signs are markers, too. Those inform us of the route, direction, dangers ahead, etc. Markers in a large building tell us of the particular office we need. or of construction in progress. Markers are everywhere. Some we pay attention to. Others we ignore often at our own peril.

Our country abounds with markers that speak of our history or of some great person. Statues, parks, buildings, road signs all call our attention to consider. Flowers are left to mark the place someone died. Grave markers give us the burial location of a loved one Markers are everywhere!

Such reminders are not new in our day. There have always been ways to mark, remembrances to call to mind, places to locate by a marker. Sometimes we pause to ask, "What does this marker mean?"

This question is one asked by the generations of Hebrews which came long after their ancestors had settled in the Land of Promise. Upon observing a pile of twelve ragged stones piled one on top of the other, they asked, "What do these stones mean?

The answer is one wrapped in their history. After hundreds of years in bondage and forty years of wandering in the wilderness due to their unbelief, God's people were about to inhabit the land they sought. As they crossed the Jordan River, their leader, Joshua, issued a command.

"Cross again to the ark of the Lord your God and each of you take a stone upon his shoulder according to the number of the tribes of Israel. Let this be a sign among you so that later when your children ask, 'What do these stones mean?', you shall say to them, 'It is because the waters of the Jordan were cut off before the Ark of the Covenant of the Lord.' So these stones will be a memorial forever." (Joshua 4:5-7)

The twelve stones which they had taken from the river were set up at Gilgal in the Land of Promise. Joshua repeated his thought again as he reminded the Hebrews of the meaning of this marker, and he gave them a reason for the remembrance.

"The Lord your God dried the waters of the Jordan before you until you had crossed just as He had done to the Red Sea which He dried up before us until we crossed. This is so that all peoples of the earth may know that the hand of the Lord is mighty, so that you may fear the Lord, your God forever." (Joshua 4: 23-24)

Perhaps as the pillar of stones was erected, the Hebrews were reminded of another pillar built many years before as a reminder of the relationship of Jacob and Laban, his father-in-law. Or perhaps they recalled Lot's wife who became a pillar of stone when she disobeyed God by looking back at all she had left behind. Each was a marker to remember an event of great historical significance.

Markers evoke memories, some good, some bad. Each marker of whatever sort reminds us of something or someone. The question then is, "What kind of markers are you making that others may notice? When noticed, will the resulting emotion or thought be one of scorn or praise? Will it be a reminder of a deed done in the Name of the Lord? We all leave markers even unintentional ones. Let it be said of us that those markers glorify God and shine His light on those who notice.

Question: What are the markers in your life, reminding you of a special occasion? Is one of these markers about your journey with God?

My Inheritance

All of us hope to inherit a family member's precious keepsakes or wealth. Sometimes this hope is selfish. At other times it may be born of the desire to preserve a rich heritage, reminders of another era and hope for the future. Because these are usually times of sorrow and loss, the emotions are all the more prevalent. We are also aware that time will reduce these treasures.

Other kinds of inheritances are less tangible, but often noticed. Do you have your father's eyes or your mother's sweet disposition? Are you tall like granddad or short like grandma? Has your mother's musical ability been passed on? So many of us have heard someone say, "He looks just like you!" or perhaps, "She has your aptitude for fixing things." Whatever the inheritance, it helps to define who we are.

No inheritance is more important than that which we have in God. It is secured in Jesus because of His sacrifice for us. The Apostle Peter wrote of this inheritance in his letter to the alien Hebrews scattered all over Asia Minor.

"Blessed be the God and Father of our Lord Jesus Christ who, according to His great mercy has caused us to be born again to a living hope through the resurrection of Jesus Christ from the dead, to obtain an inheritance which is imperishable and undefiled and will not fade away, reserved in heaven for you." (1 Peter 1:3-5)

Peter reminded them of four important things about that inheritance.

- It is imperishable, no rust or dust at all.
- It is undefiled, pure.
- It is reserved in heaven for us as believers.
- It will not fade away, be lost or disappear.

Jesus told a story about a squandered inheritance in the Parable of the Prodigal Son recorded in Luke 15. The younger son, wanting his freedom, asked for his share of the inheritance (usually received at the death of the father). Then he squandered it foolishly with no thought of the future. When he realized that his greatest loss was the security of home and father, he returned home in shame. If the story ended there it would be sad indeed, but it did not. His father welcomed him back with open arms. The son he had lost was once more home!

We must note that the elder brother wasn't so happy to have this wayward brother home. Jealousy erupted as he scorned his father's welcome and essentially scolded his father. Perhaps we have seen this played out as someone was "left out" of an inheritance or someone who wasted the inheritance selfishly.

God has our inheritance waiting for us. If we spend our lives carelessly with no thought of God, can we expect to inherit God's riches prepared for us? Will God ask for proof of our worthiness to be an inheritor?

Peter tells us what proof we will present as heirs of God's riches. He began his proof with a reminder we all need to hear'

Speaking of this inheritance he wrote, "In this you greatly rejoice even though now for a while, if necessary, you have been distressed by various trials, so that the proof of your faith, being more precious than gold which is perishable, even though tested by fire, may be found to result in praise and glory and honor at the revelation of Jesus Christ." (1 Peter 1:6-7)

For each of us that trial by fire may take a different form. Assault or scorn from unbelievers. Ostracism from a club or organization. No promotion at work, etc. Sometimes there may be physical attack as well. Each trial has a result beyond the incident. It is the measurement of our faith as heir. How we live through these hard times matters!

Question: Are you an heir of the riches of God? How strong is your faith through "the fire"?

Never Fatherless

Growing up without the strong presence of a father is becoming more and more common in these times. Absentee fathers. Abusive fathers. No known father. There are so many fractured families, split apart for various reasons. Children without fathers grow up lacking a healthy concept of the role of a father. The ideas of security, authority, role modeling, devotion to family are unformed. This has not always been true on the scale which we observe today.

In most Middle Eastern and Near Eastern cultures, including the Israelites, families were patriarchal. Family heritage and values were traced through the father's lineage. Women and children were identified by their husband or father's name. The father was the ultimate decision maker. It was he who chose his daughter's husband. There was an order to life based on the oldest man of the family the father or sometimes, the grandfather, then in marriage, the husband.

To our modern eyes such a way of life seems very restrictive; and it probably was to some. Yet, there was also security in this patriarchal headship. Indeed, community was built around this pattern. In the case of the death of a husband, the responsibility for caring for the bereft family fell to the nearest male kin. As breadwinner for the family, the man bore the burden of provision for those under his care.

We find this pictured in the story of Ruth and Boaz. A Hebrew couple, Elimelech and Naomi, had fled to Moab to escape the famine in Israel. Their sons both married Moabite women, one of whom was Ruth. In time Ruth's husband died. When Naomi, also now a widow, decided to return home, even though Naomi released her to stay in Moab, Ruth chose to go with her.

"Ruth said. 'Do not urge me to leave you or turn back from following you; for where you go, I will go and where you lodge, I will lodge. Your people shall be my people and your God, my God. Where you die, I will die and there I will be buried. Thus may the Lord do to me and worse if anything but death part us.'" (Ruth 1:16-17)

What a commitment! Here were two Hebrew women with no male covering entering a male oriented society. We know how the story ends. Ruth married a male kinsman of her father-in-law, Elimelech. His name was Boaz. The importance of this order of life is not to be missed. Ruth became a mother of a son named Obed. In the Hebrew lineage, Obed was the father of Jesse who was the father of David. Ruth became a part of the lineage of the tribe of Judah from which came Jesus, our Messiah. (Matthew 1:5-6)

In spite of the concept of fatherhood, the Israelites did not readily take to the truth of God as their Father in any personal relationship. He was seen as the Father of the nation of Israel. When Jesus was born and proclaimed as Son of God, it was hard to process the idea of a personal Father God. The people were looking for a king, a leader who would rule their country. Even the Old Testament scriptures which foretold what Messiah would be, failed to convince so many of the validity of Jesus' claims as Son of God.

Looking at the closeness of the relationship between Jesus and His Father, we can find the pattern for fatherhood. So eager to please His Father was Jesus that we are told He watched His Father to see what He was doing; and Jesus emulated that. He asked His Father for guidance, and carried to His Father the everyday challenges He faced. In death, Jesus was dependent upon His Father. Approaching the curse of the cross, Jesus prayed,

"Father, not My will but Your will be done." Matthew 26:30)

The most poignant passage in this earthly journey of Jesus as God's obedient Son is recorded in the Gospel of John, chapter 17 where we read of His relationship with His Father. In it we see clearly Jesus' trust of His Father and of their relationship as inseparable.

What of us? Whether or not we have had the security of an earthly father, we are called to trust God as our Father and entrust Him with our very lives We must believe that He has our future in His hands.

Question: What do you expect to receive in an inheritance from God as your Heavenly Father?

NOT A DOUBLE TO BE FOUND

*A*ction builds to a fevered pitch as the camera rolls. The action has reached the critical point in the plot. Everyone is alert to the impending dangers ahead. The star is waiting at the side, ready to go. Will he survive? Will the bad guys win?

Suddenly the movie Director yells, "Cut!" All action stops on cue. The star steps aside, and a well prepared double steps in to take his place. On him will fall all of the dangerous consequences of the action. Is he strong enough? Everyone holds his breath as the Director calls out, "Roll 'em!" With that, the double leaps into action. Miraculously he escapes from the super human act unscathed. Everyone applauds the daring feats.

A fairy tale? To be sure, but there is a lesson hiding in the plot. It is the scenario we may paint in our own lives when we are in great need. We look around to see who is available to rescue us from what we are certain is lacking in our own ability. Who shall we call on to do the really hard stuff? Where is the double to take our place in that moment? A parent? A friend? A total stranger? Anyone will do to take the burden for us.

All too often our last thought is to call on God. The problem is that He is not our double waiting in the wings to take our place when we are perched on the brink of disaster; but ignored as long as the plot of our lives rolls along smoothly. He isn't waiting until someone yells, "Cut!"

God is the Author of the script of each life. He has written the plan ahead of time and knows how the story unfolds. He knows the characters who will add to our stories. But most important of all, God has sent the One who truly is the Double to take our place.

His Name is Jesus! Laden down with sin, we each need someone to save us from ourselves. The Worthy One is the Son of God.

"I, John, heard the voices of many angels around the throne, and the living creatures and the elders; and the number of them was myriads of myriads and thousands of thousands, saying with a loud voice, 'WORTHY IS THE LAMB THAT WAS SLAIN TO RECEIVE POWER AND RICHES AND WISDOM AND MIGHT AND HONOR AND GLORY AND BLESSING'

And every created thing which is in heaven, and on the earth, and under the earth, and on the sea and all things in them, I heard saying, 'TO HIM WHO SITS ON THE THRONE, AND TO THE LAMB BE GLORY AND HONOR AND DOMINION FOREVER'" (Revelation 5:11-13)

Can you envision such a scene as all of creation proclaimed the worthiness of the One we call Messiah! The praises of all creation spoke of this One. What Jesus did on the cross is unmatched by any "substitute double" we may find to take our place. No one else is worthy! No one else is able! No one else can execute the plan of God! Nowhere is there to be found such a Savior!

What we must always remember is that Jesus did not escape unscathed. He was beaten, spit on, ridiculed, mocked, hated by the religious leaders and unbelieving crowd, and forsaken by those closest to Him. And then Jesus endured the agony and shame of the cross so that we might be rescued from the wrath of God against sinners.

Let us reflect in our lives the words of the Apostle Paul to the Christians in Philippi.

"Conduct yourselves in a manner worthy of the Gospel of Christ... standing firm in one spirit with one mind striving together for the faith of the Gospel. (Philippians 1:27)

Consider: What would it be like to participate in the praises of heaven to the God who literally is the one who saved us from the dangers of hell?

ORGANIC FOOD

*T*hese days the big buzz word for better health is "organic food". According to Webster, "organic" means *related to yielding a crop with the use of feed or fertilizer of plant or animal origin without the employment of chemically formulated fertilizers, growth stimulants, antibiotics or pesticides.* In layman's terms it means a higher level of purity and a lower level of harmful "stuff". Who wouldn't want that? We all want the best food to produce good health. So we look for those labeled "organic", the current buzz word for "good for you".

From the beginning God gave His people dietary laws by which to live. These laws were not meant to restrict enjoyment of eating but rather to promote health in a time when sanitation practices were almost nonexistent. Does that mean we need to do less since we have better sanitation? I wonder!

From a spiritual standpoint, let's look at this Biblically. Listen to the voice of God through the Prophet Isaiah.

> "Listen, all who are thirsty! Come to the waters and
> he who has no money, come, buy, and eat. Yes, come

buy spiritual wine and milk without money. Why do you spend money for that which is not bread and your earnings for that which does not satisfy? Listen to me! Eat what is good, and let yourself delight in a profusion of spiritual joy." (Isaiah 55:1-2 Amplified Bible)

God was speaking to people who were spiritually malnourished starved for the Bread of Life. You can hear the yearning in the heart of God to nourish His people well. He wants them to be satisfied in Him. He asks them to buy that which accepts the blessing of self- surrender.

Many years later the Messiah, Jesus, spoke about the quality of food people need as He addressed a crowd of seekers. They had come asking for a miracle as proof of His identity, using as bait a reminder of the wilderness manna their forefathers had received from God.

"Jesus said, 'I assure you that Moses was not the source of the bread. My Father was the Giver of the true heavenly bread. For the Bread of God is He Who comes down from heaven and gives life to the world. I am the Bread of Life. He who comes to Me will never be hungry, and he who believes in Me will never again thirst.'" (John 5:30-35)

Jesus was offering all who are willing to believe the opportunity to eat "healthy food", life producing nourishment. Can we understand that marvelous truth? Never hungry! Never thirsty! This is truly "organic" food!

The writer of Hebrews speaks of the progression of this food as we grow in Christ. Milk is for babies, and solid food is needed as we mature in our faith. He urges us to go on to maturity in our trust in God and His Son, our Savior. (Hebrews 5:13-6:1)

The Apostle Peter, writing to the Christians in Asia Minor also understood well the principle of growth based on the Truth of the Word. He knew this nourishment was available to all who are hungry. His encounter on the rooftop when God clarified this truth was imprinted on Peter's heart. (Acts 10:9-15)

> "Like newborn babies, all of you should crave pure spiritual milk that by it you may be nurtured and grow into a mature salvation since you have already tasted the goodness and kindness of the Lord." (1 Peter 2:2-3)

Peter is a good example of what happens when we are fed on the Word of God. We grow in our faith, in the strength to resist temptation, in our love for all mankind, in our understanding of servanthood. We grow! Growth is the sure sign that we are alive in Christ and well nourished by Him.

Question: Are you partaking regularly from the meat of the Word of God, and growing because of the spiritual health it supplies?

OUR ONE NEED

*I*f someone were to ask you, "What is the one need you must have above all others?", how would you respond? You might say it is air or water or love or health or shelter.

Certainly, each of these is important and necessary to maintain a quality of life. Other needs or wants seem secondary to these basic necessities. Sometimes what we view as a need is only a want. For example, a job or better job, more money, beauty, a new car, etc. are all wants, not needs. We are often told we "need" these things to be successful, to thrive, or "to keep up with the Joneses" Yet, the greatest need we have may be hidden behind all of our other perceived needs. What is it?

The greatest need we have, whether we realize it or not, is the need to know Jesus as our Savior and God as our Father. I mean, to really know Him not just know about Him. We need to know intimacy in relationship with our God. What is He like? What does He want of us? How shall we live in the light of knowing Him?

We need what the disciples Peter, James and John, learned on the Mount of Transfiguration. There it was revealed to them their absolute essential need as they saw the event unfold. They needed validation of what they had hoped God the Father promised in His Son who was sent to earth to be Redeemer, Savior, King. God spoke to their need with clarity.

"This is My Beloved Son in whom I am well pleased. Listen to Him!" (Matthew 17:5)

Jesus was called God's Beloved! God was well pleased with Jesus as He carried out His earthly charge! And God commanded, "Listen to Him!" This Jesus would be Savior, Redeemer, King of Kings. He would be all the awed disciples hoped for...and so very much more!

The disciples were so overcome with awe that they fell to the ground terrified. If they had been unsure before, they now knew beyond the shadow of a doubt that Jesus was the Promised Messiah. They knew they needed Him above all else. The One they had been following dusty path after dusty path for months was really Who He claimed to be! God confirmed it! This revelation was a life-changer! (Matthew 17:1-8)

It not only was a life-changer for the three on the Mount of Transfiguration, it was a world-changer. In the years to come this understanding would be the key to their ministry to both Jews and Gentiles.

So impactful was this event in the Apostle Peter's life that many years later he shared with the Jews of the Dispersion his eyewitness account of the transfiguration event.

He said, "We were eyewitnesses of His majesty. For when He received honor and glory from God, the Father, such an utterance as this was made to Him by the Majestic Glory, 'This is My Beloved Son with Whom I am well pleased.' We ourselves heard this utterance made from heaven when we were with Him on the holy mountain." (2 Peter 1:16-18)

Have you been" to the mountain"? Have you heard God speak to your heart of your greatest need, the need upon which all others rest? If not, do not delay! Go to the mountain! Hear God shift your needs focus from yourself to Him. Then live out this declaration:

My greatest need is to know God as revealed through His Son, Jesus, my Savior!

A word of caution! We cannot stay on the mountain because the test of our belief in God as our Greatest Need is found in the valleys of our lives. It is there we realize of a surety that we are living out our declaration.

Question: Whether you are currently on the mountain or in the valley, has your greatest need been God?

OUT OF STEP

We all have watched a band march by in a parade and thought, "That fellow is out of step with the rest." Somehow seeing one person measure his steps out of sync with the rest of the band is seen as messing up the whole band. "Why doesn't he correct his step? Too bad he missed the class in "how to march in step." We are, of course, measuring the band by the one who is out of step. Why is it we never consider that he might be the only one in step and marching just right?

As it is with parades, it is so in life. We tend to judge wholesale, the book by the cover, the entire basket by one rotten apple, the movie by one bad scene, the group of children by the one who is different. Is there any merit in the book? Are thee any good apples in the basket? Was the entire movie bad? Do all the children fitt into the mold of the one?

For those of us who have at times felt "odd man out", different from the rest in a situation, perhaps it is time we look at that from a new perspective. Assessing that feeling brings us to why we feel that way. Am I too shy, too gabby, less able, just plain different in thought and manner? All of these and more cause the feeling, but remember, it is only a feeling and so often divorced from reality.

Here is the reality. We are all unique. Each of us has been born with a different set of genes, traits, sizes, characteristics that make us ourselves. God made us that way. No carbon copies. That is why it is so destructive to view ourselves or others as out of step with a particular philosophy or group. God didn't create groups. He created people one by one, each special in some way.

The Biblical understanding of the word. "steps" refers to the daily walk we must have with our Creator. We must, so to speak, be in step with Him. The most important thought here is that we are created in His image, born to emulate Him in character and deed. That is the only grouping which should affect us.

The Psalmist got it right.

"The steps of a man are established by the Lord, and He delights in his way." (Psalm 37:23)

In another psalm he prays this prayer.

"Establish my footsteps in Your Word, and do not let any iniquity have dominion over me." (Psalm 119:133)

The early apostles and teachers understood the importance of our steps, our walk with God. Paul, writing to the Ephesian Christians, stated it plainly.

"For we are His workmanship, created in Christ Jesus for good works which God prepared beforehand that we would <u>walk</u> in them." (Ephesians 2:19)

Knowing that mankind's way is so often wayward and disobedient, Paul stressed the foundational thought that we were created for God's purposes alone, personal agendas aside. It was a truth emphasized by the Apostle Peter, who, of all the disciples, had experienced a few lessons in how to walk in step with the Master.

"For you have been called for this purpose since Christ also suffered for you, leaving you an example for you to follow in His steps." (1Peter 2:21)

So, consider that the only time you should feel out of step is when it is in disobedience or lethargy toward the God who created you. And let us then not consider anyone else with any other criteria. Instead, let us help others march in step to the cadence of God.

"The mind of a man plans his way, but the Lord directs his steps." (Proverbs 16:9)

Question: If you are among the "called ones", are you in step with the Master?

OVEREXPOSED OR UNDERDEVELOPED

*H*ow frustrating it is to retrieve a roll of film left to be developed only to discover that the photos are so dark that the objects and people in the prints are obscured or that they are blurry and too light! Immediately we try to figure out what went wrong so as not to repeat the mistake. Was the sun not bright enough? Was it too bright? Did the flash not go off as expected? Were the settings wrong? We are so disappointed not to have mementos of the occasion.

Note to the reader: In this digital age the use of cameras and flash bulbs is almost a thing of antiquity as we use our phones to snap a quick pic. However, the same problems exist when the lighting is not right, or the focus is skewed.

In the spiritual realm all too often the pictures people see of Christians who, though professing faith in Christ, present to the observing world an underdeveloped life of a weak or faded faith. Instead of portraying maturity in Christ, they reflect the immaturity of a child . Growth seems to have been stunted. The observer

271

surely may, at times, use a faulty set of standards in the evaluation, but the fact that unbecoming behavior is observed is nevertheless seen. What is not as obvious are the root causes of such immaturity.

To generalize, here are some of the main causes of stunted growth in a believer.

- A busy life has squeezed our schedules, leaving little or no time to read God's Word and listen for Him to speak.
- Prayer has become an "I want list" of things we wish God to attend to and fix.
- Intercession on behalf of others is a fleeting promise.
- The rigors of a disciplined life in Christ are deemed too strict and binding, so they are set aside for a more carefree approach to living.
- We have quit the journey with Christ for another, more attractive cause.

In any of these or other reasons for an overexposed or underdeveloped life in Christ, the result is tragic and life stunting.

The Apostle Paul chastised the Corinthian believers for their immaturity in their faith. He wrote of their underdeveloped life in terms we can understand.

"I could not speak to you, my brothers, as spiritual men but as to men of flesh, babes in Christ. I gave you milk to drink, not solid food, for you were not yet able to receive it. Indeed, even now you are not yet able, for you are still fleshly." (I Corinthians 3:1-3a)

For believers in Corinth, though they had heard the Word of God and pledged belief in Jesus as Messiah, their growth was underdeveloped. They were as babies, needing milk instead of adults feasting on solid food. That is quite an analogy for us.

The writer of Hebrews voiced similar concerns.

"Though by this time you ought to be teachers, you still need someone to teach you the elementary principles of the Word of God. For everyone who partakes only of milk is not accustomed to the Word of righteousness, for he is an infant. But solid food is for the mature who, because of practice, have their senses trained to discern between good and evil." (Hebrews 5:12-14)

Beware, believer, of the picture you portray! Do not appear as underdeveloped or overexposed, but as those who love and feast daily on the Word of God.

Challenge: Check the "film" of your life. Is the picture blurry, or can unbelievers see clearly your love of God?

Pivotal Moments

Often we see players running full speed, then suddenly stop to pivot to a new direction. They changed direction to complete a play or score a point. To have continued on their original course may have resulted in a foul, a collision with another player, loss of the ball, or failure to complete the play. Pivoting was the key to completion.

Have you ever stopped your motion abruptly as if by some force? It's like you heard someone say, "Pivot! Change course now." If you did, if you pivoted from your present course, it might have meant a change of direction in life. Perhaps it entailed a change of jobs or maybe it meant you stopped ambling through life and set your eyes on some purpose. In any case, when we pivot, life changes. Whether the change of direction is for the better or worse may be determined by he directional choice we make.

In Jesus' life there came such a time when He pivoted from the carpenter's shop to the role of an itinerant messenger of God. He altered the course of His early life to pursue the direction and guidance of His Father. To say that His life was thereafter different is an understatement. Nothing was the same ever again.

In the course of the three years of Jesus' earthly ministry there were numerous times when He pivoted in order to minister to some need or ease the suffering of a needy soul. Going in one direction, He was often interrupted by a request that led Him to pivot in a new direction. He walked among friends and enemies with the same focus of direction, never wavering from His Father's plan. There came a time when Jesus had to pivot away from the freedom to walk publicly among the Jews because of the hostility to Him and His followers,. He knew of their plan to kill Him.

"Therefore Jesus no longer continued to walk publicly among the Jews, but went away from there to the wilderness country to a city called Ephraim; and there He stayed with His disciples.' (John 11:53-54)

Knowing that His time on earth was short, Jesus made a change of direction. These last few days were important for those upon whom would rest the responsibility as messengers of Good News to the world. We are not told what Jesus said to His disciples during this sequestered time, but we can be certain that that it was a time of preparation for the sadness and horror of the coming days. We see no hesitation when Jesus pivoted away from the crowds. Nor do we see any negative emotion. He simply did what was needed at the time guided by His Father's instructions.

What is our most important pivotal moment? It is the moment we decide to turn from sin and the ways of the world to follow Jesus as

Savior and Lord. Suddenly for some and more slowly for others, life takes on a new point of view, a new flavor. A new horizon is revealed. Life's tenuous path is no longer viewed as something to endure as we move from crisis to crisis. The way ahead is viewed through the Word of God with greater clarity and purpose. Instead of being a confused traveler, we have pivoted into the light of God's direction for us. Sorrows are shared. Wounds are healed. Goals are changed. As with Jesus' life, there will be some changes of direction, side trips to offer healing to a friend, encouragement to a dispirited person, Good News to a lost soul. Will there be things to relinquish? Yes! And sacrifices too. There may even be a few crossroads where we must choose wisely which direction is best.

God added these words of encouragement to His people.

"I know the plans I have for you, plans for welfare and not calamity, to give you a future and a hope." (Jeremiah 29:11)

Hindsight, as they say, is 20/20. So having been urged to pivot in a new direction without fully understanding the reason, years later we may look back and say, 'Now I can see the purpose for that pivot. God had a purpose for me there." It is time to thank God for the pivotal points in our lives that have drawn us closer to Him. It is time to claim each promise of God as He directs our paths, even the pivots. Let us be willing to heed those prompts from Him and obey.

Question: Do you need to pivot? From what to what? Why?

PLANNING AHEAD

*I*n our family planning ahead has always been the norm. Waiting until the last minute and then scrambling to get things done in a "no-no". Planning ahead was the theme of each undertaking It lessened the times we had to say, "Wait a minute!". Ready to go? Oops, I forgot where I put my purse. Ready to bake those cookies? Oops! I don't have enough sugar. On a vacation at the beach? Oops! I failed to pack my swim suit. Yes, planning ahead is important to ensure the desired results.

The Master Planner is God. He doesn't just decide one day to create, change, add, answer, give and forgive. His view ahead is clear. The Apostle Paul declared this in his letter to the Christians in Ephesus.

"We are God's workmanship created in Christ Jesus for good works which God prepared beforehand so that we would walk in them." (Ephesians 2:10)

God planned, even before we were born, the agenda of our lives that would please Him. Now that is amazing planning ahead! King David said it this way.

"You (God) formed my inward parts. You wove me in my mother's womb. I will give thanks to You for I am fearfully and wonderfully made. My days were not hidden from You when I was made in secret and skillfully wrought in the depths of the earth. Your eyes have seen my unformed substance; and in Your Book were written all the days that were ordained for me when as yet there was not one of them." (Psalm 139:13-16)

God's expectation is that, having planned for us the very best, we will adhere to that plan as He directs us. As surely as we would not want to omit the sugar in the cookies or head to the beach without proper swim wear, so much more should we heed God's planning on our behalf in order to ensure a successful spiritual journey.

The Prophet Jeremiah was directed by God to show to His people their own stubborn refusal to follow God's plan for them.

"They will say, 'It is hopeless. For we are going to follow our own plans and each of us will act according to the stubbornness of our own hearts.'" (Jeremiah 18:12)

Knowing God's will and stubbornly refusing to follow the Master Planner, we know, ended in exile and separation from their Promised Land, some never to return.

What is our part in the planning process? Attention! Attention to the Planner. That is, being attuned to His plan for each of us. Will there be bumps in the road or possibly detours? Yes! Humanity, as God well knows, is prone to error...let's call it what it is, sin. The important thing is course correction back to the Master Planner's course for each of His children.

It is a daily seeking, a daily asking, a daily walk hand in hand with the One who always knows the way. He stands ready to lead us as we go about our lives. It is being available to hear His direction and what He wants for us to plan ahead that will magnify Him and execute His plan for us to be Light in a world intent on going its own way. And yes, it often requires repentance and a course correction under His guidance. That reveals a compliant and trusting heart. We must take down the funny sign which reads "plan ahe..." Due to poor planning it leaves no room to complete the thought. Let us only plan ahead under God's direction!

"For we are His workmanship created in Christ Jesus for good works which God prepared beforehand so that we would walk in them." (Ephesians 2:10)

Question: How does God's plan factor into your daily life?

POWER OF ATTORNEY

A Power of Attorney is authority vested in someone to act on behalf of another. It is a serious responsibility not to be taken lightly. It is meant to reflect the wishes and intents of the person. With the best interest in mind, the P.O.A. is to execute business with integrity. Can this power be abused? Yes, it can, sometimes to the detriment of all concerned. Can this authority be revoked? Yes, but often with disagreement and ill will of both parties. This vested power is recognized by courts, businesses, medical professionals, and family. Questions are often asked.

- How well do you know the one to whom you have entrusted this power?
- Does this power cover finances, health, purchasing, residences, business interests?
- What are the results of abdication of responsibility or misuse of power?
- Is this representative always available as needed?

Think about this as applied to God. When we accept Jesus as Savior, God charges us with the responsibility of representing Him. Jesus Himself told His followers that.

"You did not choose Me, but I chose you, and I appointed you that you would go and bear fruit, and that your fruit would remain so that whatever you ask the Father in My Name, He may give it to you." (John 15:16)

In this one declaration we see the following: calling, purpose, conditions, and results. Jesus gave those who believe in Him the legal right to use His Name with the same authority He had when He walked the earth in Human flesh.

The source of this authority is reiterated again in John 16 as Jesus declared "If you ask anything of the Father in My Name He will give it to you."

The last mandate Jesus gave His followers before Hi returned to His Father is the familiarly named Great Commission.

"All authority has been given Me. Go therefore and make disciples of all the nations, baptizing them in the Name of the Father and Son and Holy Spirit, teaching them to observe all that I commanded you; and I will always be with you always, even to the end of the age," (Matthew 28:19-20)

Up until this time the disciples had not asked Jesus for anything using the power and authority of His Name. But He did, telling them that their joy would abound. It is this same representation given to those today who are believers.

Lest we get carried away with what seems like a credit card with unlimited restrictions, we must heed the restriction which declares "Whatever you ask in My Name " Not long after Jesus ascension, Peter and John went up to the Temple to pray. At the Beautiful Gate a lame man stopped them to ask for money.

Peter turned to him and said, "I do not have silver or gold, but what I do have I give you. In the Name of Jesus Christ, the Nazarene, walk." And taking him by his hand, he raised him up... (Acts 3:3-7)

As this was taking place. people were watching in amazement. Peter was quick to explain that he did nothing on his own power but in the Name of Jesus. It was the same answer he gave to the religious leaders the next day. Later, as many believers were gathered together they prayed with confidence that signs and wonders would occur through the Name of Jesus. (v. 29)

Did you know that you also have that power of attorney placed as a responsibility on your life? You represent Jesus to others and have the command to use His Name as your P.O.A. in anything that honors Father God.

Consider: How will you use this vested Power of Attorney?

POVERTY

At no time in history has there been a people or country where poverty was absent. Hardscrabble times brought on by drought impoverished farmers. Natural disasters resulted in great destruction and ensuing times of great need. Epidemics and pandemics caused unemployment and loss of resources. Poverty has ever been with us.

Many of us have at some time experienced a degree of poverty brought on by lack of resources, abuse of our bodies, negligent habits, poor health. These times, even when temporary, cause us to grieve and perhaps rail at God as if we had no responsibility for the poverty and that b He was somehow at fault. No one enjoys such trials, yet the blame game gains us nothing unless we discover the underlying cause and determine to work to improve our situation.

Far more devastating to us is spiritual poverty, that dry, impoverished status which leaves us grasping for help. What might spiritual poverty look like?

- A deadened conscience

- Rote recitations of scripture.
- Legalistic acts
- Prayerless praying
- Overt rebellion
- A root of bitterness

Though not an all-inclusive list, you get the idea. No, these are not characteristics of an unbeliever. They are symptoms of a "deadly virus" within those who profess faith in Jesus while simply going through the motions of religiosity. It is the absence of the Kingship of Jesus over a life.

The recorded history of the period of the judges in Israel is a stark example of just such a condition. Three times we read, these words.

"Everyone did what was right in their own eyes." (Judges 3:7; 6:1; 21:25)

It was the "virus" of self. Me first. Misplaced affections. Failure to look to the Source for help. Even the brief periods when there was a Godly judge who led the people to the Lord, after he was gone, the people reverted to the ways of the world in which they lived. Forsaking their God, the Israelites tried to carve out a life of a dead religiosity, going through rituals with rebellious hearts and seeking other gods to add to their lives.

We know how that turned out. God's disapproval and, yes, His disappointment, resulted in harsh judgment. The cycle of disobedience from sin to repentance to restoration repeated itself over and over again. Apparently, no lesson was learned from their times of poverty that led them to a lasting dedication to God. So, we ask the question, "Who would want to be subjected to the severity of God's discipline because of our own spiritual poverty? No one! Not I!

The remedy? Determining to seek God in all things-finances, habits, friends, choices, daily life. This remedy will cause us to bow before our God in submission to His plan for us. It will pour the water of Life into our parched souls. It will immerse us in God's Word and cause us to kneel in obedience to what He speaks to us through His indwelling Spirit. Instead of spiritual poverty, we will dwell in the riches of God! Though physical poverty may at times be our lot, God's supply is always at hand for us.

Challenge: Read the book of Judges. Take note of what caused the Israelites to live in spiritual poverty. Ask yourself if that in any way characterizes your life. Then, act! Feed! Drink! Love! Believe! Trust! Taste the truth of a lavish spiritual life in God!

Powerless or Powerful?

*W*ho has not at some time felt powerless to control a situation or problem? We all have! There are those moments in our lives when the events render us absolutely unable to remedy the challenge before us. Having tried a variety of means, we still remain powerless to change. It is not a comfortable feeling!

On the other hand, have you ever felt so powerful that you could tackle any challenge? What a rush that feeling gives us! We know we can make a difference! We can do the unexpected! We know the answer! Instead of defeat, we experience victory. It seems as if it is through ouw own power that we were able to succeed.

It is generally thought that politics, warfare and economics folks are the power sources who change history. But, in truth, God is the One who holds the true power for defeat or victory, success or failure, wealth or poverty. Human power is not the key to historical power though it may seem so as we read the history books. Sadly, history records what men have done with power Listen to the Prophet Isaiah.

"The earth is polluted by its inhabitants, for they transgress laws, violate statutes, and broke the everlasting covenant. Therefore, a curse devours the earth, and those who live in it are held guilty." (Isaiah 24:5-6)

What a sad pronouncement on our powerless state! Many years before Isaiah, a young Hebrew woman named Hannah prayed earnestly to God for a child. God answered and gave her a son. So thankful was she that she sang a song of praise that is recorded in 1 Samuel 2:1-10. One particular verse strikes a chord with our topic.

"Not by might shall man prevail." (v.9)

Many years later the Prophet Zechariah proclaimed the word of the Lord to Zerubbabel, one of the leaders who was in the first group to return to Judah from exile in Babylon. He echoed Hannah's words.

"Not by might, nor by power, but by My Spirit, says the Lord of Hosts." (Zechariah 4:6)

In what we call the Lord's Prayer Jesus proclaimed;

"Your kingdom come, Your will be done...For Yours (Father) is the kingdom and the power and the glory forever. Amen! (Matthew 6:10,13)

It is for us to tap into the Power Source of life and see the world through His eyes. It brings delight to God if we do so.

"He does not delight in the strength of a horse. He does not take pleasure in the legs of a man. The Lord favors those who fear Him, those who wait for His loving kindness." (Psalm 147:10-11)

Thus says the Lord, "Heaven is My throne and the earth is My footstool...For My hand made all these things...But to this one will I (God) regard with pleasure; to him who is humble and contrite of spirit, and who trembles at My Word." (Isaiah 66:1-3)

Peter, the Apostle who felt the power of God sweep into him at Pentecost wrote to the Jews scattered throughout Asia Minor to bolster their faith in the One who holds all power. They, like we, needed to hear that affirmation as he spoke of Jesus.

"who is at the right hand of God, having gone into heaven after angels and authorities and powers had been subjected to Him," (1 Peter 3:22)

Jesus did not leave us powerless. He sent the Holy Spirit to indwell us as believers. His power is best perfected in our weakness. The Apostle Paul echoed thar truth.

"And He has said to me, 'My grace is sufficient for you, for power is perfected in weakness'" (2 Corinthians 12:9)

Question: When you feel weak, what is your source of power?

PRESS ON!

We all need encouragement at times, especially when faced with the hard obstacles life presents. We welcome a pat on the back, a word of support or affirmation, a helping hand, or someone to walk alongside through the darkness. We have probably seen the efforts of those running a long race, sweat dripping from them, leg-weary and thirsty. Then someone hands out a bottle of water as the runner passes by, an encouragement to press on to the finish, to finish the race strong. Even the crowd yells encouragement as the weary runners passing by. I once watched a woman crawl across the finish line in exhaustion, determined to finish the race. She was a fine example of pressing on to complete the race.

Years ago, two friends set out to climb the arduous sixteen mile trail up to the summit of Pikes Peak, a 14,000+ foot giant. One of the two had made the climb before and knew well the rigors involved. Armed with water and a few handfuls of trail mix to sustain them, they began the climb. Shortly, gasping for breath and weak in the knees, one of the duo, said, "I can't go any further! I must go back!" He lacked the stamina and determination to press on to the top.

Life is full of such moments when we feel as if we cannot endure another minute of whatever trial we are encountering. In spite of the reserves we thought we had, we falter. Thoughts of giving up invade our minds. Yet, as Christians we are admonished to "press on"!

The Apostle Paul surely knew about challenges which followed him wherever he went. Writing to the believers in Philippi, Paul sought to give witness to his relationship with the Lord. His one desire was to be found faithful by the One who is Judge. He knew that it was attainable only if he continued to press on.

"...not that I have already attained (the goal) or become perfect, but I press on so that I may lay hold of that for which also I was laid hold of by Christ Jesus...I press on toward the goal for the prize of the upward call of God in Christ Jesus." (Philippians 3:12,14)

What comes to mind when we think of pressing on"?

- Determination. That was a compelling force within that caused Paul to push on despite obstacles and much persecution.
- Obedience. Inherent in the thought is the understanding that obedience to something, Someone, propelled him onward.
- Consistency. There were no vacation days, no slacking off, one of the hardest things to confront when hard pressed to stop. It was a daily effort
- Goal. No one pushes on without a goal in mind, whether conscious or subconsciously.

- Attainability. It is foolhardy to set as a goal something we know for certain is not attainable, yet in frustration we keep at it. Paul knew with Rock-solid confidence that God would not set a standard he could reach on his own, but only with God as his strength.
- Reward. It would be worth it! Of that Paul was sure. Just hearing the "well done" spoken over him was sufficient. Paul did not leave us wondering. He said, "I am confident in this very thing, that He who has begun a good work in me/you will perfect it until the day of Jesus Christ." (Philippians 1:6)

We too must press on to become all God has designed us to be. It will be well worth the arduous climb, friend!

Question: What is your mountain to climb? Is God your daily companion on the trek?

PRIORITIES

$\mathcal{W}$e all have priorities in our lives. Some of us "list makers" have a "to-do list" on which we place things to be accomplished. Laundry. Bill paying. Dental appointment on Friday. Fix the squeaking door hinge. Buy a birthday present for Aunt Sue.

Each item on the list seems important in some way though prioritizing them may depend on a variety of factors. The desire to please a mate. The impact of neglect to heed the list. The rank of importance of a task. In the course of a day or week these priorities may be helpful in ordering our lives. For the forgetful, a list serves is a reminder.

One thing that seldom, if ever, makes the all important list is the enriching of one's relationship with God by spending time in His Word, in prayer or service to Him. Do we remind ourselves to work on memorizing a special verse of scripture which is an encouragement to us and a promise from God?

One day a Saducee who was a lawyer asked Jesus a question to test Him.

"Teacher, which is the greatest commandment in the Law?" (Matthew 22:36)

Remember that lawyers ask questions sometimes as a tactic to trip up the witness. Such was the case with Jesus. He had corrected the Saducees earlier when they misused the scriptures to try to catch Jesus in a theological trap. (Matthew 22:23-32) So, when Jesus answered as He did, the lawyer had no come-back.

"You shall love the Lord, your God with all your heart and with all your soul and with all your mind. This is the great and foremost commandment. The second is like it. You shall love your neighbor as yourself. On these two commandments depend the whole law and the prophets." (Matthew 22:37-40)

These words were the ones spoken so many years before by God through His man, Moses to the Hebrews heading to the Promised

"You shall love the Lord, your God, with all your heart and with all your soul and with all your might." (Deuteronomy 6:5)

Jesus' priority for us was stated similarly in His long teaching on the mountain.

"Seek first the kingdom of God and His righteousness, and all these things will be added to you." (Matthew 6:33)

"These things" referred to all of the blessings of God He had taught about in the minutes before. It is an awesome list of God's good toward us.

293

How can we make our spiritual priority list reflect this vital point? Let's start with a short but important list of "to-dos".

- Upon rising, thank God for the night of rest and refreshing.
- Spend quality time talking to and listening to God before reading anything else like the newspaper.
- Ask God what He has for you in the day ahead of you and promise to be faithful in that.
- Open your heart to see others as God sees them, and determine to act accordingly.
- Remember to talk to God throughout the day as you notice His creation around you.
- Close your day with thanksgiving for God's guidance and protection throughout the day.

Now add to this list as the Spirit of God prompts you. He has our priorities in mind because He has planned our days. Approach your list with a joyful heart! He will note your priorities and seek to set them in order if you forget.

Challenge: List your top five priorities. Where is God on that list?

PROCESSED FOOD

We live in an era when much of the food we consume has been "processed". That is, its original state has been altered in some way to make it more marketable, more attractive, or more convenient. Often the original is unrecognizable. The information we receive in the varied media or on the labels also seems to be "processed" through someone's opinion and fed to us as pure fact. It tells us this is the best product, the tastiest, the most health-producing. And we are expected to believe all of the marketing ads about it.

Even our bodies are "processed" by makeup, wigs, botox, surgical procedures to make us lovelier and more satisfied with our appearance. Our standard for this is often is the media, a model, or some Hollywood star holding out the latest "process" for beauty. We are led to believe that if we do not use this or that product we will remain somehow defective.

Today much of Christianity, sadly, also seems to have surrendered to "processing". Today's believers want to be happy, prosperous, entertained, comfortable in the church pews, and unchallenged by new thoughts. We seek "processed" religion taught by someone else and fed to us as processed truth. Blinded by the world's standards of a "good Christian", we seek out the new popular speaker or writer, the new book promising a fulfilled life if we will only... You fill in the blank. This too frequently bypasses the Word of God and offers instead a watered down, processed version of truth.

Perhaps this trend is because it is easier to read or listen to what has already been "processed" for us than to go to the Source and listen to the Voice of the Holy Spirit sent to teach us how to really live. We say, "It is too difficult to understand, too binding, not current in today's world." Little do we recognize that Satan is delighted to hear that.

If we truly believe that the Word of God is unprocessed truth, what then? Are we ready to consider the Real Thing? Here are some thoughts to help.

* Stand on the fact that God has the answers processed only by His Spirit within us. The truth has not been edited or watered down for easier consumption.

* Seek to understand what a passage does <u>not</u> mean, that is, anything which challenges the truth of God. Seek instead the unprocessed meat of the Word

* Allow the Spirit of God, our Instructor, to speak to us God's message. The Spirit is given to be our Teacher and Guide. He is God within us.

* Do not let someone else's opinion be your final belief as
to how to live, however spiritual it seems, until you have
allowed God to confirm its truth in your heart.

* And, most important, do not be afraid to say to God, "I
don't understand! Please help me to understand what You
are saying and what that means for my life." He knows we
often struggle to understand a passage written so long ago
and in a culture so different from ours today. He delights
in a heart hungry to know His ways.

Does that mean we should cut off all those who preach or teach the
Word? No! If they have the call of God on their lives, we must pay
due respect. We just need to listen with discernment and our own
knowledge of the Word as we take in what is said. That applies to
books written about Gid as well. When we allow unfiltered and
unprocessed truth to seep into our souls, we begin to understand
that God wants us healthy. He likes us just like we are. Who was it
that said, "God don't make no junk!"? True!

Unprocessed truth! That is what we desperately need today! God
help us to hear the pure truth and to live accordingly.

Challenge: Use your "God filter" to discern the difference in
"processed truth" and God's pure truth.

PRODUCTIVE OR REPRODUCTIVE?

*H*ow is success measured today? The words MORE, BETTER, and LARGER come to mind. We tend to measure the success of a company by its products. Are they better, stronger, cheaper, easier to obtain? Knowing it is a productive company is reassuring. We measure the success of a team by its statistics. Have they produced more wins than losses? The success of an individual may be measured by how far he has progressed up the success ladder, how productive his work life is, how much money he makes, what new idea has he produced? The report card of a school child notes the achievement or lack thereof according to whether he has produced good work. All of these scenarios are on a balance scale of sorts.

What about reproduction? One simple negative example may suffice. How often have you purchased a "knockoff" or reproduction of the real thing because it was cheaper? Some countries and companies specialize in reproductions of the original product, offering it at a discounted price. These are often made with inferior materials and cheap labor.

Sometimes we hear of an individual who has made an effort to improve on the original or to reproduce it in a more advantageous way. This may yield a better product, stronger, more reliable, more durable. Such reproduction is admired and valued. The company may grow due to the reliability of the product reproduced.

Somehow in the Christian realm we have transferred this paradigm to assess our worth as a believer. We have come to equate spirituality with productivity. Though we know the scripture reminds us that we are "saved by grace and not by works", we nevertheless conclude that the more we do for God, the more graced we will be. We look for results when we minister, count the decisions for Christ or new church members added, the number of plates we serve to the hungry, etc. The society in which we live encourages such measuring as proof that we are living productive lives. To make matters worse, we use as a measuring rod the lives of others. Am I more productive than John? Do my efforts yield better results than Sara? If not, we work harder, take more jobs at the church, visit more shut-ins. Wood, hay and stubble amassed! Isaiah 33:11 records God's words to these folks. It comes with a dire warning.

"You have conceived chaff. You will give birth to stubble. My breath will consume you like a fire... ...You who are far away, hear what I have done, and you who are near, acknowledge My might." (Isaiah 33:11, 13)

Consider how God looks at productivity. Never would He discourage our good works done with a servant heart and to build His kingdom, but He is not the Great Tabulator, sitting with pen in hand to count all which is done "in His Name". He looks beyond that to the heart.

Remember, Jesus' goal here on earth was not to preach to larger and larger crowds, multiply more loaves, tabulate how many He healed. Yes, He did all of those things and so much more. But His focus was to bring sons and daughters into the Kingdom of God. Reproduction! He came to offer the very life of God to all who would believe. Why? It was so that we might reproduce that life in the life of others as we share the Word of Truth with them.

When Jesus chose His disciples, His call was to be fishers of men, but nowhere did He tell them to tally up their results. They had heard Jesus talk of fruit bearing and understood that to bear good fruit meant backbreaking labor in the fields and orchards. First, He warned them of those who look like fruit-bearers but are only outwardly so and known by the type of fruit they bear. (Matthew 6)

He expected them to feed hungry hearts with the truth of why He came. He expected them to expend themselves as the doors opened, regardless of the cost. And their cost was great. History tells us that all of the disciples were martyred, not because of their great works but because of their great faith.

The command to us today is no different than it was to those early believers. We are to be reproducers, fruitful in all our comings and goings.

"Do not say, 'There are yet four months and then comes the harvest' Behold, I say to you, lift up your eyes and look on the fields. They are white for harvest." (John 4:35)

All around us are people who need Jesus in their lives. They need us as reproductive Christians, to step out of our comfort zones and share the love of Jesus with them, whatever the cost. And in our world today, the cost may be because of the lethargy of the church and the antagonism of the world. Let us pray for God to increase our fruitfulness in the Kingdom.

Question: What kind of fruit are you bearing? Is it nourishing to the soul?

Protect Your Treasure

In these days of increasing lawlessness, we are all aware of the need to protect those people and possessions we value the most. We subscribe to home protection services, buy a home safe, rent a safety deposit box, build a tall fence, lock our car and home at all times. Sometimes we even hide our treasure under the mattress or behind a drawer.

When someone is missing or lost, we notify the local police to put out an alert. It seems that daily there is an alert asking the public to be on the lookout for a lost child or adult. When a valuable is missing, we turn the house upside down to find it. Where is the lost treasure? We need to protect everything, especially those people or possessions most cherished.

The first question that must be asked is, "Who or what do you treasure?" Though each of us may give a different answer, the thought is the same. I must do all I can to protect those people and things I value most.

The Bible has much to say regarding treasures, what to value and how to protect them. Jesus gave a clear message about this.

"Do not lay up for yourselves treasures on earth where moth and rust destroy or thieves break in and steal. But store up for yourself treasures in heaven where neither the moth nor rust corrupt or thieves break in and steal. For where your treasure is, there your heart will be also." (Matthew 6:19-21)

To narrow our focus on treasures even more, consider what Jesus said in answer to the man who asked Him how to obtain eternal life.

"If you wish to be complete, go and sell your possessions and give to the poor; and you will have treasure in heaven. Then, come and follow Me. ...Everyone who has left houses or family or possessions for My sake will receive many times as much, and will inherit eternal life."(Matthew 19:21,29)

So vital is this truth that Jesus even told a parable about the woman who lost one coin. She searched relentlessly until it was found. Then she called all her friends and neighbors to celebrate with her. Jesus' point was not the value of the treasure. The diligence with which she searched. is what Father God does to find each and every one. He treasures people so very much! Each one! Everyone!

The greatest treasure we have is the description God gave when He created man "in His image" How can we protect that precious treasure? The Apostle Paul, writing to young Timothy, gave him some sound advice about how to live.

"Everyone who names the Name of the Lord is to abstain from wickedness...,,,,.,Flee youthful lusts and pursue righteousness, faith, love, and peace with those who call on the Lord with a pure heart." (2 Timothy 2:19-22)

Paul continues on to offer some characteristics of those who treasure God above all else.

- Be gentle when facing opposition.
- Refuse foolish and ignorant speculations.
- Do not be quarrelsome.
- Be kind to everyone.
- Be patient when wronged.

All of these are on the "to be" list and will be aided by the Psalmist's declaration.

"Your Word have I treasured in my heart that I may not sin against You." (Psalm 119:11)

Challenge: Take an inventory of your treasures? Which are those that keep you away from the riches of God, and which draw you closer to the greatest possession we could ever have, God? Are you protecting that relationship?

READ THE SIGNS

"What does that sign say?" That is a question we asked our young grandson when he was learning to read. The signs were a fun challenge to practice his skills. When he turned sixteen and was ready to drive, one of the tests he had to take was a Road Signs test. These signs would be guides to direction, warnings and cautions, speed limits and information important to helping him become a safe driver. Many were color coded to ensure attention. Some even had flashing lights. Without these aids, driving would be much more hazardous. Failure to heed the signs might often lead to accidents, injury to vehicle or driver or even death. As he prepared, we admonished him to heed the signs.

Have you ever considered that in our pilgrimage through life as Christians that there are also road signs? Spiritually we must also be able to read the "road signs" placed in our paths by God. These are designed for instruction, warning, guidance and discipline.

What are some signs God might use to get our attention?

- **U TURN** A change of direction is needed, one that will cause us to reverse direction. Such signs are sometimes welcomed and sometimes met with great consternation. This is especially true for those of us who are very single minded in our focus, determined to proceed as we have planned for ourselves.

- **DEAD END** The road we may be on leads nowhere. To continue may be harmful at worst and unproductive at the least. It is the feeling we experience when we have failed at something we hoped to do, a project we wanted to complete, a goal we had set without consulting God for the "go ahead" sign.

- **DIVIDED HIGHWAY–KEEP RIGHT** Life is full of choices, each important, some critical, lest we find ourselves going against the flow of God. We know that failure to heed His sign means we face obstacles coming straight for us. A path to sin or failure may be the result.

- **DETOUR AHEAD** These are never words we want to read, but in life they are the reality of unexpected events. Challenges, reconstruction physically or mentally, injurious ruts in the path, a sudden loss; but sometimes a detour leads to a sweet serendipitous surprise, an unexpected blessing, a new revelation from God.

- **ROAD UNDER CONSTRUCTION–PROCEED WITH CAUTION** Such signs are patience builders as we are forced to slow our pace or wait. Waiting is never a travel occurrence we welcome, but often necessary to protect us from harm. Remember, patience is a virtue! It is in the waiting that we may hear God the clearest, because we know that He often speaks in whispers only heard if we are at rest.

- **WATER HAZZARD** This sign may have flashing lights on it to emphasize the information and caution the one who wishes to hurry on his way. It is hard not to notice such warnings without making a decision to proceed or turn back. We may call this a time of considering what God has said for what it means in our lives.

- **DO NOT ENTER** Now, there is a clear "no-no". God has given us quite a few in His Word. His first was to Adam and Eve as God forbade the eating of the special tree in their lush garden. This sign had flashing lights all over it. We are the heirs of that failure to heed the sign.

- **REDUCE SPEED AHEAD** Slow your roll! Don't go rushing through life breathless and harried. Stop to smell the flowers, notice the songs of the birds. Offer thanks to God for the blessings He has bestowed. In this "fast food world" we want everything NOW! Perhaps if we slow down a bit, we may be able to hear God more clearly. We will not so often miss the words of instruction, comfort, or peace He offers freely.

- **BRIDGE OUT** Since walking on water is reserved for Jesus – and Peter – we surely must heed this sign. Getting wet may be the least harmful result we could experience.

The Prophet Jeremiah sent a warning from God to His people about the importance of signs. These were needed to correct the crooked and sinful path they had chosen heedless of the warnings of God.

"Set up for yourselves road marks; place for yourselves guideposts. Direct your mind to the highway, the way by which you went...and return..." (Jeremias 31:21)

The scenario is a familiar one to all of us. Disobedience or avoidance of the signs God places in our hearts lead to disaster. And worst of all, this willful denial of the truth of the messages leads to alienation from the God who above all wants to fellowship with His people. We live in a time when more and more people ignore God's warnings and fail to even notice His signs. We must heed His warnings! God will not leave us lost, afraid, abandoned forever. He offers a word of redemption to His people. To us because as believers We are His people, too.

"As I have watched over them to pluck up, break down, overthrow, and destroy, so I will watch over them to build and plant again, declares the Lord." (Jeremiah 31:28)

Question: Are you reading God's signs in your life journey? Do you see clearly His plan for you?

RECRUITED

The call went out in the aftermath of the tragedy of the Japanese attack on Pearl Harbor. "America needs you!" Young men by the thousands answered the call, some volunteers and some drafted. Women, too, were recruited to serve. Into the Army, Navy, Marines and Air Corps they went, off to face a determined enemy of freedom, our freedom. They did not know, nor could they imagine the hardships they would face in the days and years ahead. Roughly outfitted and briefly trained, the recruits faced challenges that would call on their inner resolve as well as physical stamina. Determination was the weapon they used in the face of wave after wave of attack by their enemies. Many thousands died as martyrs to the cause of freedom for America and her allies. The cost was enormous, but victory was won. We are free today because they paid the price for us.

Many years ago some men heard the call, "Follow Me". Recruited to a literal life or death mission, the twelve disciples of Jesus enlisted in an army which today is numbered in the millions. Like the men recruited in the World Wars, they did not know of the great challenges they would face in the years ahead. In three brief years they were trained by Jesus to meet the determined enemy of their souls who wanted to rob them of their freedom to live the life God had designed for them. Even more, they did not know the ultimate cost their Leader, the Son of God, would pay for their freedom. We are free today because Jesus faced the enemy of God, Satan, and called on the resources of His Father to defeat him.

The recruiting goes on today in the Armed Forces of the United States. Men and women are called to go to many places to ensure that our enemies do not overwhelm us. They also seek to protect others who are threatened. Recruiting also goes out to every person who will heed the call of the Master to accept the terms of service to Him and His Father. Unlike the draft, we are not conscripted. The choice to enlist in the army of God is an individual one of choice. The cost may be great. Persecution is likely. Discouragement will nag at you. Some may even become martyrs as those early disciples did.

The Apostle Paul knew firsthand what recruitment was. Jesus had met him on the Damascus Road and recruited him, commissioned him, and sent him out to serve. Paul knew all about the armor of God that he wrote about. Through many hard trials, God had sustained and encouraged Paul. I imagine there were times when Paul felt like we do sometimes when the enemy seems to plague us with unwanted challenges. But his faith in the provisions of God held him firm. And those same provisions are ours each day as we serve alongside the many others in the army of God. As Paul did, we must fight on and look forward to the crown of life for those who endure to the end.

What lies ahead? What preparation must we have? Where will we be called to go? What are the provisions we will have? These and many more are the questions we have. Here is a look at some of the answers.

- Out clothing will be the armor of God: loins girded with truth, the breastplate of righteousness, feet shod with peace, a shield of faith, a helmet of salvation, and the sword of the Spirit (Ephesians 6:11-17)
- Our marching orders are simple: It is the same order Jesus gave to Peter, Andrew, James and John. " Follow Me and I will make you fishers of men". (Matthew 4:19)
- As Jesus ascended to His Father, He left the disciples with the commission we have today. "Go ye into all the world and make disciples of all men, teaching them to observe all I have commanded you." (Matthew 28:19-20)
- Our Commander-in Chief, Jesus, will be with us wherever we are. "Lo, I am with you even to the end of the age," (Matthew 28:20)

What will be the cost? We do not know. But we must be willing to pay it. Soldier on, dear believer!

Question: What is God asking of you? What might be the cost?

REGARDING OTHERS

*L*ook out for Number One! This is the insistent theme of our times and it permeates all of life. It dictates our approach to ideas, business deals, sports, people, and even the more mundane activities of our lives. Promoted by the media and supported by those who seemed to have achieved that "numero uno" status or are hopeful of getting there very soon, we are led to believe that we must, at all costs, look after self first. The fact that selfishness and self- centeredness are encouraged is rendered unimportant. On rare occasions we may veer aside to help one another in a random act of kindness, quickly returning to our self-fulfilling lifestyle.

We have subscribed to the lie that if we don't look out for ourselves, no one else will. Citing examples, and yes, even Christians are included, reinforces our desire to see that self's needs are met first. Gone is our happy face when we feel passed over, set aside, unfulfilled, whatever that means. Cast in the role of intruder are the needs of others. When the downcast, brokenhearted, needy invade our field of vision, we pretend not to notice or turn a cold shoulder as if they have intruded on our rush to the front of the line. Not a pretty picture, is it? It surely is one in stark contrast to the life of our Savior who portrayed the totally selfless life.

Time after time we read in scripture where Jesus turned aside from His journey to offer aid and sometimes life itself, to someone in need. Here are just a few examples of Jesus' care for others.

- "Jesus was going throughout all Galilee, teaching in the synagogues and proclaiming the gospel of the kingdom, and healing every kind of disease and sickness." (Matthew 4:23)
- On His way to attend to the request of a synagogue official to heal his daughter, Jesus was touched by an unknown person. Instead of attributing it to the press of the crowd that followed him, Jesus paused. He looked around to see who had touched Him. When he discovered the woman and her great need, He said, "Daughter, your faith has made you well. Go in peace, and be healed of your affliction." (Mark 5:24-28)
- As Jesus was approaching Jericho, a blind man was sitting by the road begging... Jesus stopped and commanded that he be brought to Him. Jesus asked, "What do you want Me to do for you?" The blind man said, "Lord, I want to regain my sight" Jesus said to him, "Receive your sight. Your faith has made you well." (Luke 18:35-42)

In each instance we find Jesus, noticing someone not on the list of elites, and stopping to attend to their needs, both physical and spiritual. This singular characteristic set Jesus apart from His generation. People saw His care for the sick and downtrodden regardless of their station in life. The yearning of His heart to draw all men to Him led Jesus to put aside the privileges of heaven and assume the role of a servant. To the very last week of His earthly life, Jesus portrayed the servant example for His apostles. At the last supper He shared with them.

Jesus "got up from supper, laid aside His outer garments, and taking a towel, He girded Himself. Then He poured water into a basin and began to wash the disciples' feet and to wipe them with the towel with which He was girded." (John 13:4-5)

There is no better example of the posture of one with a servant heart than that! He had laid aside the privileges of heaven to take on the role His Father had assigned Him.

The Apostle Paul captured the essence of this selflessness when he penned these words.

"Do nothing from selfishness or unworthy ends or promoted by conceit and empty arrogance. Instead, in the true spirit of humility, let each regard others as better than himself. Let each of you be concerned, not for his own interests, but for the interests of others. Have this attitude in yourselves which was also in Christ Jesus, who, although He existed in the form of God, did not regard equality with God a thing to be grasped, but emptied Himself, taking on the form of a bond servant...humbled Himself by being obedient to the point of death..."(Philippians 2:3-8)

Giving up the race to be Number One is costly. It cost Jesus His life. Many others since then have also paid the ultimate cost of laying aside personal position and safety in order to be the compassionate hands and feet of Jesus. To the One who gives us life we, you and I, must be just that also, not counting the cost but being a servant fashioned upon Jesus' example.

Thoughts to ponder: What does this humility mean for us? How is it portrayed in our lives? And the big question is "What will it cost in time, money, reputation, career advancement, or leisure time?" To put it on a personal basis, what will others see when they observe my life? Will they see only my work ethic, exuberant life style, enthusiasm for sports, my politically correctness? Or will they see my compassion for others which reflects my love of God? Will my hands be gentle and my words kind? Will they see forgiveness, mercy, kindness reflected in my daily life?

Restored!

The old battered and scarred chest, drawers askew, sat unused in the corner amid the cobwebs. Each glance at it brought forth memories of years of use and abuse. Children's clothes, trinkets, mismatched socks, a hidden treasure, all occupied its drawers through the years long past.

One day, passing by the old chest, a flash of inspiration struck. Restore it! Bring back its former status and intended use! And so, setting to work, layers of grime and chipped paint were removed. Each drawer was repaired. A shiny, new coat of paint was applied to the exterior. And last, pretty new knobs adorned each drawer. The old, forgotten chest had been restored! Not only was the exterior restored. Its former usefulness had also been restored. Once again it would serve its intended purpose.

Such is the need of mankind, each of us born into a scarred world bearing the effects of Adam and Eve's disobedience, Even the physical world around us moans with the effects of misuse and neglect, willful thoughtlessness and abandonment. All of creation groans to be restored to its original glory.

"The anxious longing of creation waits eagerly for the revealing of the sons of God...that the creation itself will also be set free from its slavery to corruption and into the freedom of the glory of the children of God...For we know that the whole creation groans and suffers the pains of childbirth until now." (Romans 8:20-22)

This is especially true of mankind. Whether we are consciously aware or blindly ignorant, the spirit of man yearns for restoration. We all wish for a return to Eden, to intimate, in person fellowship with God, our Creator.

Even the early disciples awaited restoration of what they had lost when Roman rule put them in bondage, They had been misused, punished, jailed, criticized by neighbors and friends as they had followed the One they knew to be the Promised Messiah.

"When the disciples had come together (after Jesus' resurrection and before His ascension to the Father) they asked Him, 'Lord, is it at this time that You are restoring the Kingdom to Israel?'" (Acts 1:6)

After Jesus resurrection and appearance to them, they were hopeful of change. It is true that they were looking for an outer restoration, but soon they would understand that true restoration begins within.

That is why God sent His Son, the heir of all things, to earth. He came to show us our need and to offer restoration to all who will believe. Jesus' humanity was a pattern, a glimpse of what our restoration would look like. He revealed what we can become through the grace of God.

Jesus' sacrifice, His gift to us, is not a half-hearted overhaul of a misused and abused piece of furniture. It is the promise of a complete restoration to what each of us is intended to be. Instead of sitting idly in a corner bemoaning our scars and feeling set aside as useless, let us consider the possibility of what we can become, a restoration so awesome that the very Light of God shines in and through us. A little sanding here and there, a removal of the debris we have accumulated, a new appearance brought about by the love of the Father in us! It is not only possible. It is God's plan for His created ones. Let the restoration begin in us as we accept the full package of God's grace. God awaits our restoration!

A word of caution: Sometimes the restoration process is painful and lengthy. But it is so worth it in the end as we are clothed in righteousness.

"He who overcomes will be clothed in white garments...and I, Jesus, will confess his name before My Father and His angels." (Revelation 3:5)

Question: Are you in need of a complete restoration? Or perhaps a touch up here and there?

Scaredy Cat!

No child likes to be tagged with the title "scaredy cat" due to timidity in a situation which is perceived as risky. It is a taunt that stays long after the event is over, sometimes leaving a lifetime scar. Nor do we as adults like the feeling of fear that washes over us in some situations. Extreme height. Catastrophic weather conditions like an earthquake, fire or tornado. The out-of- control vehicle hurtling toward us on the highway. The words of a doctor offering a fatal diagnosis. A riot in our town that is violent in its destruction.

Our bodies quake, nerves shatter, hearts race, and courage flees in fear. Momentary immobility or inability to process an event in such situations adds to the fear factor. We can't seem to think clearly. We are just plain scared!

Often such fear may come as we consider the state of our city or nation that is undergoing political upheaval and unrest. This is a world-shattering fear of the future for us and for our children. Fear is a common enemy to all and as old as Adam and Eve who feared God after they had partaken of the forbidden fruit. They heard the sound of God walking in the garden and so they hid in fear.

When God asked the man why they were hiding, Adam's answer was truthful.

"I heard the sound of You in the garden, and I was afraid because I was naked; so I hid myself." (Genesis 3:10)

The Jews in Jesus' day feared Roman rule. These occupiers controlled their lives and activities. For that reason people may have clung more closely to their religious leaders for what little protection they could provide. Therefore, it is no wonder that fear was often the reaction to Jesus' teachings. John tells us that no one spoke openly about their opinions "for fear of the Jewish leaders". (John 7:13)

We are also told that many of the religious rulers believed Jesus was the promised Messiah, but were not confessing that for fear that they would be put out of the synagogue. Fear is a powerful motivator of behavior. John gives a reason for their reluctance to confess their faith.

"They loved the approval of men rather than the approval of God." (John 12:42-43)

All of these examples fall into the category of "fear of man". None address the fear of God as it is found often in the Bible. The writer of Proverbs begins our definition of the fear of God.

"The fear of the Lord is the beginning of wisdom." (Proverbs 9:10)

This is a fear that overtakes us when we consider the awesomeness of Almighty God, the One with supreme power and authority. In

Hebrew thought the word literally means "the flowing of the gut". That is the feeling we get in the pit of our stomach when we are very afraid. The word also means "reverence"

"You shall fear (reverence) the Lord, your God; and you shall worship Him and swear by His Name." (Deuteronomy 6:13)

Moses declaration may help us understand that "fear".

"Do not fear, for God has come in order to test you and in order that the fear of Him may remain with you so that you may not sin." (Exodus 20:20)

Consider how many times we fear things that are out of our control. Yet, how often do we pause to consider the fear of God? We reside in a comfortable belief in a good God who gives us good things when we are "good". But do we consider His displeasure and fear Him when we engage in sin we know He hates. Is our faith based on lethargy or truth? If we dare to trust Him, He will shatter the comfortable boxes we put Him in. Then place He will reveal to us who He really is and wants to be in our lives. He does not bring us out of the box to scare us to death. He does so to bring us into fullness of life in Him. In worship we reverence the God we know to be Almighty with confidence that He has only our best in mind.

Question: What are you most afraid of? How does God factor into that fear?

SEARCHING FOR TREASURE

Combing the beach for treasures! Discovering an old family chest full of treasured remembrances! Attending a yard sale and discovering a dusty, unused treasure! We all love to find treasures. Many of us have what we think of as treasures: aa valuable antique from Great Grandmother, a precious piece of jewelry given to us by our spouse, stocks and bonds earning interest, etc. From the media we are frequently advised to "buy gold or silver" as a way to secure our future. And who of us has not had a moment of panic when some special treasure was lost or missing?

All of these are material treasures which give us a degree of security. But do they really do that? Stock markets crash, gold and silver are devalued in worth, What we discovered and deemed treasure turns out to be only a copy of the real thing. In other words, dependence on things as our treasure is an uncertain way to live.

What then should we treasure? Or where does our treasure lie? The truth is that our greatest source of treasure, and the only one which does not go up and down like a yoyo, is God. He is the Supreme

Supplier of treasures. His riches are unlimited and are not diminished by time or circumstances.

Many years ago, Jeremiah, who prophesied during Judah's last days before their captivity, asked an important question.

"Who trusts in their treasures saying,'Who will come against me?'" (Jeremiah 49:4)

Judah's security in what they had and could summon if needed was based on false security. It was not based on the only One who could actually meet their need. When disaster struck, did their treasured resources save them? No! Jeremiah reminded the people of what God said.

"It is I, God, who will bring fear to you as your earthly treasures are destroyed...but afterward I will restore the treasures ..." (Jeremiah 49:5)

God knew that His people's trust was in their abundance and not in Him. Though this proclamation holds the hope of future restoration of material losses, of far greater importance is the understanding that God keeps His promises because we are His treasure, His creation made in His image.

This trust in earthly treasures is not confined to the time of the Old Testament. Jesus addressed the same issue to the crowd gathered on the mountain to hear Him teach.

"Do not store up for yourselves treasures on earth where moth and rust destroy, and where thieves break through and steal. Instead, lay up for yourselves treasures in heaven where neither moth nor rust destroys, and where thieves do not break in and steal... For where your treasure is, there will your heart be also." (Matthew 6:19-21)

He told them what we need to hear. What really matters in our future is how we live now. If our time and energy is focused on amassing earthly goods to the exclusion of amassing eternal treasures, then our hearts are substituting things which will eventually be gone for what is eternal riches. Later dealing with a young man seeking to know how to live, Jesus emphasized this truth.

"If you wish to be complete (in your search for God's approval), go and sell your possessions and give to the poor, and you will have treasures in heaven. Come and follow Me." (Matthew 19:16-21)

While this advise seems risky, the point is well taken that priorities must be set on God first. That young man left grieving because he had many earthly riches which did not satisfy, and he refused the offer of treasures that were eternal.

James, Jesus' brother echoed this very thought as he wrote to believers young in the faith.

"Come now, you rich, weep and cry for your riches have rotted, and your garments have become moth-eaten. Your gold and silver have rusted, and their rust will be a witness against you." (James 5:3)

It is clear! To no eternal end are the treasures we amass here on earth. What we rely on for the future is not assured. Nor will we be able to take our earthly treasures with us when Jesus returns. Someone once said, "There is no U Haul behind a hearse." We must place our search for the treasures of the Kingdom of God as our priority, and trust God to supply what we need now and in eternity. If you haven't begun the search, do so now!

Question: What is the treasure you are searching for? Will it sustain you through eternity?

Seeing Beyond the Veil

The beautifully adorned bride walked slowly down the aisle to meet the one who would soon become her husband. The wedding party was in place and the attendees were filled with anticipation. Everyone eagerly awaited the unveiling of the bride's face as she took her beloved's hand. What was hidden would be plainly seen.

What did everyone see? Was she lovely, cute, blushing, freckled? Was she smiling with delight? Were her scars revealed?

We often wait for the "big reveal", the uncovering of the not yet known. Will it be a boy or girl, twins or triplets? Will we be pleased with the present when it is unwrapped? When will we be able to see for the first time our newly refurbished home? When will the new graduates enter the auditorium to be recognized for their achievements?

So many things in our lives lie "behind the veil", obscured from view or access. The tomorrows of life may bring surprises that delight or events that bring sorrow, disbelief, awe, fear, blessing, a myriad of revelations.

As Christians we are privileged to see beyond the veil, a view not seen by the early Hebrews. For many centuries they had not been privileged to see beyond the curtains which obscured the Holy of Holies in the Temple. God's instructions to Moses had been specific.

"You shall hang up the veil under the clasps, and bring in the ark of the testimony there within the veil. The veil will serve as a partition between the Holy Place and the Holy of Holies." (Exodus 26:33)

We know that only select priests were able to enter and only once a year. When the tabernacle was completed, Moses followed God's instructions.

"He brought the ark into the tabernacle and set up a veil for the screen. He screened the ark of the testimony just as the Lord had commanded." Exodus 40:21)

It was not until centuries later when Jesus was crucified that this prohibition changed. As Jesus took His last breath on earth, something very unusual happened.

"Jesus cried with a loud voice, 'It is finished!' and yielded up His Spirit. And behold, the veil of the Temple was torn in two from top to bottom." (Matthew 27:50-51)

No longer did the veil obscure God's holy place. All could see. The opportunity to meet with God took on a new dimension. The writer of Hebrews, in speaking of the hope we have in God, spoke of the veil.

"...we who have taken refuge would have strong encouragement to take hold of the hope set before us. This hope we have as an anchor of the soul, a hope both sure and steadfast, one which enters within the veil where Jesus entered as a forerunner for us, having become a High Priest forever according to the order of Melchizedek. (Hebrews 6:18-20)

The revelation for us is that we may come humbly to the throne of grace where we may receive God's mercy and grace in our time of need. (Hebrews4:16)

God wants us to see Him for who He is and to understand His heart for us. What a revelation we have "beyond the veil"!

Suggestion: Spend some quiet time with God as you consider what He gave you when "the veil was removed".

SELF- MEDICATED CHRISTIANITY

No reliable doctor of medicine wants his patients to self-medicate when ill, and tell him later about their choices. No! The outcome could be worse than the illness. The old saying, "God helps those who help themselves", is not true. Nor is it scriptural. An appropriate medicine is needed for the best outcome. Delaying the doctor visit as the last resort may cause further complications. Have you ever been guilty of this self-medication? Not a wise choice!

This topic also applies to the Christian life as well. When we are soul sick and in need of rescuing, what is our first choice? Call a friend? Seek a counselor? Stew and fret while hoping for a miraculous change? How often is our first call to God, the One who is able to give us what is needful to set us aright. Scripture pictures God as the Great Physician for a reason. He is!

The Bible, like us, is filled with "do-it-yourself" people. Take Job for example. The story of Job's life was filled with people who wanted to be dispensers of cures for all of Job's troubles. They advised, cajoled, condemned, and blamed because they were sure they could help poor Job self-medicate. Job, however, was onto them. He knew his Source. This is what he told them.

"You are all worthless physicians. I wish you would be quiet, and that would become your wisdom...Your memorable sayings are proverbs of ashes" (Job 13:4-5,12)

Instead of trying any of the offered remedies, Job uttered memorable words in the time of his greatest distress. These words reflected his confidence in God.

"Though He slay me, yet will I trust Him." (Job 13:15)

As we read of all of the hurtful things Job was enduring, we wonder how he could remain connected to the Great Physician. The answer is a simple one. He trusted God. We know the end of the story. God restored to Job all that he had lost. But it was not before God reminded Job of who was truly in charge of life itself. In fact, God rebuked those who had tried to be substitutes for Him,

"Who is this that darkens counsel by words without knowledge? (Job 38:1)

Job's answer to all God had said was just as pointed as God's message to Job and his do-gooder friends.

"I know that You can do all things, and that no purpose of Yours can be thwarted." (Job 42:1)

The Apostle Paul said it this way.

"I know Whom I have believed and am persuaded that He is able to guard that which I have committed to Him until that day." (1 Timothy 1:12)

These words were written toward the end of Paul's life as he was imprisoned in Rome and awaiting his end. Like Job, he could not escape or delude himself into believing in release. He believed God, whatever the solution might be. In sickness and peril, he trusted. In chains and in a storm tossed sea, he trusted. In the presence of an angry mob of unbelievers, he trusted. When his words were challenged, he trusted.

Though none of us may experience the trials of Job or the dangers of Paul, we still face the challenges of illness, troubles, disasters, and loss. We may be scorned for what we believe. Life is full of opportunities to choose what kind of cure we will seek. Exercising our faith is at the very top of the list of cures. Let us affirm, as Paul did, that we trust the Great Physician as our ultimate Source of the best cure, acknowledging that is "just what the Great Physician ordered.

Question: Are you "self-medicating" or asking the Great Physician to be your cure?

SOMEONE IS WATCHING YOU!

*A*n issue of a popular news magazine contained an article about tracking devices. They called them versatile marvels with many benefits. Sadly, there are just as many, if not more, downfalls to such devices. GPS satellites track our whereabouts and those of our friends and enemies as well. Tags on merchandise help retailers trace goods to warehouses and store shelves. Those tags, bar codes, also tell them who bought the products. Mega stores know more about our shopping habits than our friends do. Emergency response times are quicker due to the ID on the phone used to call. Livestock are no longer branded. They are "chipped". Even our pets are microchipped! Instead of being clueless about where our children are or what they are watching there are devices to track them by our cell phones.

The phrase uttered in the early days of the "Cold War, "Big Brother is watching you!" is literally coming true as the battle rages over our privacy or lack thereof. When is it invasion? How far is too far? What is the latest great tracking device? The needed blocking device? So protective are we of our own personal data and space that any intrusion must be scrutinized for hazardous potential, even as we are being exposed by entities such as Facebook and Twitter. Shudder! Shudder! Not only is big brother watching. The whole techy world is watching our every move, every word, every purchase.

But, here is a thought! Have we ever been unseen? The answer is a resounding, "NO!" From the time we were a twinkle in the eye of an expectant mother, God saw us. In our less than nano-state, He had already identified us, knew our whereabouts, and even the color of our eyes, hair, freckles, and warts. He could track our course through life even as He planned our days and urged us to follow.

God is the ULTIMATE TRACKING DEVICE. No need for a microchip or bar code, a GPS or phone, or even a satellite. Longitude and latitude are not necessary for God to find us at any given time or place. In fact, He sees the "inside stuff", thoughts never spoken aloud, plans not consummated, ideas yet unborn. He knows every hair on our heads, or the lack thereof.

We need never fear being lost or of losing our identity, or having it stolen. No virus will attack our navigation through life as we are always on God's "radar". No system will shut down without God's awareness. God is always aware of our pain and knows the fear that threatens to steal our peace. It has always been so, even when He asks a rhetorical question.

"Adam and Eve heard God walking in the Garden in the cool of the day; and they hid themselves from the presence of the Lord among the trees of the Garden. Then the Lord God called to the man and said, "Where are you?" (Genesis 3:8-9)

God knew where they were and why they were hiding! If you have ever felt scolded by God, it was mild compared to the guilt and consequences the man and woman felt in the presence of God!

Elijah was hiding in a cave in fear for his life, but not hidden from God. God knew where he was and why.

"Elijah came to a cave and hid there. The Lord came to him and said, "What are you doing here, Elijah?" (1 Kings 19:9)

God knew just where to find Elijah and why he was there. Perfect deviceless tracking, I think. I think He even has the electronic age of mega spying in His hands Immanuel, "God, with us", is all the tracking system we must trust. Big Brother and our enemies or friends may be trying to track us, but they are woefully inadequate to compete with the God who made the whole universe. He is the filter through which we must go to ensure real life.

Question: Are you aware daily that God sees your every action, every word spoken, every thought? How does that thought alter your life?

Spiritual Refraction

Upon a visit to the eye doctor to have our eyesight tested, we are given an examination to determine the refraction in each eye. As accurately as possible, each eye is measured against clarity of vision in various lenses until the right one brings us to the closest standard of 20/20. Then, with prescriptive glasses, we see with a new clarity. The blurry images and squints to focus are gone.

When my eldest daughter was young, her vision was very poor. She required strong corrective lenses. One day she was able to have corrective surgery. Upon receiving her new glasses, she exclaimed, "I can see the leaves on the trees!" Suddenly things which had only been a blur before, were now quite clear. What a marvelous discovery! She had new opportunities to discover things heretofore missing. There was a new freedom.

In the spiritual realm the same poor eyesight may also prevent us from apprehending the truths God wants us to embrace. Often, as with the Pharisees of old, we see not at all. As Jesus addressed the issue of spiritual sight referring to the religious leaders, He told His disciples this.

"While seeing, they do not see, and while hearing, they do not understand..." (Matthew 13:13)

Jesus continued, quoting the Prophet Isaiah who, many years before, had addressed the same issue of spiritual blindness in God's people.

"They keep on listening but not perceiving, keep on looking but without understanding Their ears are dull and their eyes dim. Otherwise, they might see with their eyes, hear with their ears, understand with their hearts and be healed." (Isaiah 6:9-10)

The Apostle Paul, writing to the church in Corinth addresses spiritual sight this way.

"Now we see indistinctly as in a mirror; but someday we will see face to face with clarity." (I Corinthians 13:12)

He prayed for the Ephesian believers that "the eyes of their hearts might be enlightened."...

Spiritual sight is so important, so necessary. The presence of cloudy spiritual vision deters believers and unbelievers alike from seeing the truth of God. Lack of sight, or what we might sometimes call "insight" keeps us groping in the dark for answers to life's perplexing questions. We see partially, but the fog of unbelief or thickheadedness keeps from having 20/20 vision. The good news is that we can all receive "corrected vision". It is a gift from God through His Spirit. He really wants us to see Him for Who He is

As Paul prayed for the Ephesian believers, he had that in mind.

SPIRITUAL REFRACTION

"I pray that the eyes of your heart may be enlightened so that you will know what is the hope of His calling, what are the riches of the glory of His inheritance in the saints, and what is the surpassing greatness of His power toward us who believe,"

(Ephesians 1:18-19)

Eyes which see the truth of God are rewarded with the knowledge of who we are in Him. The longing in our hearts to know Him more and understand the truths of His Word are magnified. Who of us has not longed to know God more intimately! Our daily prayer should be, "Lord, open the eyes of our understanding so we may receive all You have for us." Perhaps then we will have the veil removed from our faces and see the glory of the Lord even as we are transformed by Him.

Challenge: Think of a time when you saw with new clarity a truth from God. What difference did it make in your life?

STANDING AT THE JORDAN

Forty long, hard years had passed since God pronounced sentence on His faithless people. Forty years of watching the elders die. Forty years of remembering their reluctance to trust in God's promise to give them a land of their own. Now all of the generation who had rejected God's promise, were dead. A new generation now stood on the bank of the Jordan river listening to their God-appointed leader, Joshua. None of these people, except Joshua and Caleb, had seen God draw back the waters of the sea for thousands of their ancestors to cross to safety from Pharaoh's pursuing army. But they had experienced God's provisions for them those long years of wandering. All they had to believe was Joshua's word that he had heard God say to go into the Promised Land now.

Think about it! What if they, like their ancestors, had refused to obey Joshua? What would have been the outcome if Joshua had not courageously listened to God's directions? Was their faith sufficient for the challenge before them? To be sure, God's disappointment and anger at their unbelief would have resulted in a far different outcome. We shudder to think of the cost of such unbelief!

Unbelief! A word with negative outcomes. What is the lesson here for us? We read God's Word of all of His promises and commands. Each time we understand that God is requiring us to trust Him, to stand at our own "Jordan" with a choice to obey or not. Will we hesitate? Will we let fear be the deciding factor? Has not God been faithful so many times before? It is time to recall God's faithfulness to us.

When faced with what appears to be an impossible situation, we may discover how much trust we have in God. Sadly, often we, as the Hebrews did, fail to step out into the surety that God is with us, and that He has the plan for us well in hand. Disobedience or rebellion is a costly lesson to learn, but when learned, our journey into God's favor and abundance is multiplied over and over again.

We know how Joshua's command to proceed ends. His command was not based on his own judgment but on the promises of God.

"Moses, My servant is dead. Now arise. Cross this Jordan, you and all the people, to the land which I am giving to them.—-Be strong and courageous. Be careful to follow all the law which Moses, My servant, commanded you. Do not turn from it to the right or the left so that you may have success wherever you go...Have I not commanded you? Be strong and courageous! Do not tremble or be dismayed, for the Lord, your God, is with you wherever you go." (Judges 1:2-9)

God parted the waters of the Jordan and His people set their feet at last on the land God had promised so long ago. To remember the occasion, stones from the midst of the river were set up to testify to

God's faithfulness. In generations to come those stones would be a reminder to trust God.

"When your children ask their fathers in time to come, 'What are these stones/', then you shall inform your children, saying, 'Israel crossed this Jordan on dry ground. For the Lord your God dried up the waters of the Jordan until you had crossed, just as the Lord, your God, had done to the Red Sea which He dried up before us until we had crossed. This is so all the peoples of the earth may know that the hand of the Lord is mighty and so that you may fear the Lord, your God, forever. (Joshua 4:21-24)

Today we stand at the brink of our own Jordan. The world we live in requires steadfast courage, intentional obedience, and undying faith in the God who holds us in His hands. He is the same God who parted the waters for the Hebrews. We must step out in belief that God has prepared the way for us. The words of the old hymn must echo in us.

"Have Thine own way, Lord. Have Thine own way. You are the Potter. I am the clay. Mold me and make me after Thy will while I am waiting, yielded and still."

Question: Do you dare to trust that the "waters of the Jordan" will part to allow you to fulfill God's purpose for your life?

STRENGTHEN THE BRETHREN

*J*esus' command to Peter after Peter's "trial by fire" was to be the man Jesus knew he could be if he practiced what he had been taught. At the time Jesus spoke these words Peter had yet to experience how very weak he was in his own strength. Not many days after hearing Jesus' words Peter failed to give a faithful witness about his Master. Three times Peter denied any association with the One he had followed, eaten with, listened to, pledged allegiance to for three years. His courage failed in the face of a challenge to his beliefs. We can only imagine the pain Peter experienced when he understood the impact of the words Jesus had spoken to him a short time before.

"Satan has demanded permission to try your faith to see if it I real. But I have prayed for you that in the midst of that trial your faith will not fail. When you have grasped onto your faith again, do this: STRENGTHEN THE BRETHREN." (Luke 22:30-32)

Notice that Jesus did not say "If you fail". He said, "When you fail and then grasp onto your faith again". Jesus knew the weakness in Peter better than Peter himself did. Now there is a lesson for all of us. We think we know how we will react to a given situation. But when our feet are held to the fire, what then?

Jesus' prayer began to be answered soon after His ascension to heaven. We see Peter in a leadership role, Jesus' forgiveness echoing in his mind. Luke records in Acts 1:5-26 Peter's first recorded act to solidify his witness to the life of Jesus as he suggested to the remaining disciples one to fill the place vacated by the traitor, Judas. That group of loyal followers, recognizing Peter's leadership, chose a replacement, Matthias.

As Pentecost arrived and the promised Holy Spirit descended on the disciples gathered in the room, it was Peter who "took the podium". He delivered a strong, clear explanation of the fulfillment of the Old Testament promise and of the need to accept Jesus' sacrifice. Not bad at all for an uneducated fisherman who had just gone through the painful trial of his faith!

Peter now stood as the leader of the disciples, but also as spokesman/shepherd of a huge group of new believers. Had it not been for the trying of his faith, Peter would not have understood that the Source of his strength and boldness was in Jesus, His Lord. He had been uniquely prepared to "strengthen the brethren".

The scripture records Peter's powerful message to the huge crowd of people from many countries who had heard the disciples speak in their native languages. Some who heard were confused. Others mocked the disciples with the accusation of drunkenness. Peter boldly stood and faced the crowd with words that would bring new life to three thousand souls!

Here is our lesson: PREPAREDNESS IS VITAL, AND TESTING IS A REQUIRED COURSE IN THE SCHOOL OF FAITH. Let us learn from Peter and "strengthen the brethren".

How do we go about that? We do not need to capture a large crowd in order to speak, though Billy Graham did so most effectively. For most of us, the message we have begins with the life we live as we go about our daily lives. Whether we notice or not, people watch us as Christians. Sadly, sometimes what they see or hear is not pleasant. We must let God teach us how each one of us may most effectively share the Good News. Who knows, we may be as bold as Peter was!

Question: Will you be a diligent student when God seeks to teach you?

TAKE A WALK

*H*ealth experts encourage us to put aside lethargy and walk for better health. Start with a short walk and increase the distance as you gain strength and confidence. Many of us groan at the mere thought that we might have to turn into a walker in order to gain better physical condition. This activity we see as "work". We even park our cars in the lot of a big store as near the door as possible to avoid walking. We excuse this by saying we are in a hurry. Label us lazy!

Walking has a way of calming frayed nerves and emotions. It generates oxygen to our lungs. And if we look around, we are able to see the beauty of nature God has provided for us to enjoy. The initiative to walk must be generated by the benefits we reap.

In the days before motorized transportation, people walked everywhere they had to go. If there were roads or paths, these were unpaved, dusty, rocky, muddy, and sometimes dangerous. Jesus walked such paths as He traversed the country He lived in. Never once are we told that He complained about having to do so. Actually, for Jesus, these walking adventures provided Him opportunities to teach His disciples about life in the real Kingdom, God's Kingdom. It made Him accessible to people as He passed by.

In a Biblical sense the word "walk" is used to refer to the manner of life lived as believers. It denotes one's life lived before the Lord who is worshipped.

God commanded Abram, "Walk before Me and be blameless." (Genesis 17:1)

Many years later God spoke through Moses, His appointed leader of the Hebrews. They were nearing the Land of Promise after an arduous trek through the wilderness.

"See, I have set before you life and prosperity and death and adversity; in that I command you to love the Lord, your God, to walk in His way and to keep His commandments, statutes and judgments so that you may live and multiply; and that the Lord, your God, may bless you in the land you are entering to possess." (Deuteronomy 30:15-16)

Do not miss the reminder of the adverse result of failure.

"But if your heart turns away and you will not obey, but are drawn away to worship other gods and serve them, I declare to you today that you shall surely perish. You will not prolong your days in the land you are crossing Jordan to possess it " (Deut. 30:17-18)

The first letter of John, the Apostle, reminds us of this

"If we say that we have fellowship with Him and yet walk in the darkness, we lie and do not practice the truth. But if we walk in the light as He Himself is in the light, we have fellowship with one another, and the blood of Jesus, His Son, cleanses us from all sin." (1John 1:6-7)

So, what does this walk look like? Where will we walk? What pace should we keep? Will there be rocky, hard places to navigate? Will there be dangers?

The Apostle Paul wrote to the church at Ephesus because he knew he would not again see these believers he loved and had lived among for several years. They were strong in their faith because they had walked with Paul, and they were sad that they might not see him again. Paul offered them a pattern to live by. (Ephesians 5)

- Be imitators of God as beloved children.
- Walk in a manner worthy of your calling with humility, gentleness, patience, endurance, love, diligence to preserve the unity of the Spirit in the bond of peace.
- Do not walk as unbelievers walk.
- Walk in love as Christ loved you and gave Himself up for us as a sacrifice to God.
- Be careful how you walk, not as unwise but as wise, making the most of your time because the days are evil.

As followers of our Savior we, too, must walk worthy of our calling, observing God's ways, and obeying His commandments. We, too, must imitate God's kindness, grace, patience and mercy. Our walk must take us wherever He leads, not on paths of our own making. In doing so, we will surely have better spiritual health.

Challenge: Take a walk, both physical and spiritual, with open eyes and heart. How will your fitness improve physically and spiritually?

TAKE ROOT!

Spring is such a wonderful time of the year! All the dormant plants peek their heads up out of the ground, welcoming the warmth after the freezing winter. They seem to be in a hurry to dress themselves in their beautiful colors and lush foliage. The roots that kept them safe through the winter now seem to urge them on to new growth. Spring rains come to water the tender shoots and the sun beams down in a warm smile. Trees with sturdy roots have weathered the winter winds and now their bare limbs put out so many shades of green. Not only do the plants bloom where they are planted, they also sends seeds and roots to birth new plants.

The joy of a gardener may be in the planting of seeds which will soon produce food for the family's table. Each seed is carefully imbedded in good soil and watered by rain or human hands. Sometimes a bit of nutrients are added to enhance healthy growth.

Often we are dismayed to see damage done by too harsh a winter or the careless footfall of a human or animal. Instead of the beautiful plant, we may see a misshapen and unhealthy plant struggling to survive. We hope the damage is not irreparable.

The writer of Ecclesiastes reminds us that "there is a time to plant and a time to uproot," (Ecclesiastes 3:2b) The same is true for us as Christians. We are told by the Apostle Paul that we, too, are rooted.

Therefore, as you have received Christ Jesus, the Lord, so walk in Him, having been firmly rooted and now built up in Him, and established in your faith just as you were instructed, and overflowing with gratitude." (Colossians 2:6-7)

Even as a plant that has been uprooted struggles to live, so, too, a Christian who has born the marks of damage. Disease, carelessness, unhealthy habits, or someone with bad intent, struggles to survive with faith intact. Growth may be stunted, and life may seem to be too hard to endure.

The ancient Jews lived in an agrarian culture. Not only did they raise animals for food and sacrifice, they planted what their animals and families would eat. Jesus gave such a great example of what a healthy and unhealthy plant looks like.

"I am the Vine and My Father is the Vinedresser. Every branch in Me that does not bear fruit, He takes away; and every branch that bears fruit He prunes so that it may bear more fruit...Abide in Me and I in you. As the branch cannot bear fruit of itself unless it abides in the vine, so neither can you unless you abide in Me. I am the Vine, and you are the branches. He who abides in Me and I in him bears much fruit, for apart from Me you can do nothing. If anyone does not abide in Me, he is thrown away as a branch and dries up, and the branches are burned." (John 1-2,4-6)

Not only are we are admonished to bear good fruit. We are told that this fruit brings glory to our Heavenly Father as we prove ourselves to be faithful fruit bearers. We must be like the seed that fell on good soil and yielded a bountiful crop. Jesus told a very illustrative parable about the sower and his yield. Only the seeds which found good soil yielded a good crop. The rest were eaten by birds, chocked by weeds, or lacked the proper soil. (Matthew 13:1-8)

Through the seed each of us sows as we labor for the Master, we must take care to do so within the bounds of righteousness and love. God requires that we sow, but He is the One who gives the increase as His Spirit touches lives. Bear in mind as you sow, He is the One to receive the glory, not we the sowers.

Question: Are you a sower of good seed? Or are you a lazy gardener?

Testing Your Resolve

I am resolved, that is I promise, to never do that again or I promise to start doing something good. I am resolved to be a better wife, husband, employee, team player. I am resolved to kick that bad habit. Resolve is an interesting word. When looking at a dictionary we find a large variety of nuances to define "resolve". Among them are these: the act of deciding, to declare by a formal resolution, to deal with successfully, to reach a firm decision about. Let's focus on those few.

We all know about New Year's Resolutions, things we vow to do or undo, begin or end, set as a goal or remove from our lives. And we know that usually most of those good resolutions somehow fade away as daily reality closes is. Sometimes, and after the fact, we hear of an evil resolve carried out by someone. The devastation is startling!

Our resolve is tested in numerous ways. The pleasing odor of a food we resolved not to eat. The picture of a star we know we could probably never be. The skill we have tried in vain to master. The challenges of life itself. Some of us seem to be born with more determination to do or be or achieve. We call it "grit", another word for resolve.

Now, that can be a positive asset or a negative one depending upon its use. The little baby who works with resolve to reach the floor by climbing out of her crib may be injured. On the other hand, the father who is resolved to teach his son to ride a bike, may be pleased with the results.

The question often becomes, for us personally, how much resolve do we have? Is it enough to achieve the desired result?

In the days after the Hebrews had escaped the captivity of Egypt, God spoke some very specific words to His people. These words would test their resolve to be obedient.

"If you will indeed obey My Voice and keep My covenant, then you shall be My own possession among all the peoples...You shall be to Me a kingdom of priests and a holy nation." (Exodus 19:5-6)

Moses gathered all of the elders together and set before them all the Lord had commanded him. They were all aware that God was One who frequently tested their resolve to obey Him. And they also knew that lack of resolve or disobedience to a promise would bring harsh consequences. They must hear clearly the little words "if and then".

All the people answered together and said, 'All that the Lord has spoken, we will do!"

Twice they repeated their resolve to be obedient. Again, after the giving of what we call the Ten Commandments, the Hebrews made the promise to hear and do all the Lord commanded. ((Deuteronomy 5:27)

The saddest commentary on what the Lord knew would happen to their resolve is found in the following verses. We can hear the yearning of God as He spoke.

"Oh, that they had such a heart in them that they would fear Me and keep all My commandments always, that it may be well with them and with their sons forever!" (Deuteronomy 5:29)

We know they did not do so. Their resolve melted in the face of heathen influences. It led to exile and the loss of a nation. Dire consequences!

What is our resolve before God? Do we make promises with all intentions to keep them only to renege in the face of the challenges of life? When we have lost our resolve, do we find our way to God to ask for forgiveness and restoration? The words of the old hymn echo in our ears. "I have decided to follow Jesus, no turning back, no turning back." Let that be our firm and unwavering resolve. God, help us to faithfully keep it!

Question: Are you ready to make a resolution about your walk with God? Are you trusting Him to guide you safely to the good result as you follow His "if and then" promise.

THAT DOESN'T MAKE SENSE!

*S*truggling to put the pieces of a complex cabinet together, exasperation exploded. "That just doesn't make any sense!", she shouted. All of her efforts to figure out the diagram seemed like a foreign language. Then she did what we so often do when frustration takes over. She gave up. The project lay in pieces, destined to collect dust. Does that sound familiar? All of us at some time have been exasperated by some puzzling thing which seemed beyond us to figure out.

What are some alternatives to giving up?

- Begin over, step by step.
- See the help of a friend
- Contact the maker

Let's choose # 3 and use as an example the puzzlement we as Christians feel when trying to make sense of a particular verse or passage from the Bible. Sometimes we say, "It doesn't make sense." or "I don't understand this." Realizing that we are centuries away from the times in which this was written only adds to the frustration.

Yet, what seems like a puzzle to us, made perfect sense to the ancient writers. So, what must we do?

Oh, yes, contact the Maker! God is the author of His Word penned through the lives of His people. He knows each piece intimately and is ready to help us navigate the hard-to-understand passages. It may help to remember that even those who walked and talked with Jesus during His sojourn on earth, often failed to comprehend Hs teachings. Here are a few examples of their questionings.

- Two followers on the road to Emmaus blurted out their confusion and dismay over the crucifixion of the One they had believed to be the promised Messiah. .
- (Luke 24:13-27)
- An Ethiopian who had come to Jerusalem to worship was reading from the Prophet Isaiah concerning Messiah's death. He did not understand the passage. As Philip joined him, he heard the truth about Messiah, and asked to be baptized as a believer. (Acts 8:27)
- Thomas, nicknamed "the doubter", questioned Jesus as to how they could follow Him since they did not know the way. (John 14: 1-6)

We must recall Jesus' words to His disciples just before He returned to the Father. The Apostle John heard and recorded the answer which would ease all of their confusion and questioning.

"When the Spirit of Truth comes, He will guide you into all truth, for He will not speak on His own initiative, but whatever He hears, He will speak; and He will disclose to you what is to come. He will glorify Me and will take of Mine and disclose it to you. All the Father has is Mine; therefore, I said that He takes of Mine and will disclose it to you." (John 16:13-15)

Our responsibility is to ask in patience, "What does this mean? What do You want to teach me in this puzzling passage?" It is not helpful to quit or to discount a thorny issue. Each word of God is important, even the little ones. Each passage contains a lesson to be apprehended, a truth to be shared, guidance for tomorrow, greater love for the One who comes alongside us each day.

A PhD in theology is not necessary (though at times it may be helpful). Just lean in to hear what the Spirit of God will whisper to you. Continue to seek His guidance, and don't cease seeking for the truth. Each nugget mined is preparation for life in the Kingdom of God.

Question: Have you ever read a passage of scripture and could not make sense of it? To whom did you turn for enlightenment?

THAT'S MY DAD!

That's my Dad! I see him! Where's Dad? My Dad made that for me. My Dad can do that better than your Dad. The happy, proud cries of a young child ring out, informing all who are within earshot of the exalted status of Dad. Pride swells in the young heart because he knows he is loved by the man he calls "Dad". He eagerly awaits his presence, tags along with him as he putters in the garage, begs to go with him on errands, and best of all, savors the nightly bedtime stories and good night assurances that all is well. This man is his protector, playmate, confident, teacher, and at times, his consoler. Theirs is an intimate relationship based on love and trust.

From Dad he learns how to be a man, how to love well, work with diligence, act in wisdom, live a disciplined life. The times when correction is needed are few because the child desires above all to please his Dad. He understands that what pleases Dad most is obedience. Whet the child does not know just yet, but what is everlastingly true, is that he is becoming every day more like the man he so admires. Not only does he bear his Dad's DNA, he is learning to imitate Dad in the tone of his voice, his actions, his responses to life's circumstances, his desire to live honorably for the good of others. His hours of watching Dad have shown him how to do "stuff", how to treat others, how to submit to authority, and most importantly, how to pass on that knowledge and wisdom to others.

Pretty cool,eh? Sadly,so many dads do not fit that description. The human example just portrayed is a flawed one since as humans we never achieve that "perfect" status, the underlying truth is still valid. Dad is someone we should be able to emulate and respect. There is, however, One whom we call Father who is the perfect role model for us whatever our age. It is, of course, God, our Heavenly Father, our Dad (Abba). Our relationship with Father God should exhibit many of the characteristics of an earthly Dad relationship.

- Our eagerness to meet Him
- Our delight in His Presence
- Our listening to and believing His every word
- Our desire to please Him in all things
- Our following hard after Him
- Our learning how to "do stuff" well

We bear the DNA of our Heavenly Father because we are made in His image and after His likeness. Being His children, we must learn to hear his voice with clarity and to obey with willing hearts. We do so because we know that He loves us. From God we learn how to live an honorable life, one that reflects His goodness and mercy. We learn to submit to authority, first of all, His authority and then the authority of those over us.

From Father God we learn what He expects of us as we seek to pass on what we have learned and are daily learning so that those who follow can also become sons and daughters of Father God.

Jesus left us a tangible example of what that looks like as He walked the length and breadth of Palestine during His time on earth. Daily He obediently lived out His Father's plan for Him, touching so many lives with His message and miracles. He taught His disciples principles to live by after He was not with them. His bedtime stories were truths to be followed. The relationships He built with the disciples were life-changing, life molding ones. In Jesus' last recorded prayer, He prayed for those who would follow Him, for us, that we would be the children His Father wants us to be. (John 17)

Our connection with Father God is all about our relationship with Him, Father to child. He loves us beyond measure, and expects that love to be returned in kind. Sometimes, as all humans do, we fail to be the children He wants us to be. That is where His discipline comes to bear. Sometimes we fail to love Him well., but we must keep on trying because He is our Dad. We can say with enthusiasm, "That's my Dad!"

Challenge: Read John 17 and look for characteristics of the relationships there. What are the lessons for you?

THE BEST DAY OF MY LIFE

*I*f someone were to ask you, "What has been the best day of your life?" what would you reply? Some might say it was the day I married my husband or the day my first child was born. Others might point to the day they achieved the pinnacle of their success or of the status of financial prosperity. A prisoner would surely say, "The best day of my life was when I was finally a free man again."

The term Best Day" is difficult to define because our tomorrows may be even better that the previous best. It also may vary widely depending on our priorities, achievements or goals. Perhaps we should add the words "so far" as a condition.

Let's pose that question to some of the people we find in the Bible.

- Moses: "The day I saw the burning bush and heard God speak to me."
- Abraham: "The day I finally became a father of the promised son."
- David: "The news that I would one day be king."

- Andrew: "The day I met the Promised Messiah. and introduced Him to my brother."
- Peter: "It was the day Jesus forgave my cowardly denials".
- Paul: "The day Jesus met me on the Damascus Road."

Each answer may vary, but all are anchored in some aspect of relationship with God and His Son, Jesus because these days are life changing in miraculous ways. Each encounter awakened the soul to the One who holds life in His hands.

What if we could ask Jesus that question? Do you think He would say it was the day His earthly mission was complete? Or perhaps He might answer, "Hearing My Father say, 'Well done'"

Our answers as Christians may be varied as to the time and event, but surely the answer would have to be the same. "The best day of my life was when I realized my condition as a sinner and gave my life to Jesus. He took up residence in me, and my life has never been the same."

Each "best day" may look different, but none surpasses the realization that we can become new creations in Christ and join Him as the heir of the riches of our Father, God.

The Spirit Himself testifies with our spirit that we are children of God, and, as children, heirs also of God and fellow heirs with Christ, if indeed we suffer with Him so that we may be glorified with Him." (Romans 8:16-17)

James, leader of the fellowship of believers in Jerusalem also told us the same thing.

"Listen, my beloved brethren, did not God choose the poor of this world to be rich in faith and heirs of the kingdom which He promised to those who love Him?" (James 2:5)

The very best day for us is yet to come. It will be the day when the Kingdom of God is established and Jesus reigns as King of Kings! Can you imagine the excitement you will have of meeting the Savior face to face as the disciples had done! Or the joy of meeting the saints of old whom we meet in the Bible! Or of rejoining loved ones and friends in joyful worship of our Lord! What a day that will be, the "Best Day of all".

Question: How do you rate those days which we may consider "best"? What is your "best day" so far? Why?

The Benefits of Imprisonment

What? There are benefits from being imprisoned? Surely that cannot be a good thing There are many kinds of imprisonment besides police custody. The prison of a severe disability. The prison of unwanted circumstances. The prison of mounting debt. The prison of a habit that is wrecking health and endangering life. While these may not be actual prisons, they do certainly make us feel as if we are in shackles and bound. We whine, complain, and struggle against the unfairness of it all. Worse, we listen to the lies of Satan who wants us to believe we are not free. Could there possibly be any value in such bondage?

We need to hear the words of Isaiah, the prophet, whose calling from God was this.

"The Spirit of the Lord God is upon me, because the Lord has anointed me to bring good news to the afflicted...to proclaim liberty to captives and freedom to prisoners...that He may be glorified." (Isaiah 61:1b, 3b)

Jesus, our Messiah, who chose these words to read in the syna-gogue in His hometown of Nazareth, are recorded for us by Luke in 4:16-18 On another occasion, speaking to those who believed in Him addressed the idea of freedom.

If the Son sets you free, you will be free indeed." (John 8: 36)

So, if we are imprisoned by something, are we still free? Are there still benefits to be gained? An enigma? No! Benefits, yes! Twice in his letter to the believers in Ephesus Paul identified himself as "a pris-oner of Christ Jesus". This he proclaimed while being in chains in a Roman jail. (Ephesians 3:1; 4:1) He wrote letters of encouragement to believers all over Asia Minor. Pouring out his heart on behalf of their growth in the Lord, Paul's own testimony strengthened them.

"Be assured that my imprisonment has actually served to advance the spreading of the Gospel so much that throughout the entire Imperial Guard and to all the rest here, my imprisonment has become generally known to be in the cause of Christ. And most of the brethren have gained fresh confidence in the Lord because of my chains." (Philippians 1:12-14)

Instead of bemoaning his fate, Paul used the time as an opportu-nity to share even with his captors the Good News of the Messiah Believers, many of whom were new in their faith, were encouraged and emboldened to share their faith with others as they realized Paul's powerful testimony of peace. Unbelievers came to understand that Paul was not in bonds because he had committed some heinous crime, but because of his faith in Messiah and his desire to share that message. What a powerful testimony of God in one's life "in prison"!

While we may not literally be in chains, some of our brothers and sisters in other countries are. There are many circumstances of life in which they are imprisoned. Abject poverty, disabling disease, civil wars, persecution because of their faith, absence of freedom to come and go as they wish. All make them prisoners.

Fear should not render us immobile. Habits should not deter us from sharing the truth of Jesus. Illness is not an excuse to darken the light of Christ in us. The question then becomes: How will we respond to our imprisonment? Will we become embittered, adopt a "poor me" attitude? Will we rail against the unwanted bonds? Or will we, as Paul did, be able to put the chains in God's hands and recognize the opportunity to share the Light of Christ to a dark world that is truly imprisoned by unbelief? Are we able to consider our present bondage as a vehicle through which we can share in the sufferings of others who also wear bonds?

Ours is a choice based on faith in God who enables as He sustains us with His grace. We are bound to Christ, yet free indeed. We must choose to emulate Paul as we witness to the love of God. We must choose to say as Paul did

"I am put here by the grace of God for the defense of the Gospel…for me to live is Christ and to die is gain…For me to live is Christ and to die is gain." (Philippians 1:16, 21)

Question: What imprisons you in some way? Is it bondage for the sake of Christ?

THE ALIENS HAVE LANDED

In these days there is much talk about aliens, not the E.T .kind but the title given to the many who pour across our American border seeking asylum. Some are refugees displaced from their native countries, having fled for their lives. Some come seeking an education or better health care or to experience the "land of opportunity" for themselves. So many are children without any family member with them. Many come to escape from poverty and homelessness And some come for nefarious reasons. Whatever the reason, they come with only what they can carry with them. Most have left family and possessions behind.

Everyone seems to have an opinion about this influx of aliens. Are they welcome? Do they seek citizenship? Will they be productive? Will they be scorned and abused? How will they find housing and jobs, especially since most do not speak English? Some express animosity toward the aliens. Others express sympathy. Some hope to use them for personal or political gain. Most wonder what should be done about the vast numbers coming to America.

We have forgotten that all of us, either ourselves or our family before us. came from another country. Some came fleeing religious persecution, some escaping lawless acts, some hoping for freedom from an oppressive government, some for the adventure, and yes, some came against their will as slaves. They were aliens seeking life. We are a country of former aliens, speaking a variety of languages, and embracing a number of societal and religious differences. Have we all made the leap into "likeness"? No, yet, here we are co-existing and getting along...mostly.

Aliens have been around since the creation of the world. The very first aliens were Adam and Eve after they had been cast out of the lush, safe Garden of Eden into a life of hardship and danger. The first use of the word is found in Genesis 23:4 where Abraham calls himself a "stranger and alien" in the land of Canaan. Two generations later, Isaac, Abraham's son, addressed his own son, Jacob, with these words.

"May God give you and your descendants the blessing of Abraham so that you may possess the land of your sojourning." (Genesis 28:4)

Not many generations after Jacob, God's people found themselves aliens in Egypt where for hundreds of years they were enslaved and mistreated. This was not their last such status. As sin overtook them, they later became aliens in Assyria and Babylon. There they were alienated from home, country, customs, and the Temple which was their center of worship. Psalm 137 records their lament.

"By the rivers of Babylon we sat down and wept when we remembered Zion. There we hung our harps on the willow trees... How can we sing to the Lord on foreign soil?"

King David clearly understood his status as an alien. Listen to his words.

"Hear my prayer, O Lord, listen to my cry. Do not be silent at my tears. For I am a stranger with You, an alien like all my fathers before me." (Psalm 39:12)

As Christians we, too, are aliens and sojourners on the earth. We face many of the same difficulties and choices all aliens face. Will we thrive or just survive? Will we "hang our harps on the willow trees" because we find life too fraught with troubles? We are called to thrive, and like Abraham, look forward in faith to the place even now is prepared to house us eternally. In that day the Hebrews and we who are covered by the blood of Jesus will no longer be aliens in a foreign land. Our pilgrimage will be over. We will be HOME!

While we wait, let us extend mercy to those who seek to call America their home and refuge.

Challenge: Consider your status as an "alien". What do you look forward to?

The Art of Letter Writing

$\mathcal{I}$n this day of technological advances we have set aside so many of our long time customs and habits. Since the days of the Pony Express, and probably before that, people wrote and sent letters to friends, family, businesses, government officials, etc. We wrote letters and notes of encouragement, information, request, sympathy, and just plain "how are you". Each communication was treasured for its worth, especially the personal ones to distant friends and family. Children sent letters to Santa. Leaders sent information to their constituents. Most mail had the expectation of a return reply. Many eagerly awaited the postman's visit to deliver paper lifelines to the outside world.

These days electronic devices are used to email, tweet, relay information, send a photo, and are often written in short speak abbreviated terms leaving the receiver to decipher intent. No personal touch is used or expected. We pass electronic messages to people we have never met with the same fervor that we address friends and family. Anyone can snatch the messages and read them without our permission. These sometimes personal messages are critiqued by strangers who neither know or care about the sender. The personal touch is lost.

However, in days of old the Apostle Paul had no such quick conveniences. In fact, letter writing itself was a daunting task complicated by availability of materials, a literate secretary who could take down the thoughts of the illiterate and semiliterate, and of course the distance and time it took to send and reply to any communication. Messages were written on scraps of parchment, animal hide, a piece of stone or clay, a piece of cloth, whatever was available. So precious were these epistles that they were shared with many others who hungered for news. Often these messages were carried long distances to be shared with others or copied to spread the news to a wider audience.

The striking thing about Paul's letters is the personal touch with even those he had never met. Such is the letter to the Romans. Paul cared deeply for them. Romans 1 reveals Paul's feelings with phrases like "I long to see you..." or "I am eager to preach the Gospel to those in Rome."

So eager to share with these long distance believers, Paul wrote that both he and they might be strengthened. He prayed that he might be allowed to come to them as he realized that times were hard for those who professed faith in Christ and sought to live for Him. Moreover, Paul felt an obligation to do so.

There is something about holding a piece of paper in hand and reading words that soothe the troubled soul or comfort a sad heart, or just remind a friend that you still care even though miles or time separate you. Often letters written long ago, when found, reveal the heart of a lover, an absent friend, a long term friendship. Even today these warm our hearts.

At the risk of being called old-fashioned, let me pose a question or two for us modern day communicators.

- When was the last time you wrote, pen in hand, a letter of encouragement to someone?
- When did you pen an offer to intercede in prayer for a distant friend or family member?
- What would you write to a fellow believer who lives in a hostile environment?
- What would God have you share with someone struggling to believe God?

There is no need to be an accomplished writer to undertake such a task. It requires a response to that inner thought about somebody who needs a reminder of his or her worth. It requires only the willingness to really communicate beyond a quick tweet or email. That personal touch is a treasure still valued even by " texters and posters" Thankfully we don't have to search for animal skin or a stone to do so. Nor do we need the Pony Express. USPS is sufficient. Paul's letters to the Christians scattered throughout Asia Minor are read and reread today as letters of instruction and encouragement. Perhaps yours will as well.

Challenge: Choose someone who appears in your thoughts frequently, and write a letter or note of encouragement to that person.

THE DISASTROUS EXCHANGE

"What are the charges?" the man asked. A policeman had pulled him over as he was driving. Thinking he had not transgressed any law, the man was concerned over the event. When asked for proof of license, the man quickly pulled it out for review. Much to his dismay, he found that he was driving with an expired license, therefore was a law breaker. He protested loudly that he had not realized it was expired. Nevertheless, he was guilty, and as the exchange accelerated, the end was more severe than just the original offense.

Whether "accidently" or purposefully when we sin, it is still the same judgment. We are guilty of breaking the law and judged accordingly. To protest too loud, denying responsibility, may result in disaster for us spiritually.

The Prophet Jeremiah heard the Lord say, "I will contend with you." This word "contend" literally means <u>to bring charges against.</u> We can sense the sadness and anger of God as He gave evidence of the many ways His people had blatantly disregarded His laws and taken His blessings for granted. It was toward the end of the time of freedom for the people of Judah. Sensing God's analogies as a pre-amble to what was to come, Jeremiah listened intently as the Lord commanded him to go to Jerusalem and proclaim God's message.

God addressed the former devotion of His people and then their continued disobedience. God calls the time of faithfulness "the devotion of your youth", meaning when Israel was becoming a nation unto God. On and on through chapters 1-3 God describes their sinful ways and complete disregard for His laws. The list is long, but here are a few of the sins of their disobedience.

- They forgot all God had done for them throughout their time of wilderness wandering.
- The priests who handled His Law did not really know God.
- The rulers had sinned against God by ruling unjustly.
- The priests prophesied by Baal, a false god.
- God's people had forsaken Him to go their own selfish ways.

God reminded them, "You have brought this judgment on your-selves by forsaking Me."

Later God reminded His people again.

"In the day of your trouble you will cry to Me to arise and save you. But I will say, 'Where are your gods which you made for yourselves? Let them arise and save you.'"

All of this is recorded for us in Jeremiah 2-3

Our hearts grieve for the Israelites who had turned their backs on God. They were sinfully "driving without a license".

What does that mean to us today? It means that we are now expected to abide by God's standard of righteousness. We must not allow our gaze to be diverted to lesser gods.

Taking a look at our own country, America, we see the retreat from obedience to God and to an adoption of "idols" in His place. We bow down to beauty, fame, wealth, popularity, harmful substances and many more things. Recently a group of people, in rebellion against Christianity, erected signs which said, "In God we <u>do not</u> trust". In an effort to become "politically correct" we have become disobediently unrighteous.

Failing to heed God's warnings and disclaiming His right to "tell us what to do" we make our choices based on our own selfish wants and desires. Think about what that may mean for our future. What will be the result of such disregard for God?

To echo God speaking through the Prophet Jeremiah we read many times in Jeremiah's recording that Israel will become captive because of their sinful behavior toward their faithful God.

Have we made the disastrous exchange of Judah?

Suggestion: Read Jeremiah chapters 2-3 and think about it in the light of your own life of obedience or disobedience to the laws of God. Are you guilty, even unawares, of a disastrous exchange?

THE FAMILY BUSINESS

*I*n days gone by, though infrequently today, the expectation was for the eldest male child to carry on the family business. Often young children worked alongside their father to learn the skills required. Sometimes the son was apprenticed to someone more skilled to enhance his abilities. Personal wants to launch out in another direction were set aside because the expectation and family welfare were at stake. It was deemed an honor when someone said, "Your Father taught you well."

The term "family business" applies well to the life and ministry of Jesus, Son of God. Though we have no details of Jesus' early training in his earthly father's business, we must assume that he filled that role until He began His public ministry because He was called "The Carpenter". We do know of Jesus' childhood training in God's accepted laws for living.

At the age of twelve, the time a Jewish boy was considered a man, Jesus accompanied His parents to Jerusalem to celebrate Passover. When his family and other relatives of the area called Galilee left to return home, Jesus remained behind. Dismayed at finding their son absent, Mary and Joseph hurried back to Jerusalem to search for Him. After three days they found Jesus in the Temple among the teachers, listening to them and questioning what they said. When asked why He had treated them that way, Jesus gave an answer that was confusing to them, especially since He did not see a reason for their great concern.

"Why is it that you were looking for Me? Did you not know that I had to be concerning Myself with My Father's affairs?" (Luke 2:41-49 CJB)

At the age of twelve Jesus had a keen interest in everything about His Father's business, He did not refer to Joseph when He spoke of "Father's affairs". We are told that He returned to Nazareth to resume His responsibilities as eldest son as He "grew in stature and in favor with God and man".(Luke 2:52)

Now we must ask the question, "What was Jesus' Family Business"?

- "I can do nothing on My own initiative. As I hear, I judge; and My judgment is just because I do not seek my own will, but the will of Him who sent Me." (John 6:30)
- "I glorified You on earth, having accomplished the work You gave Me to do." (John 17:4)
- "I have manifested Your Name The words You gave Me I have given to them (the disciples) " (John 17:6,26)
- "It is finished!" (John 19:30)

Jesus came for one purpose: to do His Father's bidding, to speak what He heard Father say, to be Father's hands and feet to all He met. He sought to make God real to a people who considered God remote and far away. Not once did Jesus disobey His Father's will or shirk the assignment given Him whether the encounters were hard or easy. We never read where Jesus expressed fatigue or reluctance. He was about His Father's business.

What is the lesson we must take away from this? What is our Father's business that we are expected to carry on? In many ways our business is akin to Jesus' Family Business. We are to reveal the truth of our Father. We must go where He tells us to go with a singleness of purpose. That is to teach people about God, and ask the Holy Spirit to draw them to Him. It was His commission to His disciples and to us. (Matthew 28:19-20)

He has a training program for us as we soak up His Word in preparation to follow His leading. Obedience is the key. Nothing less will do. May we say, "I must be about my Father's business."

Question: Have you apprenticed well so that you can be about your Father's business?

THE GREATEST DREAM OF ALL

"I have a dream." These words from Rev. Martin Luther King still echo in our ears. He dreamed big and lived his life to make that dream a reality. Even in death his influence is felt by so many because of that declaration.

We all dream, both asleep and awake. Little girls dream of being princesses. Little boys dream of super human feats. Teens dream of mates. Young adults dream of the ideal job. As adults we dream of that perfect house with the perfect mate to share it. We even dream of the perfect body, flawless and strong. Some of these dreams are fulfilled, but many fade as years pass and the realities of life take over.

Is it wrong to dream? No! Often from dreams come ideas, positive changes, new insights, creative juices. Even the unrealistic dreams give us insight into ourselves. Some of our dreams seem silly or far out of the realm of possibility. Yet, some of them do become a course of action or an important factor in our decision making.

In the Bible we read of many instances when God spoke to His people and to His enemies in dreams as to future acts or consequences. As examples consider these.

- Joseph's dreams, recorded in Genesis 37, were life changing and history making as they came true.
- Pharaoh had a dream which Joseph was able to interpret. (Genesis 41)
- Jacob's dream gave him wise advice. (Genesis 31)
- Daniel was able to interpret two kings' frightening dreams. (Daniel 2 and 4)
- Joel records God's promise of the Holy Spirit's outpouring and says, "Your old men will dream dreams and your young men will see visions." (Joel 2:28)

Dreams! These were not the ones caused by that extra slice of pizza or the fear of tomorrow. These dreams were the ones God placed in the hearts of those He sought to bring to Him. They were life challenging, earth moving dreams! Dreams were meant to stir someone to action, to reveal one's sins, to plan for the future, to realize the hand of God on history. These were not the trivial, "What crazy thing did I dream last night?" kind of dreams.

Such pointed and directional dreams from God are not common these days. However, that is not to say dreams are insignificant. Some are! There may be any number of reasons why this is not the usual now. One that seems reasonable to consider is this. As we read the Bible, we see the unfolding of people's perceptions of God as He showed Himself strong on their behalf. They needed clear guidance because they did not yet have the Holy Spirit within them. We know that after Pentecost the Holy Spirit came to indwell believers. We have the Spirit of God within us now to give us direction and information. We sense His presence guiding us as we seek to follow God's path for our lives. So our need for dream directives lessens.

The greatest dream we can dream, awake or asleep, is to know God and what He has planned for our lives. Now that is the dream we should live out, knowing that God goes before us to make the way plain. He walks alongside us as our constant and faithful companion. He leads us to the goals He has prepared for us. Yes, some of these dreams are very challenging, even daunting in scope. Yet, dream we must, knowing God speaks today, even as in the past, to bring His loved ones along in His prepared path. Some may say dreams are silly or just a nighttime occurrence. Some may not believe that God still speaks in that way. It is a grave mistake to box God's actions into our framework of our disbelief. Be open to consider what you recall of a dream. Ask God to let you know if it is important. He will! And if it is from Him, He will be the One to help you see it to its conclusion. Dream on and listen for the voice of God!

Question: Have you ever had a dream when asleep or awake that you thought was from God?

THE IMPERTINENCE OF ARGUING WITH FATHER

*H*ave you ever had a heated, impassioned argument with your father? Plead though you may, whine and cry, fathers usually maintain the upper hand. Trying to bargain doesn't help either. Fathers have the last word, and often the first word as well. Our arguments, in the long view, seem petty and even silly. Why did we ever think we would win?

What about the arguments we pose with God, our Heavenly Father? Have you ever tried that? Plead your cause, tell of your innocence, whine at the injustice of a matter? Try to bargain with the Almighty? Offer a "foxhole bargain" like this? :God, if you will just get me out of this mess, I will go to Africa as a missionary" How did that work out for you? Did God suddenly change His mind and agree with you? Hmmm...

Listen to Job. He had suffered the loss of everything; material goods, family, friends, and even his health. He was in misery and grief. Now we know that Job was a faithful, God-fearing man, upright in all of his ways. God said as much. We find Job at a loss to explain to his wife and friends that he was not being punished for unbelief or some hidden sin. So, we hear Job begin his argument before God.

"Oh, that I might find God. I would lay my case before Him and fill my mouth with arguments...Would He then plead against me with His great power? No, He would listen to me." (Job 23:3-4)

Job continued to argue with God, beefing up his plea and citing all he had done. For three chapters, (29-31), Job continued as he was laying before God all of his righteousness.

"Oh, that I were as in months gone by, as in the days when God watched over me, when His lamp shone over my head and by His light I walked through darkness" (Job 29:2-3)

Job's friends were no help either. They were sure Job had done something awful to deserve such harshness from God. Their advice only made matters worse. Finally, God had listened to Job and his so-called comforters quite enough. So He responded, and not as Job had expected. Job got an earful and then some Wow!

God said, "Where were you when I created the world, placed everything where it was supposed to be, ordered the seasons, provided for the needs of all of My creation? Tell Me, Job...Will you contend with the Almighty? If you dispute Me, give Me an answer." (Job 38-41)

God's reply encompassed 4 chapters and left Job in grief that he had the impertinence of contending with God. To all that God had said, Job's answer was the correct one.

"I know that You can do all things and no purpose of Your can be thwarted...Therefore I have declared that which I did not understand, things too wonderful for me which I did not know.....But now my eyes see You. Therefore, I retract and repent in dust and ashes." (Job 4 2:1-5)

Job's response is the one God seeks from us when we challenge His authority and whine at Him for some perceived injustice. Do we really seek to change God's mind? Our impertinence is sinful, and our lack of trust in Him is revealing our level of faith. Who are we to challenge the Almighty?

Isaiah said it well as he recorded God's conversation with Cyrus who ruled over the Hebrew exiles.

"I am the Lord and there is no other. Besides Me there is no god...I am the Lord and there is no other, the One forming light and creating darkness, causing well being and creating calamity. I am the Lord who does all these...Woe to the one who quarrels with his Maker, an earthenware vessel among the vessels of the earth! Will the clay say to the potter, 'What are you doing?' (Isaiah 45:5-7, 9a)

Lest we forget, let us remember Job. God said it. That settles it. I believe it! One final word from God.

"It is I who made the earth and created man upon it." *Isaiah 45:12)

Question: Have you ever been impertinent before God, demanding your way or expecting His immediate attention?

THE KINGDOM OF ME

We are a self-centered people, more so every day. Just take a look around and listen to what bombards our eyes and ears. For example, a popular gas station has as its jingle these words. "I want it and I want it now!" That seems to be the theme of life in our world. Add to that the desire, we want to "do it my way". Short cuts to a goal notwithstanding, we seem bent on having it all and as soon as we can manage to grab it. Faster food delivery, package by overnight mail, shorter lines at the grocery store because we are in a hurry. No one wants to use snail mail if another option is available. We hate to be inconvenienced in any way.

Perhaps this has been true from the beginning. After all, didn't Adam and Eve want more than God had provided for their welfare? It was not enough to have a lovely garden, plenty to eat, freedom to walk about without danger, and a close communion with their Creator. More! More! Did they feel as if God was withholding something from them? Was His Presence not enough?

If that sounds familiar, remember the Israelites, God's chosen people. God had led them out of slavery, provided a leader, protected their leaving, dried up the waters for them to pass safely through, led them by night and day with His Presence, and led them to the land He had promised them. He called them to be set apart and their lives to be ordered by His laws. He promised abundance if they would be faithful to him.

Yet, here they came years later and demanded they be allowed to have a king to rule over them. They wanted to be like their neighbors, thinking this would provide added protection from their enemies. Major mistake! Wasn't that what God had been doing for them? They had gone through a period when judges offered leadership, but this period had not increased their faithfulness to God. The last verse of the book of Judges gives a sad commentary on that era.

"In those days there was no king in Israel. Everyone did what was right in his own eyes." (Judges 21:25)

It was a period surely illustrating evidence of the "kingdom of me".

God's prophet, Samuel tried to warn the people that having a king was a bad idea. He knew that the people despaired over their tendency to make their own way by their own pattern. Perhaps they had begun to realize that the "kingdom of me" would never result in peace. The "me" life had resulted in lack of harmony within and enemies in abundance. Yet, persist they did. "Give us a king!". God knew the result, but He gave them what they asked for, a kingdom, but not His. Kings in the years to follow would lead Israel away from God, not closer to Him. It resulted in a divided nation, and eventually exile by both the Northern and Southern Kingdoms. The worst consequence was hundreds of years without hearing His Voice. The period between the close of the Old Testament and the Coming of the Messiah was a dark period indeed in the "kingdom of me".

As we live now over 2000 years after the coming of the Messiah, are we any different from the Israelites who wanted it their way? Do we not so often follow our own selfish desires and rule over our own "kingdom of me and mine"? This is an era when we hear so many say, "I will set my own rules according to what I want. I will be in charge of my own life. I don't need anyone else to tell me what I should and should not do." Have we forgotten what happened to Israel as a result of their own selfish desires? In exile, they mourned for a kingdom lost and a land called home. They missed the guidance of the God who had been faithful to them even through their selfishness.

Let us learn a lesson from this. Who of us would ever want to be in captivity as a result of our own selfish desires? Perhaps some of us already are captives and do not realize it. That is truly sad! Let us repent and turn to being the people of God. Let us listen for His voice and heed His instructions for our lives. Let us choose to live in the Kingdom of God instead of the "kingdom of me".

Question: Which kingdom do you live in? Is it one of your own making or of God's design?

The Measuring Stick

Standing in the corner of the room is a yard stick, commonly recognized as a three foot measure of one yard. By it we measure the length of a board to be sawed, the length of a piece of cloth sufficient for our next sewing project, the height of our little children standing tall against the door post. But this "yard stick" is four feet long! To use it assuming a yard measure is to assure a wrong result. Too long! Too much!

We are constantly measuring something in our lives. We may measure our height or weight. (I'm the shortest in my family) We measure as we cook, as we sew or saw or paint. We measure our own success against another's achievements. We measure our beauty against the gorgeous movie star. We take the measure of a man by how he acts in public.

Does it ever occur to us that we may be using the wrong measuring stick? Who deemed this much money is what we must have? Who standardized the perfect body type? Is there only one way to make a delicious chocolate cake? Does one size fit all in clothing? (If you think that, try finding the right fit for you!)

What is the only measuring stick by which we should measure to be assured of good results? It is God's measuring stick! The Prophet Amos heard God say He was going to use a measure we today are unfamiliar with because of our tech age. He would use a plumb line usually used to determine the squared up lines of a building.

The Lord said to me (Amos), "What do you see?" And I said, "A plumb line." Then the Lord said, "Behold! I am about to put a plumb line in the midst of My people Israel. I will spare them no longer." (Amos 7:8)

God went on to tell Amos what would occur as a result of His measuring. Nothing good but judgment needed! What caused God to say that? The first two chapters of Amos tell us that God's people had cast aside the measurements God had set for them, and instead were using their own rules.

As we read the Bible it is clear that God is the one and only measuring stick by which righteousness is determined. He is the One with authority to use a measuring stick on us. This is revealed from the very beginning and continues to the cross.

Adam and Eve were measured against their disobedience. The people of Babel measured to build a ziggurat, but forgot to measure God's demands on their lives. Abraham was measured by his faith in the promises of God. God's standard of measurement matters!

"You shall not have in your house differing measures, one large and one small. You shall have full and just weight that your days may be prolonged in the land the Lord, your God, has given you." (Deuteronomy 25:15)

The New Testament echoes that same thought. Jesus said, "By your standard of measure, it will be measured to you..." (Mark 4:24)

The correct measuring tool matters eternally! He has commanded us to be holy, using Himself as the standard. He includes His people in this standard to be aimed for. "Be holy as I am holy." (Leviticus 11:44-45) This is the highest standard! We are to be holy, set apart, distinctive people, different from the world's standard. It sounds daunting unless we remember that the God who set the standard of measurement is the One who will help us achieve it.

Challenge: Measure yourself! Are you growing in grace and faith in God? Is your life a reflection of God's standard of measurement?

THE OWNER

*O*nce upon a time there was a cat who roamed the neighborhood. One lady decided to adopt it. So she began to set out food and water for the cat. (Let's call him Tom) Each day Tom came to dine. Down the street another lady, also seeing that the cat appeared ownerless, decided to claim him too. She also set out food and water. An opportunist at heart, Tom became accustomed to visiting each home to dine, selecting whichever meal suited his taste for the day. One day Tom failed to show up for his food at the first lady's house. Worried, she began to call, "kitty, kitty!". Now Tom had discovered that lady number 2 had set out a special meal for him, fresh fish! Finally, in hopes of discovering Tom's whereabouts, lady number 1 began to walk the neighborhood in search of Tom. Seeing him asleep on the porch of a neighbor's house, she rapped on the door to ask, "Why have you stolen my cat?"

Perplexed, the neighbor replied, "Your cat? He is mine. I adopted him after I saw him roaming free." Oh dear! It seems Tom had claimed both owners as his suppliers. To whom did he belong? You guessed rightly if you said, "Whoever had the best meal."

This humorous story is an analogy worth asking, "To whom do you belong?" Is it the thing or person which feeds your appetite best ? Does that change from time to time when you discover "a better meal"? You may even choose several "owners", as Tom had. Which of these offers the thing you most desire today? Do you even recognize that you visit several sources to be satisfied? And the most important question is, "Do you realize who or what does own you?" As Christians, is the choice of ownership ours to decide?

Jesus was clear about ownership because He knew that whatever we treasure most will capture our time, attention, and resources. It will be what feeds our wants.

"Where your treasure is, there will your heart be also." (Matthew 6:21)

"No one can serve two masters. Either he will hate the one and love the other, or he will be devoted to one and despise the other. "You cannot be faithful to God and to another owner." (Matthew 6:24)

How can we identify the "meal we like best" on any given day? The answer may be as clear as choosing what relieves the pain. It may be what we call "comfort food". Or perhaps, we feel owned by a person who dominates or seeks to control our thoughts and actions. Perhaps it is a job, a hobby, or media addiction which owns our time and attention. Whatever the source, this ownership issue is an age-old problem to be addressed.

The Apostle Paul understood this principle well. He knew each of us must choose. In his letter to the Christians in Rome, he identified this very issue.

"Do you not know that when you give yourselves to someone (or something), you are enslaved by the /thing you choose. The result is either sin leading to death or obedience leading to righteousness." (Romans 6:16)

As Christians we can only faithfully belong to one Master. He is the One who feeds us, guides us, protects us. As believers we are not free to roam from "house to house" feeding from different sources. Like Tom, who eventually chose what was best, we are to choose God. We must do so because His way, His truth, His plan for our lives, is not only the best. It is the only way to satisfy all the needs of our lives. It is the way which leads to life.

Question: Who or what has mastery over you?

The Proof is in the Tasting

We are obsessed with food! Restaurant business is booming. Food shows on television give us recipes and tips for greater flavor and appeal. Food magazines tell us what we should and should not eat if we desire good health. We have tasting parties with friends. "Do you like the taste? Is it good?", we ask. Peering into the refrigerator we spy a container of left-overs and ask, "Is it still good to eat?"

In each scenario, the proof is in the tasting. Does the left-over dish still taste good? Did the cook add the right seasoning? Is the meat cooked to my taste? Will I like this new dish? Which restaurant has the best tasting food? Does the product advertised really enhance the flavor of my food? Must I buy the new set of cookware in order to cook tastier meals? We want proof.

Let's apply this thought to our lives as Christians. All around us every day are those who "taste" the flavor of our lives to assess whether we really are what we say we are. They seem to ask. "What proof is there that he or she is a truly a Christian?" Our words of confession are not sufficient when offered as evidence. The proof is in how we live out that confession. Many years ago the Psalmist spoke of our taste.

"O taste and see that the Lord is good. How blessed is the one who takes refuge in Him! The young lions may lack food and suffer hunger, but they who seek the Lord shall not be in want of any good thing." (Psalm 34:8.10)

How can someone assess our good "taste"? Matthew recorded Jesus' answer.

"You will know them by their fruits...Every good tree bears good fruit, but the bad tree bears bad fruit...So then, you will know them by their fruits." (Matthew 7:16-20)

We may call those who take note of our lives "fruit inspectors". Is there good fruit to be found as they" taste" our lives? Is the fruit of his life good for me? Our lives are offered as proof. The Apostle Paul described the fruit we should exhibit in our lives.

"The fruit of the Spirit is love, joy, peace, patience, kindness, goodness, faithfulness, gentleness, and self- control. (Galatians 6:22)

In writing to the Ephesian believers Paul pictured what those fruits would look like lived out. In our world today.

- Be light. Take no part in deeds of darkness.
- Live purposefully
- Make the most of each opportunity to be light.
- Have a firm grasp of the will of God.

- Be filled with the Spirit
- Talk about the Word of God to each other.
- Be subject to one another out of reverence for Christ.
- At all times and in all things give thanks to God

The proof is in the tasting of our lives as lived in the truth of God. The writer of Psalm 119 went to great lengths to tell us how very important God's truth is. In one section he lays before God his requests for a fruitful life.

- Teach me, O Lord, the ways of Your statutes.
- Give me understanding that I may observe Your Law.
- Make me walk in the path of Your commandments.
- Incline my heart to Your testimonies.
- Turn away my eyes from looking at vanity.
- Establish Your Word to Your servant as that which produces reverence for You.

(Psalm 119:33-38)

Question: When people "taste" your life what flavor is it? The flavor of sin or of righteousness?

THE RETURNS AND COMPLAINTS DEPARTMENT

*E*very store has one...a Returns and Complaints Department. It is the place where dissatisfied customers go to return unwanted merchandise or register a complaint and demand satisfaction. Too large. Too small. Doesn't work as advertised. Lacks a part. Tastes bad. And so it goes . Some businesses have employee satisfaction personnel on hand to settle office disputes, field complaints and smooth ruffled feathers. It seems there are a growing number of complaints these days. Somehow it had become our "God-given-right" to voice our opposition to perceived injustices. Riots, angry outbursts, scorching letters to the editor, withheld grace, snap judgments all cascade around us. Turning away from calm reasoning we turn instead to soulish desires and quick "fixes". Long held convictions are often cast aside in our efforts to have our complaints justified.

Sadly, this is often the way we treat our God, the One who wants to grace His people with peace. We demand:

- Where were You, God when..?

- Don't You care...?
- Why did You let this happen to me?
- She didn't deserve...
- He's a good guy, so why...?
- You should have answered my prayer!

We treat God as if He is in charge of the Returns and Complaints Department, hired on to make right our perceived wrongs, heal our wounded egos, get the guy who did us wrong. When God doesn't act as we demand or as quickly as we wish, we either amp up the volume or look to an alternate source of help.

It should come as no surprise that we are not the first generation to have such attitudes. God's chosen people, the Israelites specialized in complaining as God led them out of captivity. They whined over lack of food and water, perceived dangers, Moses leadership, etc. Even though God more than met all their needs, they whined and grumbled, accusing Moses, God's appointed leader,

- "Is it because there were no graves in Egypt that you have taken us away to die in the wilderness? " (Exodus 14:11)
- The whole congregation of the sons of Israel grumbled against Moses and Aaron in the wilderness. 'We wish we had died by the Lord's hand in the land of Egypt when we had plenty of bread and meat to eat. You have brought us out in this wilderness to kill the whole assembly with hunger'" (Exodus 16:3)
- "The people thirsted for water and grumbled against Moses and said, 'Why have you brought us up from Egypt to kill us, our children and livestock with thirst?'" (Exodus 17:3)

- "As for the men Moses sent to spy out the land, they returned and made the whole congregation grumble against him by bringing a bad report." (Numbers 14:36)

At one point, Moses pointed out to them that their complaining was not really against him but against God Himself who was their Provider. (Exodus 15:112)

Sometimes we are asked by a Christian whose faith is weak to explain God's perceived lack of help' Or we may be ridiculed by an unbeliever and asked to provide proof of God's caring as if we are somehow appointed to be God's defender. News Flash! God does not need anyone to defend Him! We are not His Press Secretary sent to soothe critics and solve grievances. God is more than able to defend Himself.

Why can't we just accept the truth that, regardless of our situation, our complaints, our perceived injustices, God is always for us? He is always for His people! Always! Does that mean that He jumps at every complaint to satisfy us? No! His is a much larger and grander plan than just to soothe our wounded egos and wavering faith. He does not exact immediate justice on every slight, though He does comfort the wounded heart. He is called "the God of all comfort." God Himself, speaking to Isaiah said, "I, even I, am the One who comforts you." (Isaiah 51:12)

What then should we expect of God? Or should the question be, "What does God expect of us?" He expects that we will trust Him. It is just that simple. Not easy, but simple. Trust the loving Father who has promised to carry us "under His wings". Our daily confession should be, "God, I trust you with my life, all of it every day!"

Question: How long is your complaint list against God? What is His complaint about your life?

THE SAMSON SYNDROME

Everyone, whether we acknowledge it or not, seeks purpose and meaning in life. We sense potential that seems out of reach, but attainable if only... In futility, we reach,, and much like the writer of Ecclesiastes, we may express our feelings.

"Everything is meaningless, utterly meaningless! What do people get for all their hard work? Generations come and go, but nothing really changes...Everything is so weary and tiresome. No matter how much we see, we are never satisfied. No matter how much we hear, we are never content. History merely repeats itself. It has all been done before. Nothing is new under the sun." (Ecclesiastes 1:1ff from NLB)

What pessimism! Yet, we seek on. Rick Warren's best selling book, "The Purpose Driven Life" offers hope for those who seek meaning and offers suggestions to that end if only... Further evidence man be seen in the "cafeteria style" approach to religion. Many take a little of this and a little of that to make a plateful of scrambled beliefs and ideas. In the end, we remain unsatisfied and unfulfilled.

We may suffer from the Samson Syndrome. No, that is not some disease unless you call the state in which so many live a "diseased state". A brief look at Samson's life is quite revealing because it portrays a picture of unfulfilled promise. God had told Samson's parents before his birth that he would have a special calling on his life. He was to live a purposeful life and drive the enemies of Israel, the Philistines, from their land.

But Samson's life as a judge in Israel was a litany of sinful, willful mistakes. He married a foreign woman and then shacked up with a harlot. When his wife was killed due to his actions, he married a Philistine woman named Delilah. She was a big nag and betrayed him, causing him to be captured by the Philistines. They gouged out his eyes! Blinded, he was made sport of by the drunken partygoers of the king. In one last attempt to be the man God had wanted him to be, Samson in his great strength, pulled down the pillars of the building, killing all of the Philistines inside and himself as well. (Judges 13-26)

Why tell all of this about Samson? It is because we understand that he failed to live the life God had planned for him. The picture of Samson is a mirror image of so many of us today. God, before we were even a twinkle in our mother's eye, had already a plan for each of us. We were called to a life of grace and truth. Instead, earthly satisfactions and the lure of forbidden fruits draw us away from that purpose. Like Samson, we focus on self-satisfying human desires rather than seeking to please God.

Samson prostituted the design and purpose of God by continuing to live with the ungodly. His life is an example of what not to do. We must avoid the pitfalls of Samson. How can we do that?

As a starting point let us heed the admonition of the Prophet Isaiah.

"Seek the Lord while He may be found. Call on Him while He is near. Let the people turn from their wicked deeds. Let them banish from their minds the very thought of evil doing. Let them turn to the Lord that He may have mercy on them. Yes, turn to God, for He will abundantly pardon." (Isaiah 55:6-7 NLB)

Second, we must heed the command of Moses .who gave God's people this admonition.

"Love the Lord, your God. Walk in His ways. Keep His commandments and statutes and His judgment that you may live." (Deuteronomy30:16 NAS)

And third, heed the pleas of the Apostle Paul.

"And so, dear Christian friends, I plead with you to give your bodies to God. Let them be a living and holy sacrifice, the kind He will accept... Don't copy the behavior and customs of this world, but let God transform you into a new person by changing the way you think. Then you will know what God wants you to do, and you will know how good and pleasing and perfect His will really is." (Romans 12L1-2 NLB)

As the chosen and called people of God, let us live with His purpose and meaning to His honor and glory!

Question: Do you sometimes suffer from the "Samson syndrome"? It may be contagious to those around you!

The Whole Truth

Some years ago there was a television show entitled "Truth or Consequences". So popular was the show that a town was named for it. To tell anything other than the truth was to experience some type of consequence. There was another show called "To Tell the Truth". In this show contestants were asked to discover which of the panelists was actually telling the truth.

In a court of law as we stand before a judge we are asked to swear that we have told "the truth, the whole truth and nothing but the truth, so help me, God". We must answer in the affirmative and keep our oath, knowing that there will be serious consequences if we lie or "rearrange" the truth". Our word becomes our pledge to be truthful in what we say. Each witness called to testify is asked to give the same oath

As sinful humans we stretch the truth, manipulate the truth, twist the truth, tell a partial truth or hide the truth. We have metaphors based on truth, such as "I'm dying for a cup of coffee." Really? Often there is outright denial of the truth of a matter. Alfred Tennyson said, "A lie which is half a truth is ever the blackest of lies."

Jesus said, "I am the Way, the Truth and the Life." (John 14:6)

The Apostle John declared that truth came through Jesus Christ. (John 1:17)

When Jesus was on trial for His life, He stood before Pontius Pilate, Roman ruler and was asked, "Are You the King of the Jews?" Jesus answered truthfully.

"My kingdom is not of this world. If it were, my servants would be fighting so that I would not be handed over to the Jews, but My kingdom is not of this realm... I came into the world to bear witness to the truth. Everyone who is of the truth hears My voice." (John 18:36-37)

Pilate's response was quite revealing of his lack of understanding of truth. He said, "What is truth?" (John 18:38)

What then is truth? Your truth? My truth? Do they differ in meaning and intent? Is truth based on a particular situation? What we do recognize is that a half truth is a lie. A matter is either true or it is not. To engage in other than that is called situation ethics, That is using truth as the situation demands. And there is no such thing as a" little white lie". All lies are black. A lie is a lie whatever the size.

In his letter to the Christians at Ephesus, Paul wrote, "Let our lives express truth in everything." (Ephesians 4:15) That includes speaking the truth, dealing truthfully with others, living the truth of our confession, and standing for truth at any cost. To be sure, at times speaking the truth can be costly, even dangerous. Yet, we must be people of truth. To engage in anything less is to be a liar.

Jesus said, "You shall know the truth and the truth will set you free. (John 8:12)

We are free from the inclination to lie to cover ourselves. Free from half truths. Free from distortions of the truth. We are free in Christ to be truth bearers so that no one can question our validity. The Spirit of Truth lives within us, giving us the power to be truthful. The best freedom of all is the freedom to believe the absolute truth of the Word of God. Upon that rest any and all truth we embrace.

Challenge: Read John 8:12 again. What is the truth, the absolute truth, to which Jesus referred?

THE WOW FACTOR

*D*riving west through middle America, we were caught in a hail storm. As the storm increased in intensity. we took shelter in a farmer's barn with the cows in attendance. This was not just a little hail storm, It was gigantic as evidenced by the pounding on the tin roof of the barn. When the storm was over we ventured out to an amazing sight. The ground was literally covered with baseball sized hail stones! WOW! Was all we could say, followed by a thanks to God for safety1.

The same reaction comes when we experience an earthquake, a volcanic eruption, a violent hurricane. We are wowed by these natural phenomena. These days we seem to need the awe factor in our everyday lives. We are constantly searching for the bigger, higher, better, newer thing to wow us. The wildest rollercoaster just opened! Don't miss this scary movie. It's a hair raiser! Try this extreme sport. It's thrilling! I dare you to jump off the ledge!

Even the ads which assault our senses every few minutes on the TV are designed to wow us with the best ever product we can't live without. "You can't live without this. It will change your life!", so they say. Oh, and don't miss this new tech product which is so much better than the one you recently paid big bucks to own. You will be will amazed what it can do! That longing in our gut never seems to be satisfied as we want more, more, more. Why is that?

Perhaps it is because we are not looking in the right way. We should look no farther than the "Most Awesome of All„the Almighty Triune God! He revealed His awesomeness in Himself, His Son and His Holy Spirit all through scripture. Imagine the WOW factor present in the Hebrews as they watched God roll back the waters of the sea so they could cross over on dry land. And then He returned it, destroying the enemies who threatened them. Wow! That was awesome!

As we read through the New Testament we find so many WOW events. People were continually being amazed by what Jesus said or did. Early in His earthly ministry Jesus went to the Synagogue in Capernaum on a Sabbath day. We are told that the people were amazed by the power of His words because He spoke with such authority. Never had they experienced the Spirit behind those truths which Jesus shared. The listeners became even more amazed when Jesus exorcised the demon in a man, and did so with only a command.

"And amazement came upon them all, and they began talking with one another saying, 'What is this message? For with authority and power He commands the unclean spirits and they come out!'" (Luke 4:36)

So amazed were they that their report of this event spread all over the area. The news was so good it had to be shared by eye witnesses of this power from a carpenter from Nazareth.

There was much discussion as to who this man, Jesus, was. Some said He was the Prophet. Others said He was surely the Christ only to be challenged because Jesus came from Galilee and not Bethlehem as the prophecies foretold. They did not know He had indeed been born in Bethlehem. The Temple guards were listening to all of this and dared not arrest Him because they too were amazed by Him. When they came before the Chief Priest and Pharisees, they were questioned.

"Why did you not bring Him in?" The officers answered, "Never has a man spoken like this man speaks." (John 7:46)

When is the last time, or only time, you have ever had that intense WOW feeling when you heard someone speak about Jesus? Not just a really good sermon or a great revival, but a spine-tingling, hair raising response to something so powerful that you were rendered unable to carry out your duties...

If we are not wowed by the works of God, the miracles He causes to happen, the thrill of His promises to us wayward children, perhaps we should check our pulse to see if we are alive. So awesome is God that we must bow in amazement before Him!

"Let all the earth fear the Lord. Let all the inhabitants of the world stand in awe of Him!" (Psalm 33:8)

Question: Have you ever been Wowed by something God did or said? Why or why not?

THREE LITTLE WORDS

*H*ow does the old song go? "Three little words, eight little letters spell "I Love You". So much is said in a few letters and yet so full of meaning. Perhaps the message is even enhanced by its brevity. No flowery phrases or idle promises. Just a heart message spoken out loud. Implied in these words is the intent to prove it. Haste or over familiarity may make this simple declaration overlooked, undervalued or even forgotten. The real value may be lost through neglect.

This is true when reading the Bible. In an effort to read all of the story or to search for a hidden meaning, we often overlook the little words so packed with meaning. I offer three such words as examples: **IF AND BUT** So important are these three little words that the listing of them in a concordance requires many pages.

Example Number 1: Deuteronomy 30

The Hebrews had travelled many long years through the wilderness. They had come to the time when they would be able to cross over into the land God had promised to their forefathers. God, through His chosen spokesman, Moses, spoke, preparing them for life ahead.

"Then the Lord your God will prosper you abundantly in all the work of your hands, in the offspring of your body and of your cattle, and in the produce of your land; for the Lord will again rejoice over you for good just as He did for your fathers." (verse 9)

But the message does not end there. The next little word is so very significant.

"**IF** you obey the Lord your God to keep His commandments and statutes which are written in the book of the law; **IF** you turn to the Lord your God with all your heart and soul. For this commandment which I give you today is not too difficult for you, nor is it out of reach." (Verses 10-11)

There is more from God about this promise, little words not to be dismissed.

"**BUT IF** your heart turns away and you will not obey, **and** you draw away to worship and serve other gods, I declare to you this day that you shall surely perish. You will not prolong your days in the land where you are crossing Jordan to enter and possess it." (verse 17)

God's call to His people was repeated many times in this form as He sought to anchor them in Him. The result of dismissing God's warning brought catastrophe over and over again to the Hebrews as they turned from God to serve other gods.

Example Number 2: Matthew 16:24-25

The Apostle Peter had just rebuked Jesus for saying that this Messiah he had followed for three years would suffer at the hands of the religious leaders and be killed. He did not understand at all the plan of God for His Son. Jesus called Peter a stumbling block to what would surely come. Then Jesus spoke these words to all of the disciples.

"**IF** anyone wishes to come after Me, he must deny in himself **AND** take up his cross **AND** follow Me. For whoever wishes to save his life will lose it, **BUT** whoever loses his life for My sake will find it."

The powerful promise captured in those three little words is meant to be imprinted on our hearts as they surely were in the days ahead for the disciples. Neither they nor we have a picture of what the future may hold as that commitment is made. What we can know is that life will be lost or saved as we choose to ignore or embrace Jesus' statement.in the IF, AND, BUT of His message.

Question: If God has spoken to you in this message, will you choose life?

Time to Plant My Garden

*S*pring is a wonderful season because it speaks of life. After the winter's bareness Spring says, "Let's party!" The soil must be readied to receive the seeds and young plant shoots. Weeds must be removed and fertilized added as necessary. The choice of which seeds or plants to use is carefully considered, remembering the requirements of each type. Then anticipation of the harvest of blooms and delicious fruits and vegetables to come delights the soul.

But what happens if the soil is not good? Too rocky, devoid of needed minerals, infested with weeds, lacking a water source. Has the land been prepared properly? We know that poor soil rejects good seed. Can we expect a good return for our labor if care has not been taken in preparation? Probably not! If the drought doesn't kill them, the weeds may choke them out. If the soil isn't fertile, growth may be stunted.

The same is true in thinking of ourselves. We do what we must to remain healthy and free from blemishes. We bathe, use body care products to combat dry skin, carefully groom unwanted hair, take vitamin supplements to be certain we are fortified. To do less is... well, let's just say, "It is not a pretty picture."

Luke, the Physician recorded a story Jesus once told that we call "The Parable of the Sower". In the story seeds fell in three types of places.

- The roadside where the birds ate the seeds
- Among thorns or weeds where the seeds were choked out.
- Good fertile soil where the seeds produced an abundant crop

Jesus then compared the seeds to those spiritually sown in three types of people who received the seed. (Luke 8)

- Those who allow Satan to dissuade them from believing that God's Word is true. The truth is dismissed.
- Those who receive the Word of God and embrace it for a while. Then the cares of the world encroach and choke out the seed so that it never matures.
- Those whose hearts are open to receive the truth of God's Word and then use it to keep on growing in grace. The seeds are watered by time in the Word, communion with God in prayer, and fellowship with other believers.

We are reminded that in the beginning God, the Master Gardener, gave us the seeds and the directive to cultivate them well. (Genesis 1:29-30)

The Apostle Paul described this planting in another way, referring to the seeds of truth that Christians scatter as they go about their lives every day. It is a shared task.

"I planted. Apollo watered. But God gave the increase." (I Corinthians 3:6)

The Apostle Peter called the seed that God plants in the life of a believer "imperishable". What does that mean? It means that the truth we receive when we become Christians is a living, growing entity, forever able to bear fruit. (1 Peter 1:23-24)

That brings our attention to bear on the responsibility we have as Christians to be faithful seed scatterers. These seeds of truth must not be a mixture of types or rotten or tainted. They must be healthy seeds of truth. As farmers know, planting and harvesting is hard work, constant work, but rewarding work. So too must be our seed sowing in the lives of those God puts in our paths each day. The Master Gardener expects a good harvest!

Question: Are the seeds you plant good, healthy seeds and tended as the need arises?

To What Shall I Compare This Generation?

*W*hat superimposed title does your generation have? Are you a "baby boomer", Gen X, Y, or Z? Are you among the "old timers"? All of these categories are based on when you live, the year or century in which you were born. And each seems to be tagged with a different set of characteristics compared to the generations before it.

Comparisons are interesting based on the standard we use. I am short compared to my daughters. He is strong compared to the couch potato. The cook is more talented compared to the originator of the recipe. We are poor compared to that millionaire or rich compared to the slum dweller.

Comparisons are not new. They have been with us since the onset of time. Many years ago Jesus, addressing His followers within earshot of the religious leaders of the day, asking an important question.

"To what shall I compare this generation? What are they like?" (Matthew 11:16a)

Answering His own question, Jesus continued., addressing the crowd around Him.

"They are like children who sit in the marketplace calling to one another, saying, 'We played the flute for you and you did not dance. We sang a dirge and you did not weep.' John the Baptist came eating no bread and drinking no wine and you said he has a demon. The Son of Man has come eating and drinking, and you say 'He is a glutton, a drunkard and a friend of sinners.'" (Mathew 11:16-19)

The hypocrisy and animosity of the day was revealed in the comparisons made to an artificial standard. It referred to the artificial rules and regulations imposed by societal leaders. This was not the only time Jesus addressed this same issue. Once He likened the Pharisees to "whitewashed tombs, beautiful on the outside but inside full of dead man's bones". (Matthew 23:27)

These two examples provide food for serious contemplation of today's societal and religious leaders and people in general who proclaim their spirituality and yet fall short of God's standard of measurement, His Plan A. Either by pretense or delusion, certain man made standards of comparison are being used. There is a blindness, a failure to see hypocrisy for what it is. Sin!

It is easier to adhere to the standard of the day than to take a stand at the Plan A line. It is easier to put on spiritual clothing, whatever that might be. After all, we go to church regularly, read our Bibles daily, give some money to the church, avoid places of ill repute, and even give a bit of our time in service. We are "good" Christians. But are we" Plan A" Christians?

Compared to what? This generation? That famous preacher? The latest popular Christian writer? That pile of wood, hay and stubble we have accumulated as we did "good stuff" for God? Our standard of measurement matters greatly, even eternally. The cost of pretense or ignorance of first century cover-ups, and of ours today, is fatal at worst and sad at the very least. Our standard of comparison should always be God's standard spelled out clearly in His Word. Jesus is our Standard Bearer. A look at His earthly life gives us a clear look at what God expects of us. All pretenses aside, Jesus lived by His Father's Plan A. Never did He choose His own path. Even facing certain death, in the Garden He submitted to His Father's Plan A.

"Going a little ways beyond His disciples, He fell on His face and prayed, ' Father, if possible, let his cup (of suffering and sacrifice) pass from Me. Yet, not as I will, but as You will.'" (Matthew 26:39)

Can you imagine what that prayer meant? Hours of torture, agony, blood spilled, great thirst, pain, and eventually death. All of this was done that we might, as a Christian,, be able to live out God's best plan for our lives. Our responsibility as Christians is to seek out and execute God's Plan A for our lives individually, never forgetting the price which was paid for us.

Question: What is your generational tag? Are you a typical member?

TRADITIONS

What is a tradition? It is a custom handed down through the years. These traditions make us feel more connected in a way to ancestors or cultural norms. When asked why we do something a particular way, we may respond, "We've always done it that way. It's a tradition in my family, church, country." Often these traditions were begun with no aim except to fit the current situation or event, not as a "hard and fast rule" to be followed just because Great Grandmother Alice did it that way. While many traditions are based on some needful action, many are simply born of a desire or need of bygone days with no real connection to life today. They may even become burdensome issues causing division in families, churches, communities, and countries.

Such was the case in Jesus' day. Mark records an incident in which the religious leaders confronted Jesus with scorn at the lack of tradition keeping among His disciples.

"The Pharisees and the Scribes asked Him, 'Why do Your disciples not walk according to the traditions of the elders but eat bread with impure hands'" (Mark 7:5)

This was a man-made rule which had to do with ceremonial cleansing and was handed down orally as customs to be observed. Over time the religious leaders had added their spin on the original laws given by God for healthy and holy living. Why they felt it necessary to burden the people with hundreds of add-ons, we do not know. From a modern point of view, hand washing before a meal is a matter of control of germs and not to satisfy our elders' traditions. Jesus' answer to the religious leaders is a rebuke as true in His day as it had been in the time of the Prophet Isaiah.

"Isaiah spoke rightly when he heard God say, 'These people honor Me with their lips, but their heart is far from Me. In vain do they worship Me, teaching as doctrines the precepts of men...thus invalidating the Word of God..." (Mark 7:6-13)

This accusation by the religious leaders was only one of numerous times when they either confronted Jesus in person, or mumbled and complained to anyone who would listen, about all of the things they faulted Jesus for. We might say that they were gossips spreading their own opinions of the rules they deemed broken. It is interesting to note that after this confrontation, Jesus spoke openly to the crowd. The essence of His words strikes at the heart of traditions.

"Listen to Me, all of you and understand. There is nothing outside a man which can defile him. It is the things which proceed out of man which defile him." (Mark 7:14-15)

After this Jesus continued on to list some of the sinful things a person may harbor within his heart. It is not a list anyone would want said of him. (see verses21-23)

What about us today? In our churches we find many man-induced traditions, some of which have become burdensome to the point of impeding the presence of God to speak to those present. For example, length of service, type of music to use, when to sit and stand, whether to bow heads and close eyes when praying, whether one may raise hands in worship, etc. Are such traditions bad in themselves? No. Might some actually be helpful? Yes. But here is the question. Why do we do as we do? Is it by default, habit, desire to honor our ancestors, simply because we don't want to upset the establishment? Or are our traditions based on the Word of God? Do they serve to honor Him? So many churches have been split apart by disagreement with some tradition they believed contrary to the Word of God. Grace goes out the window as rules come in the door. Often some of these man- made traditions were begun by well- meaning elders However it is so important to take the time to separate in our minds the difference between tradition and the Laws of God. Tradition does matter if it is based on the Word and intent of God and is not used to shackle our souls. Perhaps it is time that we paused to ask God which is His way and which is man made tradition. Then we will not end up on the list of the religious Pharisees. We may decide wisely and with grace if the traditions which engulf us are worthy of keeping. Let us pray to that end!

Question: In the church you attend which customs or traditions do you think are helpful to your growth as a Christian? Are there some that are man-made?

TRANSITIONS

*L*ife is replete with transitions, another word for change, leaving one thing for another. Child to adult. Single to married. Student to employee. Worker to retiree. City to city. The list is very long. Each of these examples begins with a point of reference. Often transitions begin with the little word "if". It is such a small word, yet so impactful as we transition.

For example, if I am no longer a child, what is expected of me? If I am not a student, where will I find employment? If I retire, will I have enough money to sustain me? If I move to another house or city, will I like it there? Some transitions are easier than others and go almost unnoticed by us. For this we are thankful. Others require a major upheaval, a brand new mindset, a change of occupation, a new living status.

The word "upheaval" describes the transitions in the life of the Hebrews. God's chosen people throughout their history. Their lives were, and still are today, a definition of transitions. Being a nomadic people in the early years, they transitioned from place to place is search of water and pasture for their flocks. These were rather ordinary occurrences. The first huge transition occurred when they found themselves as slaves in Egypt. There they lived subject to new culture, new language, new religions, new customs, new rules for life. Leaving the familiar to embrace another way of life is never an easy or smooth transition.

Their next monumental transition came as they were able to leave Egypt to return to their Promised Land. The transitions they faced in the 40 years of wandering were harsh elements, lack of food and water, and most of all, the security of a routine, if not easy, life. They met the reality that God was their only Source. They could not depend on themselves. That lesson was learned and relearned as they traveled north.

As if these transitions were not enough, the Hebrews transitioned from no rulers to judges and then to kings. What we can see from that is that sometimes we get what we ask for as God seeks to teach a lesson. The next huge transition came as both Northern and Southern Kingdoms were destroyed by their disobedience, and were carried into exile. There they faced a new set of transitions. New language. New culture. New religions. New rulers. Sound familiar?

Years later some of the Hebrews returned to their land to find a harsh transition called rebuilding a nation. Their homes and cities, their Temple, their family structures. The time was laced with hardships, causing a focus on the laws God had set forth so many years before.

The next transition came with the Advent of the Messiah, so long promised. This confrontation with Pure Truth and the validity of God's promise was one of life's most difficult transitions. That transition continues today as so many Hebrews still do not embrace the Messiah of God's promise.

There is One who never transitions, never changes. He is Almighty God. It was God Himself who reminded us of that.

"I, the Lord, do not change." (Malachi 3:6)

"Jesus Christ is the same yesterday, today, and forever." (Hebrews 13:8)

For all of mankind, including God's chosen people, the last great transition will come when Jesus returns to claim His kingdom rule over all.

"When the Son of Man comes in His glory and all he angels with Him, then He will sit on His glorious throne. All the nations will be gathered before Him. and He will separate them from one another." (Matthew 25:31-32)

Jesus went on to tell us about the separations which will occur as everyone transitions to one inheritance or another. Perhaps we need to practice making smoother transitions so we will be prepared to delight in Jesus' Royal Reign. What about you? Are you ready for the best transition of all?

Question: Have you handled the transitions in your life with grace?

WHAT ANSWER WILL YOU GIVE?

When someone asks a question that may not lend itself to an easy or quick answer, what will you say? Will you hesitate, start and pause, deliberate? If I say this, then... But if I say that, then... Especially this may be true when someone these days asks for a political opinion or to take a side favorable to popular opinion. Not wanting to be criticized for an opinion, you may think twice before blurting out a response. Or you may counter with a question about what was asked. No one, it seems, wants to be on the wrong side of an issue requiring an honest and heartfelt answer.

The reply we make may reveal more than we are willing to openly admit. It may uncover a lack of solid belief on an issue or an opinion at the time very unpopular with the "in crowd". Such was the case as Jesus was confronted by the religious leaders as He walked in the Temple courtyard.

The day Jesus had entered the Temple He found dishonest money changers set up to cheat those who came to attend the Passover celebration. He drove them out of the Temple with the following words.

"Is it not written, 'My House shall be called a House of prayer for all nations'?, but you have made it a den of thieves." (Matthew 21: 12-13)

Not long after that as He entered the Temple to teach, the religious leaders approached Him and posed a question.

"By what authority are You doing these things, and who gave You that authority?"

Jesus countered with a question of His own as He addressed them.

"I will also ask you one thing which, if you tell Me, I will also tell you by what authority I do these things. The baptism of John was from what source, from heaven or from men?"

So the religious leaders began reasoning among themselves.

"If we say 'from heaven, then He will say "Why did you not believe Him?' "But if we say, 'from men', we fear the people because they regard John as a prophet." So they answered, "We do not know."

Jesus said, "Neither will I tell you by what authority I do these things."

(Matthew 21:23-27)

Fear of God and fear of man caught the religious leaders in a net of unbelief. Their hearts were exposed for all to see that those who professed to have all the answers, indeed did not. Answering a question with a question proved to be the real answer to the original question, "Who gave You the authority?"

That brings us to the crucial question for each Christian. What answer will we give when confronted by someone about our Christian beliefs? Will fear of censure silence us? Will fear of rebuke or ridicule cause us to hesitate or hedge our answer with a "non-answer"? Will we stop to weigh the possible consequences of our reply? Might we lose a friend or possibly our job? Might our neighbors shun us or a club or organization ban us? Might we be refused that desired promotion?

Or will we stand firm as witnesses to the truth as we know it from the Word of God? In a society that is more each day becoming non-religious, will we be lights in the darkness and straightforward with our answers when questioned, Why do you believe that?" Eternity may record our answer, so consider well what answer you will give.

Question: When confronted as to your faith in God, how will you answer?

WHAT'S YOUR PASSION?

What are you passionate about? What thrills you more than anything else? What makes you want to be a participant rather than a spectator? Sports? Music? A special place? A Hobby? Politics? Grandchildren? Which of these do you defend most vigorously, support most consistently, think about most often? Whether we can readily identify it or even admit to it, we all have something we are deeply passionate about, invested in, or centered on most.

Though the word passion may conjure up a myriad of emotions from love to hate, most would agree that it is a quality which well expresses where our hearts are. Webster's Dictionary defines the word as an intense driving or overmastering feeling or conviction, a strong liking for or a devotion to some activity, object, concept; an object of desire or deep interest. Some synonyms are: fervor, ardor, enthusiasm, zeal. Of these words, <u>zeal</u> most nearly portrays passion without the emotional overlay. Zeal is an energetic, unflagging pursuit of an aim or devotion to a cause. It speaks of allegiance, loyalty, and obligation.

In the spiritual realm the passionate heart of Christianity is our relationship with our Savior, Jesus Christ. Our salvation begins and ends in Him. He is the reason for life itself. Paul, the Apostle, knew this, and as he faced his own death, he wrote to the believers in Philippi.

"I count all things as loss in the view of the surpassing value of knowing Christ Jesus, my Lord." (Philippians 3:8)

This was his goal, his passion, to know Christ and be known by Him. Paul was always a passionate person, though early in his life, his passion was wrongly and sinfully placed. Before his encounter with Jesus on the Damascus Road, his passion was aimed at the persecution of those who were followers of the Messiah. That evil passion was quenched in an instant as he was confronted with the reality of Jesus. His encounter quickly set upon him a new passion, to tell everyone about the truth of Jesus. It caused him to declare words which bring us to realize the cost of such passion.

"For me, to live is Christ, and to die is gain." (Philippians 1:21)

He lived thereafter passionately pursuing a life lived for and through Christ, seeking hungry hearts with which to share the Gospel. He defended the truth rigorously, a costly venture often resulting in physical harm to himself. Beatings, shipwrecks, prison, stoning, loss of former friends, suffering hardships wherever he went did not deter him or diminish Paul's passion for his Lord. In all things he passionately labored for the One Truth, Jesus crucified and resurrected for the salvation of sinners.

That same zeal he passed on to believers all over Asia Minor and even from a prison in Rome. His letter to the believers in Philippi was written from there in the last days before his life was taken for the cause of His Savior.

All of the things we enjoy are hopefully good things in some way, but none of them may elicit the passion, zeal needed as a Christian. The kind of passion for the things of God that we need is the kind which drives us to our knees in humble submission to whatever the Lord has for us in each and every day whether0r not it is hard or beyond our understanding. Some days we may need to confess what the Psalm writer said.

"My zeal (for God) has consumed me because my adversaries have forgotten Your words." (Psalm 119:139)

Let us be those who embrace Pauls' declaration to count everything las oss in order to know the One who holds our lives in His hand.

Question: What is your greatest passion, the one thing which totally captures your heart? Is it God?

What Can a Nickel Buy?

A little girl lived in an apartment not far from her school. Each day as she walked to school, she passed a candy store. Each day she stopped to look in the window at all the delicacies, wishing for a taste. One day Mama gave her daughter a shiny nickel to spend at the store. Finally, the day had come when she would be able to taste those sweets. Entering the store the girl approached the row of bins of different candies, each marked with its name and the price. She noticed that some were a penny each, some were two for a penny, and one was five pieces for just one penny. The store owner would not bargain with his customers. Wanting a variety meant that there must be careful choices in order to get the most for her precious nickel. Finally, her selections were made, and the little girl left the candy shop with a bag full of assorted candies. Today, of course, a nickel wouldn't buy much of anything as prices are much more for just one piece of delicious candy. But the question remains. How much will your money buy?

One day a man set on evil intent went to the religious leaders of his day. He had decided to ask for a reward for the deed he would offer to do. Surely he would be richly rewarded for such a risky act! Going to the Chief Priest he asked his question.

"What will you pay me to betray Jesus to you?" (Matthew 26:15)

The answer was swift as the religious leaders had for a long time been seeking a way to trap the Man they considered a danger to their status. They would not recognize Jesus for who He claimed to be in spite of hearing Him teach and witnessing His miraculous acts. Thirty pieces of precious silver were counted out and given to Judas.

Judas was one of the twelve disciples chosen by Jesus. He had travelled with Jesus up and down the dusty roads of Palestine, listening to Jesus' words, witnessing His compassion, and miracles. Jesus knew what was in the heart of Judas, and still He loved him. Judas was the treasurer of the group, in charge of buying their food as needed. He loved the idea of riches. Once as he and the other disciples had gathered for a meal at the invitation of Simon the (former) leper, a woman came in with a vial of costly perfume made of nard. She broke the vial and poured the perfume over Jesus' head. The response from Judas and some other disciples to such a precious act?

"Why has this perfume been wasted. It could have been sold and the money given to the poor!" (Mark 14:4-5)

What had her money bought? It had been purchased to bless the One who would soon pay the ultimate cost for her life and the lives of the disciples as well. Jesus scolded His disciples, reminding them of the value of her act in anointing Him beforehand for His burial.

We know what the thirty pieces of silver bought Judas.

"When Judas, who had betrayed Him saw that Jesus had been condemned, he felt remorse, and returned the money to the Chief Priest and elders, saying, "I have betrayed innocent blood." But they said, "Why should we care?" So Judas threw the money into the Temple sanctuary and went out and hanged himself." (Matthew 27:3-5)

The Chief Priests gathered the silver, and because it was deemed "blood money", they used it to buy a piece of land suitable for a burial place for the poor. It was called Potters' Field. Today it is called Field of Blood.

Judas' money did not buy him peace or satisfaction. It brought a sad ending to a selfish life.

Jesus had said, "Where your treasure is, there will your heart be also." (Matthew 6:21)

That was a teaching Judas had missed. His heart was set on getting what he wanted, not in service to his Master.

Question: What will your money buy? Things and more things? The newest fad? Food for a feast? A cemetery plot like the Potter's Field? Or will you maximize its worth by investing it in the lives of others, the needy, the homeless, the widows and orphans, the lost souls who need to hear the Words of life?

What Happened to Simon?

$\mathcal{H}$ ave you ever heard someone say, "What happened to _____? He's not the same person I knew. Where did the old _____ go?" Sometimes the difference is so radical as to even change one's countenance. The puzzlement continues when we cannot figure out the cause of the radical change. Sometimes this change is for better. and sometimes for worse. Let's focus on the positive as we look at the life of Simon Peter, one of the twelve chosen by Jesus to carry the message of redemption to the world after He had returned to His Father.

Simon was a rough, uneducated, brash, impulsive," blue-collar" fisherman. He and his brother, Andrew, were in the family business. How did Simon undergo such a radical metamorphosis? What changed this rough fisherman into a solid, eloquent, mighty apostle in the years after Jesus ascension? The word *metamorphosis* suggests a change from one thing to something entirely different. For example, a little worm crawling around on short legs nestles securely in the cocoon and, unseen by human eyes, undergoes a radical change. Emerging from its cocoon, we see no more the creeping caterpillar, but a beautiful butterfly, All of this is engineered by the Creator.

Such was the case of Simon, renamed Peter by the Master. There is but one explanation, and that explanation is the same for every person who dares to become a "butterfly". Peter became a new creature in Christ. Did it happen overnight? No, the seeds of change were planted in the three years he followed Jesus along the dusty roads of Palestine. Those days were laced with setbacks and course corrections Day by day as Peter listened with open heart to Jesus, he soaked up the truths of a new life. These truths penetrated deeply into him, changing how he worshipped and lived. In the process, Peter questioned, pondered, and even denied the Truth.

- At the last supper Jesus would share with His disciples, He offered a picture of servanthood by washing the disciples' feet. When He came to Peter, Peter said, "Never shall You wash my feet!" Brash Peter did not understand what Jesus was trying to show him. (John 13:5-8)
- As the meal concluded Peter sensed that Jesus was leaving them. He said, "Lord, where are you going? ... Why can I not follow You now? I will lay down my life for you." (John 13:36-37) Peter's brash statement would pierce his heart in a few short hours.
- Temple soldiers had come to arrest Jesus to begin the trial and persecution which would follow. Peter, hoping to defend his Master, "drew a sword and struck the Hight Priest's slave, cutting off his right ear." Jesus' words to Peter embraced His understanding of the events to come. (John 18:10-11)
- As Peter waited to see what would happen to Jesus at the court of the High priest, three times someone recognized Peter as one of the disciples of Jesus. Three times Peter

denied his allegiance to Jesus, as Jesus had predicted he would. (John 18:16-27)

We see in these examples the brash, impulsive Peter who had yet to learn the path of transformation.

On the Day of Pentecost everything changed for Peter. Brashness was replaced by humility. Impulsiveness was replaced by a steady focus on what he had been taught. Insight came slowly, but at Pentecost the coming of the Holy Spirit to indwell believers, turned brash, impulsive Peter into the mighty speaker of the truths he had absorbed those three years of walking with Jesus.

Into an open heart came the Holy Spirit, promised by Jesus, bearing the key to a new life for all who dare to believe, to receive, to embrace, to let die the "old man" in order to make room for the new. At Pentecost Peter spoke with boldness and hope to the crowd before him, proclaiming what he now saw through new eyes. With eloquence and courage Peter told the people what had transpired for them.

As time passed, Peter's strength bolstered the young believers as he wrote words of encouragement to Jewish exiles scattered throughout Asia Minor. Even as he admonished them to stand strong in the face of great persecution, Peter must have remembered the time when he did not do so. The lessons learned the hard way remind us of the progress made. Metamorphosis indeed! The lowly fisherman had been transformed into a new creature in Christ.

Such is the transformation which comes to all who put their trust in Jesus. With the guidance of the Spirit of God we, too, undergo metamorphosis. Our lives are never the same. Yes, Peter continued to grow in grace, and so do we, as we absorb the Word of God and live it out day by day.

Question: Are you a butterfly yet or still in the cocoon? Get ready to change!

WHAT IS THE PURPOSE?

*W*andering through the kitchen section of a store I often look at an item and wonder, "What is the purpose for that?" In other words, "What is its use?" When an item is invented and manufactured it is with a clear purpose in mind. Sadly. Sometimes that use is ignored and the item may be used wrongly. Have you ever done that? Couldn't find a screwdriver, so used a knife. Oops! I got cut! Didn't have a hammer so used a shoe. Oops! Broke the sole! Often such efforts do end badly, causing injury to us, or destruction of the original item. The maker's instructions ignored, we find ourselves disobeying the instructions.

Everything has a purpose. Every tool, machine, piece of clothing, money, laws and regulations, and so the list goes. We may often ask ourselves the deeper question. "What is my purpose in life?"

In thinking about this application to our lives as Christians, consider the words of the Apostle Paul as he wrote to encourage his young friend, Timothy.

"The purpose of the commandment is love from a pure heart, from a good conscience and from a sincere faith." (1 Timothy 1:5)

We can assuredly say that Paul had answered that question faithfully and to the best of his ability. Sometimes, in fact often, he answered it in the midst of great peril.

"Five times I received from the Jews thirty-nine lashes. Three times I was beaten with rods. Once I was stoned. Three times I was shipwrecked, spending a night and a day in the deep water. I have been on frequent journeys in dangers from rivers, robbers, my own countrymen, Gentiles, whether in the city or wilderness, at sea, or among false brethren; in labor and hardship, through many sleepless nights; in hunger and thirst, in cold and exposure. Add to all of that my concern for the churches." (2 Corinthians 11:24-28)

Probably, not a one of us would have traded places with Paul! His life was filled with purposeful challenges! Yet his devotion to the commandments of God and the call of God on his life were set in stone. We are not told if there were times when he wondered if he had heard rightly or if he felt like giving up. What we can see as we read his many letters is the portrait of a man whose gaze was fixed on God's purposes.

For us, as well as for young Timothy, the commandments of God are for His purposes. He has carefully and fully considered our needs, our condition, and His plan for our lives, and has made everything for a purpose so that we may live as He intended. When we abuse what God has designed for our good, the results are wasteful and harmful. Lack of abundant harvest. Disease and sickness.

Unproductive lives. Selfish gain. The results aren't pretty! They are in a word, "SIN"

However, there is a promise we must embrace.

"Every scripture is God breathed and profitable for instruction, for reproof and conviction of sin, for correction of error and discipline in obedience, for training in righteousness in conformity to God's will in thought, purpose and action so that the man (or woman) of God may be complete and proficient, well fitted and thoroughly equipped for every good work." 2 Timothy 3:16-17

God has written His laws on our hearts to guide us to holy living before Him. As the scripture reminds us, these words of God have a purpose. They are given to completely equip us for everything God asks us to do and be. Let us consider Paul's advice. Guided by love, may our lives become productive, useful, fulfilling God's intended purpose. Isn't that what we really desire?

Question: Dos your life have as its goal God's purpose for you?

WHAT KIND OF HOUSE WILL YOU BUILD FOR ME?

Building a house is an arduous and lengthy task. It requires much planning and skilled hands. Design is the first issue. What will it look like on the outside? Will it be two stories or just one? How many rooms will there be, and what will be their function? Will it be an open or closed floor plan? How tall will the ceilings be? Do you want a porch or a deck? A basement? This is a short list of things to consider.

Then there are the materials to be chosen: siding, roofing, trim, flooring, window type, colors inside and out, number of electrical outlets etc. How many things did we forget? Oh yes! Be sure to ask the woman of the house about her requirements for the kitchen. (voice of experience here)

The most important issue is the choice of a builder. Is he licensed? Does he have the necessary skills to do the job? Can he supervise a work crew effectively? Does he have an eye for details? All of this and more is essential in building a house we would be pleased to live in, one that will endure the test of time.

Before any of the above can take place, there is the site preparation. Are there trees to be removed or transplanted? What kind of grading must occur? Where will the plumbing and electrical lines be routed? Is the soil foundation stable? Is there proper drainage? There are so many things to consider when building a house!

In Matthew's Gospel we read the parable Jesus told about the wise man who built his house on a rock foundation and the fool who built his house on the sand. When the rains came the house on the sand was destroyed, but the house built on the rock stood strong. (Matthew 7:24-27) The meaning is clear. The stone which the builder rejected, Jesus, is the Cornerstone of our faith. His Name is Jesus. The house must be built on the Rock, Jesus. To build on anything or anyone else, we do so to our own peril.

Many years ago, in the time of the Prophet Isaiah, God's people had sinned themselves into a soon coming exile. God had continued to spread out His arms to them to urge them to repentance. Refusing to repent and return to God made Him ready to exact punishment . But God's faithfulness to His promises is always present. He reminded them of a time when all things would be restored to their intended status. There would be a new heaven and a new earth. The people would once again build houses and dwell in them instead of foreigners taking possession. Then God asked an important question.

"Thus says the Lord, 'Heaven is My throne and the earth is My footstool. Where then is the house you will build for Me and where is the place that I may rest?'" (Isaiah 66:1)

What did God mean by that? New Testament scriptures shed light on the meaning. We see that what God was asking had to do with the place He would reside in our hearts. This same question was asked by Stephen, the first Christian martyr, as he testified about his faith in Messiah. Reminding the religious leaders of all that God had done for them, he spoke to them about their sin and God's faithfulness. His final words were enough to send him to his death by stoning.

"Solomon built a house for God. However, the Most High God does not dwell in houses made by human hands as the prophet Isaiah said, 'Heaven is My throne and earth my footstool. What kind of house will you build for me?'" (Acts 7:47-49)

The Apostle Paul, writing encouragement to the believers in Corinth said,

We know that when this earthly tent which is our house is torn down, we have a building from God, a house not made with hands, eternal in the heavens," (2Corinthians 5:1)

It matters greatly, this "house" we build of our lives. On earth it must be a house where God dwells, where He is the real Owner of our lives. Its rooms must be cleansed by repentance and adorned by the Spirit.

"Unless the Lord builds the house, they labor in vain who build it," (Psalm 127:1)

Question: What kind of house are you building fit for the Lord to dwell in? Check your foundation. Is it based on Jesus, the Cornerstone?

WHAT LANGUAGE WAS THAT?

*H*ave you ever been in a crowd and heard nearby a language you did not recognize? Or have you listened to an interview on television when the one who answered spoke in a foreign language? Perhaps you have, as have I, wished to be fluent in another language in order to communicate with someone. Often when information is given by a government official on TV, a person using ASL was there to translate to the deaf or hard of hearing. Did you understand the signs?

Even in our own language there are those times when we fail to understand what is being said perhaps due to accent or speech pattern or vocabulary. Language starts wars, makes peace, keeps us safe, informs us, educates us. The language of words is unique to the human species. Language is so very important.

According to the Bible there was a time in human history when only one language was spoken. We do not know what that language was, but we may assume that everyone could understand the words relayed. After the flood, when mankind began repopulate the earth they still spoke only one language. That is, until Babel. Genesis 11 is the account of the confounding of languages. The people of Shinar made bricks and used them to build a tower "that would reach to the heavens" so they could make a name for themselves. God saw their sinful ways and acted.

The Lord said, 'They are one people and they all have the same language...Now nothing which they purpose to do will be impossible for them. Come, let us go down there and confuse their language so that they will not understand one another's speech." (Genesis 11:6-7)

Thereafter, the place was called Babel. Can you imagine the frustration when suddenly no one could understand anyone else? The people scattered across the earth, no longer able to be understood or to understand. Ever since that catastrophic event, communication has been difficult.

Consider language from God's point of view. He speaks all languages, you know. The communication was clear as Jesus hung on the cross, Pilate has a sign placed above Jesus. It read "Jesus of Nazareth, King of the Jews". The remarkable thing about the sign was that Pilate had it written in the three languages common in that day. Travelers from all over the area who were in Jerusalem for the Passover could read the message in Hebrew, Latin and Greek. There was no missing the message. The One on the cross was the King of the Jews. For three years Jesus had travelled the dusty roads of the land telling people who He was. Some believed, some didn't. But on that fateful day, the thief on the cross beside Jesus read the sign and believed. We are not told if others also got the message, but they did realize what a terrible day it was through the earthquake and the darkness that covered the land in the middle of the day. Now, that was God's communication with mankind!

Not many days after Jesus had ascended to heaven, God sent His Spirit to fill the Apostles. They spoke to the crowd in many languages and the people gathered heard the Good News in their own languages.

"When the day of Pentecost had come, they were all assembled in one place. And suddenly there came from heaven a noise like a violent rushing wind, and it filled the whole house where they were sitting. And it appeared to them like tongues of fire that rested on each one of them. And they were all filled with the Spirit and began to speak in other languages as the Spirit gave them the ability." (Acts 2:1-4)

The people were amazed to hear their own native languages spoken in a foreign land. God had spoken as only He can!

How does God communicate with us? With you? Through a breathtaking sunset? In time of great need? On a joyous occasion? Does He shout so loud the mountains quake? Does He whisper as He did to Elijah? Does He send a dream as He did with Joseph? Does He use another person to be the messenger with a word from God as He did with the prophets? Does He lay a message on the heart of a pastor who will shake your lethargy? By whatever means, God wants to communicate us in a language we can understand. Like the thief on the cross, we must "read the signs" and listen to what God has to say. Our response must be as the thief's was. "I believe."

"They who revere and worship the Lord will enjoy His sweet, satisfying companionship. He will show them His covenant and reveal to them its deep inner meaning." (Psalm 25:14)

Question: In what way does God most often communicate to you?

WHERE DID THAT COME FROM?

*H*ave you ever gotten a letter in the mail with no return address or postmark? Where did it come from and from whom? Even better, to receive an anonymous present left on your door step. Hmm! Wonder who put it there? Discovering a bruise on our body, we wonder where it came from as we can't recall an injury. Often those of us in the "older" generation pull out a quaint expression once commonly used but now whose origin is a mystery. Life is full of such instances when we pause to wonder where something came from.

This is true when we think of our current spiritual beliefs. Most of us cannot identify the source as we are asked the question, "How did you come to believe that?" We just believe, never having considered its origin. There are several apparent sources to consider.

First, one's parents who may carry a little or much spiritual fervor from their own heritage, plant seeds of their beliefs in us. Our parents probably would say that their own family planted those seeds in them, and their parents before them. Hopefully, such beliefs contain some grains of truth amidst the colored or skewed beliefs.

Second, our teachers at school or church planted seeds. Again, these were diluted by the passage of time and their own influencers. As decades pass and culture invades our lives these truths become diluted or skewed by the current fads.

Third, as we are attracted to people of influence in person or via media, we are drawn to what they believe. These folks, heroes of a sort, present humanly flawed snippets of truth gleaned by their own education and influencers. One such hero may even be a pastor or spiritual leader who is also carrying a mixed bag of truths and untruths passed on to him through the years.

The circumstances of life also mold our beliefs, especially about God, because of the hard things we encounter. Molding our beliefs on these times often tend to erode present beliefs or draw us away from truth.

As vital as people are to us in our lives, none contain the pure truth. The source of that is the Word of God and God Himself as He enlightens us. Bit by bit and day by day we read and hear pieces of the greater truth. God's Word becomes more than enjoying eye-catching phrases and seeking words of comfort. These truths are etched in our hearts to bring life to us. They form our beliefs from a Source which answers the question, "Where did that come from?"

As we feed on the Word, the Spirit of God who indwells us, translates and enriches truth into a knowing who our Master is and what He wants of us. Believing the One who declared Himself to be "The Truth and the Light" opens us to the path of worship, obedience, and completion found nowhere else. Shaped by God, we are becoming the image He intended from the creation.

Honoring those who came before us and imparted some truth, we then become the repositories of those truths to be passed on to others. Others are impacted, even when we are not aware. This should propel us to search diligently to purify our beliefs so we do not pass on error. How is this done?

- Psalm 1: 2 In describing the ones who are blessed, the Psalmist says, "His delight is in the law of the Lord and in His law he meditates day and night."
- Psalm 63:6 David, in the wilderness of Judah said, " I meditate on You in the night watches."
- John 8:31 Jesus said, "If you continue in My word, you are truly disciples of mine." (We must add that the definition of disciple is not follower but one who learns as a student of the teacher)
- .1 Peter 2:2 The Apostle Peter, writing to the persecuted refugees in Asia Minor said, "Like newborn babes, long for the pure milk of the Word so that by it you may grow in respect to salvation."
- James 1:22 "Prove yourselves doers of the Word and not hearers only."

The message is clear. If we are to answer the question posed at the beginning, we must immerse ourselves in the Truth of God as recorded in His Word. A final thought.

"Be diligent to present yourselves approved to God as workmen needing not to be ashamed, but accurately handling the Word of Truth." 2 Timothy 2:15

Challenge: Examine your beliefs about God to discover if you may have acquired any diluted or skewed truths about God, especially in His relationship with you.

Where Do You Belong?

"I don't belong here!" Have you ever had that thought? A place that is new or somehow doesn't seem right? A situation that causes unease? A turn in the road missed and a feeling of lostness? Cast away on a lonely isle? The need to belong to someone or something is as fundamental as life itself. This great need is born within us. Sadly, so many people search a lifetime and never satisfy that need. Always seeking, striving, backtracking, wondering, but never feeling comfortable in our belonging.

Can we even define what that feeling of belonging would be? What would satisfy that longing to really and truly forever belong? A human relationship like Daddy's strong arms or Mother's tender caress? A forever best friend? Membership in that special club or organization? As wonderful as all of these might be, there is always the possibility that some day each of these may disappoint us or disappear. In some way all human relationships will at some time render us alone, and in a place called "need to belong".

It is an age-old problem. Throughout history we may read stories of those who had no place to belong. The Bible offers numerous illustrations of this in the lives of God's people.

Esau's twin, Jacob, had stolen his birthright, the inheritance which would have been his as the eldest son. Esau was understandably angry. He felt unwanted, out of place in the family. His anger led him to make life choices which invalidated his faith in God's laws. He married foreign women, hoping to bring heartache and punishment to his parents. That missing sense of belonging forever separated him from his people. (Genesis 28)

Jacob, his brother, fled to Haran to escape Esau's wrath and ended up marrying the daughters of his kinsman, Laban. Ultimately Jacob felt he no longer belonged there, and so he snuck away with his wives, children and all of their possessions. (Genesis 31)

Jesus told a story which illustrates this issue of belonging. It is called the Parable of the Prodigal Son. This son's dissatisfaction led him away from the place called home and into a world where belonging was absent. His thirst for freedom was never satisfied. One day he realized that where he really belonged was at home with his father and brother. When he arrived, the welcome he received from his father was what he had been missing all along, belonging. (Luke 15:11-24)

The Psalmist wrote about the two sides of belonging.

"A Father for the fatherless and a judge for the widows is God in His holy habitation. God makes a home for the lonely. He leads out the

prisoners into prosperity. Only the rebellious live in a parched land."
(Psalm 68:5-6)

Moses knew this as he gave his last instructions to the Hebrews
before they entered the Promised Land. As a man who had lived
in a palace and in a barren wilderness too, he knew where he
truly belonged.

"The eternal God is our dwelling place and underneath are the everlasting arms." (Deuteronomy 33:27)

If you have ever experienced that lack of belonging, that desolate
feeling of aloneness, where did you turn for comfort? For all of us
there are those moments when we feel as if we don't belong. It is only
when we run to the arms of our Creator that we find the truest sense
of belonging. We, as Christians, belong to Him. He is our refuge,
our strong fortress in times of need.

Question: Have you ever experienced that "I don't belong"
feeling? Did you ask God to help you understand and be healed?

WHICH PATH SHALL I TAKE?

*W*hich way shall I go? That question is asked many times as we try to find our way to a destination. Even with the assistance of GPS, we still wonder which way is best. Should I look for a shortcut? Is there an alternative route with less traffic? I've made a wrong turn, so how do I get back on the right pathway? Whether we are driving or walking in the woods, we need to know which way to go, the one most direct or less dangerous.

As we look at history through the eyes of the Word of God we find several paths followed.

The Path of Philosophy and Learning

This was the path chosen by the Greek culture in Bible times. The Apostle Paul commented in his letter to the church at Corinth of the Greeks search for wisdom. (1 Corinthians 1:22) This was said in acknowledgement of what he had observed on his trip to Athens, the seat of Greek culture.

Paul stood in the midst of the Areopagus and said, "Men of Athens, I observe that you are very religious in all respects. For while I was passing through and examining the objects of your worship, I also found an altar inscribed, 'To an unknown God'. (Acts 17:22-23)

They were seekers but on the wrong path to truth.

The Path of "Some of this and That

The Samaritans' path was a mixture of Jewish and ancestral beliefs with a little of the culture and religion of the people who had inhabited Samaria during the Jewish exile. That had corrupted their beliefs. The woman Jesus encountered there was on that path.

She said to Jesus, "Our ancestors worshipped God on this mountain and you people say that Jerusalem is the place where men ought to worship." (John 4:20)

The Path of Religiosity

The Jews living in Palestine had been subjected to the numerous rules and prohibitions imposed on them by the religious leaders. These were not the Laws God had given His people to live by. So rigid were these rules that any small infraction resulted in punishment. When Jesus came as Messiah He was labelled "lawbreaker" since He did not follow their rules. In spite of witnessing the many miracles Jesus performed, the religious leasers wanted more proof that He had the authority He claimed.

"Some of the scribes and Pharisees said to Him, 'Teacher, we want to see a sign from You.' But Jesus answered, 'An evil and adulterous generation craves a sign, yet no sign will be given except the sign of Jonah, the Prophet.'" (Matthew 12:38-39)

The religious leaders missed the message, as Jesus was referring to the three days Jonah spent in the belly of the whale and the three days He would be in the grave before His resurrection. Jesus had already labeled them "whitewashed tombs which on the outside appear beautiful, but inside they are full of dead men's bones and all uncleanness." (Matthew 23:27)

<u>The Only Right Path</u>

Jesus proclaimed, "I am the Way, the Truth, and the Life. No one comes to the Father except through Me." (John 14:6) The early disciples had heard Jesus say, "Follow Me". It was the same direction He gave to all who accepted the truth of who He was.

"My sheep hear My voice and I know them and they follow Me" (John 10:27)

This is the path we must choose whether it is smooth or rough, hard or easy, peaceful or turbulent. Any other path taken will lead us wrongly away from truth. It will corrupt our lives. God created us to be followers of the path to righteousness and truth. The writer of Revelation, observing the many gathered around the throne of God, said, "These are the ones who follow the Lamb wherever He goes," (Revelation 14:4)

Let us make the declaration of the Psalmist.

"Your Word is a lamp to my feet, and a light to my path."
(Psalm 119:105)

Question: Are you following GPS, God's Perfect Salvation?"

WHO CARES?

ne day while watching an ASL teacher explaining to her deaf student the need in his life for the Savior, Jesus, I kept seeing him use a sign I did not recognize. Later I asked, "What dies this sign mean?" Her answer prompted this writing. He said, "I don't care!"

Have you ever had that thought about something? Sometimes we say this over the most trivial matters which really do not make a difference. But sometimes we say or think these words concerning a matter of vital importance. Listen to what the Prophet Isaiah said.

"Now the Lord saw that" truth had stumbled in the street and it was displeasing in His sight that there was no justice. He saw that there was no man who cared, and was astonished that there was no one to intercede." (Isaiah 59: 15b-16)

The heart cry of God recorded by the Prophet Isaiah penetrates ones very soul. Note well what God had pointed out. No truth was to be found. No justice had been served. And no one seemed to care enough to intercede for change. In other words, belief in God did not factor into their life choices.

Truth and justice had vanished and God's people were defenseless against the onslaught of the world in which they lived. On all sides they were beset by alien gods, heathen influences, undesirable life-styles. They were immersed in a pagan culture and did not seem to care enough to try to combat it.

In God's view the problem is larger than the inaction or ignoring the injustices. God was displeased that no one had stepped up to intercede on behalf of these injustices, these sins which permeated all of life.

In prior verses 7-15 Isaiah listed the characteristics of his times.

- Violence in the streets
- A bent to evil
- Perverse and evil thoughts
- Lack of peace
- No justice
- The shedding of innocent blood
- Turning away from God

As Isaiah had said "Truth had stumbled in the street."

If that sounds familiar, it is because that might well describe our world today. We moan and rant over the injustices we see. The news media keeps us in a snit over this person or that thing which just isn't right. "How can that happen?" we ask. "Why doesn't someone step up and do something about that?" we cry. "Doesn't anyone care?"

Such is the day in which we live. With the use of so many electronic devices, we hear a myriad of voices giving opinions as to the causes. There are many critics but few intercessors What has made this condition so prevalent? Has it always been this way or are we seeing history repeat itself? When we look back into history, we can observe the disastrous results of such a condition of life. It is not a pretty picture. It is also true that there has always been a voice crying out for justice, and at times, pleading for mercy.

If we would be among these true intercessors in the battle for truth and justice, we must not turn our prayers into criticisms. Instead we must cry out to God for our lives to be characterized by truth, energized by His Spirit, and focused on making a difference. The injustices around us must not characterize our own lives. Instead, we must seek truth and speak it with courage. When we see injustice, we must try to rectify it... When we are victims, we must turn upward to God, not inward to pity. Most of all, we must be prayer warriors on behalf of justice lest we experience again God's discipline and wrath as His people, the Hebrews did.

Prayer: O God, forgive me for my lack of intercession on behalf of all of the injustices in my world. Let me shine for you so the Light of truth will illuminate the darkness. I plead for truth to penetrate the hearts of those who need to hear it. Use me as You will to do that. Amen

WHY THE REACTION?

*W*hat causes us to react when we experience something out of the ordinary? Doubt? Fear? Scorn? Criticism? Rejection? Conviction? Acceptance? Are the reactions caused by the severity of the matter or the incredibility or even the contradiction of what we may believe? Is it gossip or truth? Is it an over-reaction? In the days in which we now live not a day passes without opportunity to react to news on the media. Any statement with which we take issue encourages our reaction... Here is the important *question*: Will our reaction line up with the severity or importance of the occasion? Most importantly, does it line up with the Word of God that we profess?

Examining several passages of scripture we find some of these "normal" reactions

- Jesus and His disciples were in the process of sailing to the other side of the lake when a storm arose. Remember, as we examine this, that the disciples had previously witnessed miraculous things at the hand of their Master. Now as Jesus slept peacefully in the stern of the boat, the disciples quaked with fear at the ferocity of the storm. They awakened Jesus with this question,

"Master, don't You care that we are in danger of drowning here?" Jesus' response addressed their level of faith.

"Why are you so timid and afraid? How is it that you have no faith?"(Mark 4:35-41)

We may think this an appropriate fear given the severity of the storm. It never occurred to them that Jesus, the eternal Son of God would have also drowned had they been thrown into the sea.

- Having seen some of Jesus' miraculous works, a group of Pharisees and Scribes had come to admonish Jesus because His followers "broke the rules" of ceremonial hand washing before meals. This in our modern language would be called "making a mountain out of a mole hill". Of all the things they could have reacted to, how important was this man-made law?

"Why don't Your disciples follow the traditions of our forefathers by eating with purified hands that are ceremonially cleansed?" (Mark 7:5)

Using a passage from the Prophet Isaiah (Is. 29:13) that would have been very familiar to the religious leaders, Jesus reminded them of the hypocrisy of following the traditions of man and ignoring the commandments of God. The verses that follow include Jesus' teaching to the listeners about the source of uncleanness being within the heart and not what pollutes from without.

- On this occasion Jesus went into the Synagogue on the Sabbath and began to teach. The reaction of the listeners was astonishment as they heard the wisdom and authority in Jesus' teaching. Their second reaction was to question His right to be so authoritative.
""Where did this man get these things, and what is this wisdom given to Him. and such miracles performed by His hands. Is this not the carpenter, the son of Mary and brother of James, Joses, Judas, and Simon?" (Mark 6:2-3)

  Jesus tells us that He marveled at their reaction of unbelief. They couldn't fathom someone who had been their neighbor could be so wise. What a sad reaction to someone who spoke only the truth!

- A great crowd had just heard Jesus teach. The disciples had witnessed the miracle of the few loaves and small fish which fed the multitude. Jesus told the disciples to go on ahead of Him to the other side of the lake while He sent the crowd away. As evening came Jesus saw the disciples struggling to row the boat. The wind had increased. Stepping out on the water, Jesus walked to them. Seeing Him, the disciples' reaction was to scream, "It is a ghost!" Fear filled them. Jesus continued toward them and offered encouragement.
"Stop being alarmed and afraid! Take heart!" (Mark 6:45-52)
As Jesus entered the boat, the wind ceased. Their reaction? Astonishment! So soon after the miraculous scene on the grassy slope when Jesus multiplied the little to make enough and leftovers!

Question: What can we learn from these reactions? Rate your level of faith in the God of miracles.

WILDERNESS SKILLS

*A*s many have discovered, wilderness treks and camping require both knowledge and skills. To set out unprepared or ignorant of possible dangers is foolhardy to say the least. As challenges come, and they will, one may be called upon to draw from that storehouse of skill and knowledge combined with a dash of courage, too. There may be at least two possible outcomes when wilderness challenges occur.

1. The failure to ensure safety, inviting harm
2. Reliance on our knowledge or skill, ensuring safety

It is not hard to choose which outcome we want. Safety is important!

When the Hebrews left Egyptian captivity and entered the wilderness, they were totally unprepared for the challenges they would face. For hundreds of years they had lived in a relatively secure place even though life was hard. "Egypt" lived inside of them. As difficult as life had been before, at least the trials they faced were familiar.

What did they do? As we read the account of their wilderness trek the predominant response to challenges was whining and complaining. As we know, those characteristics did not help them meet the dangers ahead. It is an unproductive habit for that to be the first response to some wilderness challenge. Read for yourselves some of the following passages. (Exodus 14:10-12; 16:3;17:2-3; 32:1)

Faithless, and unwilling to trust their God, they paid a severe penalty for all the unpreparedness and whining. In spite of all God had done for them as they traversed the arid lands, they did not rely on Him, their Sure Provider. Forty long years they wandered in the wilderness while a whole generation died never realizing the promise of a real homeland.

What lesson is there for us when we find ourselves in a season of dry and dangerous wilderness time? The answer is obvious, but not easy to maintain.

- We must trust the One Who has promised to be our help and safety. He has promised not just once but over and over again as He did with the Hebrews.
- We must refute the darkness which encroaches upon us.
- We must move at God's command, trusting Him to lead us out of the wilderness and into His strong arms. He has promised us a kingdom prepared for us from the onset of time. Let us enter in with the preparation of the Word of God as our instruction manual.

James, leader of the Church in Jerusalem, says it this way.

Listen, my beloved brothers and sisters, didn't God choose the poor and downcast of this world to be rich in faith and heirs of the kingdom He has prepared for those who love Him? (James 2:5)

God knew we would face many wilderness days in a lifetime, so He promised to walk with us through each one. He is the best guide we could ever have and the ultimate supplier of solutions to protect us.

In life there are also "wilderness" times or seasons when we feel as if we are wandering in an unknown and danger-filled place. The question then is, "Am I prepared to deal with this in a way in which the outcome is beneficial?"

Question: What wilderness have you faced that made you doubt your "wilderness skills" to undertake it? When you relied on God for safety and solution, was He thee? I know He was!

WILL IT NEVER END!

*P*eace in these times is an illusive quality. All around our world there are riots, wars, dissensions among opposing views, hostility among neighbors, divided political parties. Angst, bitterness and anger seem to be the prevalent emotions. Thorny relationships, petty disagreements, biased opinions all cause us to wish for peace. It seems like good times are fleeting and bad times last forever, Even when we find a snippet of peace, it is not lasting. We ask "Will it never end? Will peace never come? Why can we not settle the issues that divide us? "And the BIG question, "Where is God in all of this?"

The real issue is one of perspective. When we look inward or on a parallel plane to find answers we are left with confusion. We have forgotten to check our perspective. We look at our situation and try to lay it out as we see it, deeming it unredeemable at worst and tragic at the very least.

When we stop to consider what God's plan is and the futility of trying on our own to end the strife, we have made a giant step toward the solution on a personal level. That is where the unrest must end.

The Prophet Jeremiah, during a very difficult time of war and hostility among peoples, had a word from God which we must ponder today.

"I (God) know the plans I have for you, plans for your welfare and peace and not for calamity, to give you a future and a hope. Then you will call on Me and I will hear you." (Jeremiah 29:11-12)

When it seems as if the hostilities will never end, we are reminded that "God has got this!" It all hinges on our trust of Him. Will we continue to have wars? Will hostilities continue? Will anger and bitterness remain? Sadly, the answer is "Yes". We live in a fallen world. Sin has ravaged mankind and the physical world too. The end is not yet in view.

However, we can lay down our own strife and seek peace within. How is that done? Listen again to God's answer.

"You (God) will keep him in perfect peace whose mind is fixed on You because he trusts in You. So trust in the Lord forever, for the Lord God is an everlasting Rock" (Isaiah 26:3-4)

As Jesus prepared to face the cross, surrounded by hostile voices of condemnation, He spoke these words to His disciples.

"Peace I leave with you. M y peace I now give you, not the world's kind of peace. Do not let your heart be troubled." (John 14:27)

Several things leap out at us in Jesus' words.

- Jesus said this as He was facing the worst day of His earthly life.
- The kind of peace available for His disciples then and for us today is the quality of the peace being given. It is perfect peace.
- We have the will within us, if we are trusting in God, to chase troubled thoughts and emotions out of our hearts...

Listen to a final word from the Apostle Paul which may solidify that peace within.

"Let us live in a manner worthy of the Lord, desiring to please Him in all things, bearing fruit in every good work and growing and increasing in the knowledge of God. (Colossians 1:10)

Consider: Describe "perfect peace" as you wish to find it in your life.

WINNING IS EVERYTHING

*W*inning is everything! Failure is not an option! A coach spoke these words to the players sitting before him as he prepared them to take the field for the most important game of their season. No one in the room doubted the message or what would be required to achieve that. The team they were up against was noted for its superb offense and strong defense. They were well equipped and very prepared. Yet, the coach had given his team not just some encouraging words but a truth to build a victory upon. Nothing less than their best effort would be required. They would leave it all on the field.

An army sent to the battle field does not go with the attitude that it doesn't matter who wins. The determination of an army is to be so well equipped and trained that the outcome will be victory. Decisions and planning are intense. Orders are obeyed. When the battle has begun, every soldier must be focused on the goal of victory over the enemy.

This winning mantra is the prevalent philosophy of our day. The aim of every business mogul, every magazine editor, every film producer, every sports team. This trickles down to every small shop owner, blog writer, little league child. Indeed, all of us are inoculated by the thought that to be successful we must win at something, be the best at a skill, talent, or product. To do less seems like a failure, unacceptable.

Our personal reconnaissance is imperative. We must know they enemy's strength, position, weaknesses. Will our opponent surprise us? What weapon will be used against us? Are there weaknesses we have that might be exploited? Have we done all we could do to be prepared for success? What price will we have to pay in order to come out on top?

The greatest battle ever fought is the battle for the souls of mankind. The enemy is illusive, deceptive, alluring, well versed in human weaknesses. The Bible tells us who he is and what he does. Among his many names are these: Serpent, dragon, prince of the power of the air, adversary, accuser, Beelzebul.

"Be on the alert Your adversary, the devil, prowls around like a roaring lion seeking who he may devour." (1 Peter 5:8)

From the very beginning our enemy has sought to dissuade us, lure us away from victory. He began with Eve in the Garden of Eden and has continued to assault the forces of truth and righteousness ever since. Using lies, half-truths, "luscious fruit" that pleases the soul, he pushes against the defenses of those he hopes to enlist in his army...

We have the best equipment available. We have God's command to attack!

"Be strong in the Lord and in the power of His might. Put on the full armor of God that you may be able to stand firm against the schemes of the devil." (Ephesians 6:10-11)

To be certain we know what that equipment is Paul tells us.

- Truth, whole and pure
- Breastplate of righteousness protecting the hearts
- Preparation of the Gospel of peace
- Shield of faith against the enemy's lies
- Sword of the Spirit, our weapon of offense
- Helmet of salvation protecting our minds

Paul continues to remind us to pray at all times in the Spirit and to be alert. We cannot win if we are "out of shape" spiritually or lack sufficient equipment for our defense. We must recognize the enemy in whatever garb he wears and whatever the lure. There is One whose victory at such enormous cost gave us what we need to win. Jesus paid the price that we might be victors. In the Kingdom of God, winning is assured if we will follow Him.

Question: Are you prepared for the battle ahead?

WORDS MATTER

When we speak we uncover something of ourselves, what we like or dislike, what we enjoy or value, what we believe, who we are in the depths of our hearts. Words, spoken or written, are powerful, often life changing. They have the power to kill or cure. In the days in which we live we carelessly post words on line to be read and dissected by anyone, whether they know us or not. Examples of the negative results of what we "speak" on line are abundant and many times hurtful to us. Our words matter!

The writer of Proverbs, King Solomon, spoke often of the power of words.

- "A soothing tongue is a tree of life, but perverse words crush the spirit" (Proverbs 15:4)
- "Death and life are in the power of the tongue." (Proverbs 18:21)
- "He who guards his mouth and tongue guards his soul from trouble." (Proverbs 21:23)
- "The tongue of the wise brings healing." (Proverbs 12:18b)

The writer even proclaimed that God hates sins of our tongue. He calls this a "lying tongue". We can almost hear King Solomon reviewing his own use or misuse of words as he wrote.

In the New Testament James, leader of the believers in Jerusalem, when writing to the Jews who were dispersed throughout Asia Minor because of persecution, warned them of having an "unbridled tongues" which damage our lives. It is a great description of the power of words to harm or heal.

- "If anyone thinks himself to be religious, and yet does not bridle his tongue, this man's religion is worthless" (James 1:26)
- 'We all stumble in many ways. If anyone does not stumble in what he says, he is a perfect man, able to bridle the whole body as well." (James 3:2)
- "The tongue is a small part of the body, and yet it boasts of great things...The tongue is a fire...and sets on fire the course of our life." (James 3:5-6)
- "No one can tame the tongue. It is a restless evil and full of deadly poison. With it we bless God, our Father, and with it we curse men who have been made in the likeness of God. From the same mouth come blessing and cursing." (James 3:8-10)

The Psalmist, David, understood the grave importance of God's words.

- "The word of the Lord is as pure as silver tried in a furnace on earth refined seven times. You, O Lord, will keep them" (Psalm 12:6)
- "How sweet are Your words to my taste." (Psalm 119:103a)
- "The unfolding of Your words give light and understanding to the simple." (Psalm 119:130)

When God speaks, the purity of His words reveal Himself as our Lover, Disciplinarian, Protector, Strong Rock of Refuge, Counselor, Life Giver to name a few of the characteristics of God. Each word God speaks brings with it life, His life.

The writer of Hebrews declares this regarding Jesus, the Word of Life.

"God, through the ages, has spoken through the prophets, but now He has spoken through His Son." (Hebrews 1:1-2)

We know that Jesus is called the Word. The Apostle John had no doubt as to that title.

"In the beginning was the Word, and the Word was with God, and the Word was God." (John 1:1)

He came to speak to us of His Father's grace extended to all who will believe His Word. So precious is this gift of the Word, Jesus, that we have life through Him. In addition, we have been given the indwelling Spirit of God to speak to our hearts what God wants us to know. Our responsibility is to listen, heed, and relay that truth through our daily lives. Let our words be these. By our kind and gentle words let us repel the bitter and angry words we hear or read.

"Let the words of my mouth and the meditations of my heart be acceptable in Your sight, O Lord, my Rock and my Redeemer." (Psalm 19:14)

Challenge: Do a "word review" of your speech. Does it pass God's standard?

YOUR PERSONAL TRAINER

When you join a gym or health club, one of the benefits is the services of a personal trainer. This is someone who helps you design a regimen which will propel you to better health and fitness. Steady and frequent training builds stronger muscles and greater lung capacity Skipping sessions and a lazy approach to training does not bring about wanted results. It does reveal frustration and an "I quit" attitude.

There are many kinds of personal trainers available to us: an athletic coach, a teacher or professor, a wise older person, a dietary specialist, Mom and Dad, etc. In each is the responsibility to provide specialized training in some way as best fits our needs both then and in the future.

However, you and I have a Trainer that excels in the very best personalized training available in every area of our need. God, our Father, the One who created us to reflect His image, has a plan suited to the needs of each person. Knowing what life may bring and which challenges will be the hardest, He gives us the opportunity to train as if for "combat". It is our choice to follow His instruction in a disciplined manner...or not.

A very wise man, King Solomon, admonished those to whom fell the responsibility of training their children.

"Train up a child in the way he should go, and when he is old he will not depart from it." (Proverbs 22:6)

The seeds of the Word planted in a young life take root and grow. Though Solomon did not follow his own advice, we must. Training in righteousness should begin as soon as possible to ensure a healthy life both spiritually and physically.

This same idea is echoed by the writer of the letter to the Hebrew Christians who were unprepared for the harsh challenges their future held. He had heard about or had observed the undisciplined condition of some of those who professed belief in Jesus. He knew the root cause was their lack of training in the Word of God. He called them "infants".

"Though by this time you ought to be teachers, you have need again for someone to teach you the elementary principles of God. You have need of milk instead of solid food,...Solid food (the "meat" of the Gospel) is for the mature who because of their practice have their senses 12- to discern good and evil." (Hebrews 5:14)

He knew the cause and effect of a life untrained in the principles of God. They were unprepared to meet the harsh challenges of life in an unbelieving world.

A very good example of that training is found in the story of Daniel, a young Hebrew exile who was living in a culture very alien from the one in which he was trained. He and several other young men had been carried into captivity in Babylon. Selected to be trained in kingdom ways, they were soon faced with a choice that was unhealthy. Daniel chose to follow his training from God's Word. On behalf of himself and his three friends, Daniel offered an alternative choice. The choice was not easy because it could have cost him his life. Instead, he set an example that resulted in enhancing his righteous standing in this idol worshipping culture. His adherence to his training in God's Word was evident in the years to come as Daniel served with wisdom and integrity even when he faced death. (Daniel 1:3-18)

Here is the question the Psalmist asks and the answer he gives.

"How can a young man keep his way pure?" Here is the answer. "By keeping it according to Your Word. Your Word I have hidden in my heart that I may not sin against You." (Psalm 119:1,3)

This entire Psalm speaks of the benefits of "eating" the Word, hiding it in your heart, meditating on it day and night, studying its truths. To do so trains your heart for obedience to God and provides insight as to the path of life He has for you.

The Apostle Paul, writing to his young protégé, Timothy, gave this admonition.

"Discipline/train yourself for the purpose of Godliness." (I Timothy 4:7b)

Paul knew that his time was short and that he could no longer train Timothy. So concerned was he that he took this opportunity to remind Timothy of the importance of a disciplined approach to life.

Preparation and training equals righteous living and obedience to the Word of God. Let us heed that advice and submit to the training God offers. It is found in His Word and enlightened by His Spirit as He trains us.

Question: Who is your personal trainer?